MOUTHPIECE

MOUTHPIECE

A LIFE IN —
AND SOMETIMES JUST OUTSIDE —
THE LAW

EDWARD HAYES WITH SUSAN LEHMAN

WITH AN INTRODUCTION BY
TOM WOLFE

BROADWAY BOOKS

NEW YORK

PRINTED IN THE UNITED STATES OF AMERICA

BROADWAY BOOKS and its logo, a letter B bisected on the diagonal, are trade-marks of Random House, Inc.

Visit our Web site at www.broadwaybooks.com

Book design by Diane Hobbing of Snap-Haus Graphics

Unless specified otherwise, photographs are from the private collection of Edward Hayes.

Library of Congress Cataloging-in-Publication Data
  Hayes, Edward, 1947–
    Mouthpiece : a life in—and sometimes just outside—the law / Edward Hayes
  with Susan Lehman ; with an introduction by Tom Wolfe.
      p. cm.
    1. Hayes, Edward, 1947– 2. Lawyers—New York (State)—New York—
  Biography. I. Lehman, Susan. II. Title.
  KF373.H389A36 2005
  340'.092—dc22
    [B]   2005047046

ISBN 0-385-51111-6

First Edition

10 9 8 7 6 5 4 3 2 1

To Tom Wolfe
Except for my family, this life has given me no greater gift than his friendship.

INTRODUCTION: "GET ME HAYES!"

BY TOM WOLFE

When Si Newhouse, the multibillionaire monarch of the Condé Nast publishing empire, realizes somebody's stalking him—

When rapper R. Kelly lies flat on his back at 3:00 a.m. in New York's St. Vincent's Hospital with Mace in his eyes after a beef at a nightclub with his fellow rap name-amputee, Jay-Z—

When Andy Warhol dies at 6:30 a.m. on a Sunday in New York Hospital after a routine gall bladder operation, and his business manager, Fred Hughes, suddenly has half a billion dollars in art and real estate to protect, starting *now*—before the sun comes up—on a Sunday—

When Anna Wintour, editor of *Vogue*, is sued for $10 million as a result of her nanny's claims that negligence in the fashion lioness's home renovations caused her to contract asbestosis—

When it dawns on visionary architect Daniel Libeskind that to win the visionaries-only competition to design a vision-of-the-future skyscraper to replace the World Trade Center's twin towers he will need a New York political infighter to watch his back at street level with his eyes locked on the here and now—

When Stephen Caracappa is arrested and depicted as a rogue cop who used the power of his badge to set up eight men for murder by the Mafia, and the tabloids predict "the trial of the century"—

When New York police commissioner Bill Bratton, architect of the most radical and successful anticrime strategy in the history of American cities, finds himself nevertheless in danger of losing his job in a clash of egos with Mayor Rudy Giuliani—

When rich-kid PR girl Lizzie Grubman mows down sixteen people in front of a nightclub with her black Mercedes Darth Vader SUV and flees the scene—

When yet another rap name-amputee, a member of Sean (P. Diddy) Combs's posse going by the lone tag Wolf, flees the scene of yet another nightclub, after yet another melee, in yet another black Darth Vader SUV, viz., Combs's Navigator, and is stopped by cops and arrested for illegal possession of a .9 mm handgun—

Oh, they come in every breed, every color, every station in life, don't they! Lowlifes—and high livers! The lawless—and the law men! Artists alive—and artists dead! Brutes who gibber away without knowing the third-person singular present tense of any verb in the English language—and beauties and cuties personal-trained and carb-starved until the tendons in their necks stand out taut as banjo strings—*every* sort of human creature, as I say—and yet—

—once they're in a jam, it is as if all speak with but a single voice, crying out:

"*Get me Hayes!*"

In sum, the man who is about to tell us the story of his life, the 210-pound, iron-pumped-up fifty-seven-year-old lawyer in the chalk-striped brown unfinished worsted suit and snap-brim fedora on the jacket of this book, Edward W. Hayes, Esq., is the Tommy Corcoran, the Edward Bennett Williams of our time. He is what is called the go-to guy. He's the lawyer who will Batman out into the dead of the night to rescue any wretch, rich or poor—or, rather, any rich wretch and any poor wretch with a relative, a sister or an aunt, say, willing to wring a second mortgage out of her two-family (Maspeth talk for a house housing the owner and one tenant) in Maspeth to pay the Counselor's retainer fee. For while he is famous for representing policemen, firemen, and their families, such as the widows of 9/11, and charging next to nothing, he tells the rest of his clients, "I want you to remember two things. First, I do this for money. Second, I'm not your friend. I'm your lawyer. But I'll do more for you than your friends."

Like Donald Trump or Russell Simmons, Counselor Hayes is what is known in New York as a colorful character. In New York colorful refers not to what a celebrity does in his work (if any) but to his ability to stamp his personality upon the scene. Robert De Niro is a riveting movie actor and Woody Allen a vastly amusing movie writer and director, but talking to them is like interviewing a raindrop. Afterward no one can ever remember what they were wearing. In the case of Counselor Hayes, on the other hand, no one ever forgets. The Counselor was born and raised in Jackson Heights, Queens, one of those outer-borough New York neighborhoods where the houses are separated only by alleyways upon which, in the heart-penetrating words of Jimmy Breslin, God looks down at night and sees a thousand points of light—those being the glowing red tips of cigarettes lit by the husbands who smoke them leisurely out in the alleyways to give their wives time to go inside and get into bed and feign sleep so that when the husbands come into the bedrooms, the possibility that they might use beds for reaching anything other than the Land of Nod is already consummately moot. The Counselor has clung tenaciously as a terrier to his Queens street accent. When he enters a room, he turns his high-wattage eyeballs on above a warm grin, leans forward, and beams the eyeballs at you as if searching for what it is you want most of all in this world and conveying his commitment to getting it for you, puts out his hand in a curious way that makes it look as if he has just thrown a sidearm curveball, and says, "How yeh doooooin?" Every man in the room whom he knows he greets with, "Ayyyyyy, the big mehhhhhhn," just the way Richard Widmark said it when he played Tommy Udo in the movie *Kiss of Death*. On the streets of Jackson Heights, and in the mouth of the Counselor to this day, the word *law* has an r on the end of it—*lawr*—and *forward* has no rs at all—*foe-ud*. Immediately those Jackson Heights rs, the interlopers and the lost, clash with the Counselor's clothes, which are strictly Savile Row British in cut. Some of the Counselor's tailors actually have shops on London's Savile Row, although his *egregio* maestro in the esoteric world of chalk-striped brown unfinished worsteds, peaked lapels, inverted pleats, envelope pockets, hand cutting, hand stitching, raglan sleeves, and sleeves with real buttonholes that button and unbutton is the fashionable tailor Vincent Nicolosi of Madison Avenue in New York. The Counselor has more custom-made suits than anyone I've ever known; also more custom-made shoes, shoes of crocodile hide, pigskin, century-old Russian calfskin found on a shipwreck at the bottom of the Atlantic, shoes brogued, half-brogued, Tuczek-toed, monk-strapped, gilly-laced, the lot.

When his wife, the five-foot-ten former supermodel Susie Gilder, is along, she and her hurricane of long blond Category 5 curly hair and her just-you-wait-buster laugh, she doubles the amplitude of the Counselor's presence. The pair of them glisten at night on the hot-boîte circuit of Wevar and Tribeca, which is, as the great medievalist Johan Huizinga put it in *Homo Ludens*, "where things are happening" currently. Glisten . . . and nothing more, for the Counselor is not a carouser or a cutup. Thanks—bitter thanks—to a figure we will meet immediately in the pages ahead, he does not drink. He does not smoke. He does not ingest caffeine, nicotine, cocaine, crank, crunk, or crystal meth. He does not try to be funny, but he does have a pressurized laugh at the ready to make *other people* feel amusing. The laugh begins with a virtually silent but obvious buildup of pressure, which he then releases from the solar plexus: *eghh eghh eghh eghh eghh eghh eghh eghh.*

The Counselor's manner has a certain manly haunch-to-paunch charm, but charm is not the same thing as social grace. The Counselor is not a Southern gentleman (I, on the other hand, am), even though he spent four years at the University of Virginia and was tapped by the exclusive TILKA Society, whose Southern boys found New Yawk street charm exotic. In company, at the dinner table, at home or at Churrascaria Plataforma, this month's restaurant of the century, the Counselor is unable to hide it when he's bored. His eyes fasten upon some invisible point in the middle distance. Then they go blank, or, rather, transparent, so that they look like two windows in an empty house at night. Even so, this is an improvement. When bored in days gone by, he used to turn his chair about and present his back to the table. After three or four minutes he would stand up and walk away, muttering something over his shoulder about making a telephone call.

I used to think this telephone call business was nothing more than a rude and rather juvenile fib. I was wrong. It was merely rude and juvenile. It wasn't a fib. He would leave the room and make a telephone call or, just as likely, five or six. For such is the Counselor's peculiar social art. At playing that instrument, the telephone, he is a virtuoso.

In no small part thanks to telephone virtuosity, the Counselor became a maestro of networking long before that term had even entered the language. Whenever he meets someone of special interest, he calls him up the next day—not with a question or request or an invitation but with a . . . "How yeh doooooin?" Gradually it dawns on you that this man Hayes wants nothing more than to let you know he has a congenial interest in how yeh doooooin. There is absolutely nothing you can do for him . . . *now*. The next week you may very likely receive two such calls . . . "How yeh doooooin?" He will keep in touch every week from then on. Rare is the ego that minds having a new friend, particularly one who is worthy of ink by the barrel from the press yet who calls up from time to time just to show his delight in *your* existence on this earth.

I would eventually discover that the Counselor calls up each of his clients about eleven o'clock at night—two hours past what local protocol decrees as the cutoff time for nonemergency nighttime telephone calls. He wants each of them to know that what monopolizes his attention right up to the moment he turns in for the night is . . . *you* . . . From time to time the Counselor convenes members of his network for dinner. At one point he used to assemble ten or twelve of them on Monday nights at a big round thick slab of an oak table at the Manhattan Café, a steak house, *steak house* being a big thick slab of a term that disguised the fact that this was actually Eddie Hayes's salon, *salon* being one of the many French expressions that were gaffes in conversation on the streets of Jackson Heights. *Gaffe*, being French, was a gaffe, too. At the same table one would find Si Newhouse; John Gotti's burly lawyer, Bruce Cutler; New York police commissioner Bill Bratton (now police commissioner in Los Angeles); his deputy commissioner, John Timoney (now chief of police in Miami); New York *Daily News* columnists Michael Daly and Mike McAlary; investment bankers Tom Guba and Alex Porter; the Counselor's brother, big-time show business lawyer Steven Hayes; and Tom Wolfe. Any attentive soul could have picked up enough material for a novel at the Manhattan Café every Monday night.

In the pages before us the Counselor tells a saga's worth of tales of the city. As the saying goes, he's got a million of them. God knows I helped myself to my share and then some when I wrote *The Bonfire of the Vanities*. Here in his own book we are about to meet rogues and rascals and learn how politics *really* work, at street level and below. To borrow a conceit from Freud, the politicians' grand issues, their grand "stands" on the issues, their ideologies, philosophies, programs, causes, initiatives, judicial decisions, fiscal debates, legislative votes—all such things are, in the Counselor's telling, the parlor furniture of politics. In this book the Counselor crooks a finger and says, Come, follow me, and I'll take you down into the cellar and show you the greasy machinery, the furnace with its torn lagging of asbestos, the sweating water pipes, that actually make this house run.

Startling as much of it is, it is no more than what one might hope for from the Counselor. What truly startles *me* in this book is what the Counselor reveals about himself, things he has only obliquely alluded to in my presence, and we have been close friends for thirty years. I daresay all of us will be surprised by how often this man who has tangled with every sort of thug, con man, mobster, jezebel, and homicidal husband in the billion-footed city, this man so tough looking that boys who come by to date his teenage daughter tremble for fifteen minutes even after they leave the premises with her, confesses to have broken down and cried, sobbed—*sobbed!* blubbered! boohoo'd! snuffled! gasped! sighed! cried himself a river that comes coursing down over the rise of his cheekbones! These helpless jags, we will learn, began in childhood and certainly did not abate over the past decade even as he became known as Get Me Hayes. He confesses to having been in psychiatric therapy for most of his adult life. His inconsolable agony has deep roots, and he strips them down, before our eyes, to their very last cilia.

This, the story of his inner life, is the greatest tale of the city the Counselor has ever told. It is breathtaking, heartrending to see a man of his prominence lie down before you, supine, at the mercy of your judgment, denuded of all pretenses and defenses. This is not merely *I Pagliacci*, a story of tears wept over love behind the mask of a clown. *Mouthpiece* is a story of a man whose metastatic anguish is primal.

Or, as the Counselor himself puts it in the first words of chapter 1: "I learned as a child not to expect to be loved for myself." Offhand I can't think of a more gripping opening line written in my lifetime. Personally, it is my key to a man who loves his friends in the same way he loves his children and will fight for them with an extraordinary loyalty . . . and ferocity.

It is my pleasure to present . . . with a single turn of the page . . . Counselor Edward W. Hayes himself.

"I don't like your manner," Kingsley said in a voice you could have cracked a Brazil nut on.

"That's all right," I said. "I'm not selling it."

— Raymond Chandler, The Lady in the Lake

PROLOGUE

There are snakes in the basement.

King snakes. Rat snakes. Pine snakes. I don't know the first thing about snakes or about South Carolina either, but I know there are snakes in the basement of the two-story brick ranch house in Greenville and I am fucking terrified.

Boom. My dad, fat, stinking of beer, comes in wearing the cheap suit he wears to work at the Sperry plant outside Greenville—so many hundreds of miles from Jackson Heights, Queens, where I played in the alleys behind the rows of single-family brick town houses with kids who came from the same world I did, took pride in the same heritage, and went, on Sundays and on holy days, to the same church, St. Joan of Arc on Eighty-sixth Street. That was where my mother danced with my father at age fourteen, fell madly in love with him, and married him five years later, completely unaware that he shared the Irish predilection for drink, the result of which would be that every day of her life and ours would contain elements of violence and terror and blinding rage. Now we might as well have been on Mars. My dad slams open the kitchen door and walks, in cheap brown shoes, across the linoleum floor, opens the cupboard, grabs a glass, smashes it on the counter, and says, "What are you looking at!?"

I'm eleven. I'm not looking at anything.

"You don't say hello when I walk in?"

First of all, I'm not glad to see my father. Second, I've learned that a lot of times it's best to keep quiet.

"Look at me, you little shit. I'm your father!"

His big, thick hand hits the side of my head. Thwack! I'm on the floor, looking at the linoleum.

Smack! His shoe smashes into my side. I guess I'm going to die here.

No, I'm not. With his beefy hand, my father picks me up off the floor and carries me across the kitchen to the basement steps and, holding me tight by the arms, lifts me down the first four steps, then throws me down the remaining stairs into the dark, wet, snake-plagued basement. The door at the top of the stairs shuts.

All is quiet.

Then the basement door opens.

Crash. Crash. Crash.

What the fuck is this?

Loafers fly down the steps. Oxfords. More loafers. Scuffed wingtips from Sears. All the shoes in the house come crashing down the steps.

"Shine the shoes, goddamn you."

My father slams the door closed.

My mother is upstairs. So is my brother, Steven, who is fifteen months younger than me. They can't do anything to help me and I don't expect them to. I don't scream. I don't say anything at all. I just lie there for a while, and then start polishing the shoes in the dark, scared to fucking death I'm going to run into a black-headed rat snake or yellow-eyed king snake.

I am going to climb out of this basement and I am going to have what I want out of life—the best relationships, the best family, the best everything, including shoes, that money buys. In the inarticulate thoughts of an eleven-year-old child, this is what I vow as I shine all those shoes in the dark. "I'll show you." That's my response to the basement and to all the beatings that came before and that will come afterwards. "I'll show you what the best is."

And I did.

And there is probably no one in the world who has better shoes than I do.

CHAPTER 1

I learned as a child not to expect to be loved for myself.

My father was a very good teacher.

I don't have a single good memory of him, not one, but he taught me a lot of useful lessons. A merchant marine during World War II, my father had gone on missions to Murmansk and Malta on a tanker and he told me how, during those voyages, American destroyers rammed German subs and the subs torpedoed the tankers and, in the end, the water was full of sailors who had been blown to bits or were on fire. They fought to the death. I remember thinking, *That's the way life is: somebody goes home and somebody does not, you try to avoid the latter, but that's how life is.*

I learned this early on, and also that people are weak and can't control themselves and you have to protect yourself from that.

All in all, pretty useful things to learn, especially if you live in New York. New York, this City of Ambition, is brutal, unrelenting, dense, neurotic, always alive, and, if you're willing to take a chance and pay the price, you can get what you want here, or at least close enough. The whole city is full of guys who can take beatings, guys who got beaten somewhere else but crossed the ocean to get here and take another one and who will get up tomorrow to do the same thing.

———

I was born Edward Walter Hayes on November 3, 1947, at Physicians Hospital in Jackson Heights, Queens. It was a difficult breech birth and the doctor, who was Jewish, had to reach in and ease me out, which saved my life and was my first good experience with Jews. But my breathing was strange and Dr. Goldberg didn't think I would live long. So Father Cunningham, the priest who had married my parents a year before, was dispatched to baptize me right away.

My mother does not know where my father was at the time, but he wasn't there, for either the birth or the baptism. My mom says he was probably out in the waiting room, fainting or drinking.

I made little squeaking sounds,—"Ehhhh"—and couldn't cry for four months after they got me home from the hospital. My mom worried about this and about some trouble she thought I seemed to have eating, but she says my father was not too concerned. About this, my father's response seems to have been just right: after a while the squeaking stopped; I have never had trouble eating *or* crying since; and the years we lived in the four-story red brick house on Eighty-sixth Street were the best of my childhood.

The house cost four thousand dollars. My aunt Nonie bought it courtesy of Bill Fitzgibbon, who worked at Grant's department store and had nice cufflinks and silk shirts and may have been the first Irish affirmative action hire in the history of New York and who for years courted Aunt Nonie until finally she agreed to marry him. Fitzgibbon promptly became a hopeless drunk and died an awful death a year later, but he left Aunt Nonie with the four thousand dollars she needed to buy the brick town house on Eighty-sixth Street.

In Jackson Heights, there are tales (true, partly true, or not at all true) that are told and retold so many times they eventually take shape as actual, incontrovertible fact. They're called *Irish facts*. Aunt Nonie was orphaned ten years earlier when her father, Francis Mc-Cade, a tombstone cutter, died of consumption; Nonie was dispatched to a wealthy family, the head of which was a fashionable dressmaker who taught Aunt Nonie her craft. Is it an Irish fact that Nonie first caught Bill Fitzgibbon's eye as she bent her pretty head over a sewing machine? No idea, but I know that Fitzgibbon supplied Aunt Nonie with her one chance at love and that she took it; it didn't turn out well, but the story introduced an idea central to the rest of my life: everyone, even an orphaned seamstress, gets at least one shot at something and you're a fool not to take your chance when you get it; it might not work out, but there could be a house full of happy memories in it for someone.

Decades of white-boy history ran down Eighty-sixth Street and all the other streets in Jackson Heights, a neighborhood of garden apartments and family homes inhabited then—as now—mostly by immigrants hungry for a taste of some chicken-in-every-pot, car-in-every-garage-type American prosperity.

Brits Out. Before any of us Irish kids had any idea what it meant or even who the Brits were, this was pretty much the first thing any of us who ran around the streets and the alleyways behind our garden apartments had to say about anything. We all went to the same parish church and held the same beliefs. Chief among these was the idea that the worst thing you can do is rat out a friend, and that if you did you would (and should) be killed, and that life is cruel and harsh and the best you can do is die for your faith, and that the point of life is to know God and be with Him forever and the purpose of this life is for the next. Also God will forgive you for everything, but I don't have to. (He will forgive you. I will blow up your car.) We were also told from early on that Jews killed Christ. But that was very long ago in some messed-up place with camels, so who cared? And besides, we didn't know any Jews.

The Italian kids had good food, the Germans had decent pastry, and the Irish had neither, but we kids had the same heroes: Frank Gifford, firemen, cops, baseball players. Right from the womb, everyone knew about the charming and brilliant Irish military leader Michael Collins, who helped start an uprising in 1916, when he joined a small force of Irish guys enraged at the British Empire encamped in the Sackville Street General Post Office in Dublin, in particular. Though British troops instantly surrounded the post office and fired mercilessly, the ragtag team of Irishmen held their ground and fought it out for days and days, choosing to fight long past what common sense or honor required rather than retreat or give even an inch. When, exhausted but triumphant, they finally surrendered, the British soldiers fucking hung every single one of the leaders (though not Collins), including Joseph Plunkett, who led the whole thing, and his little brother, who was just along for the ride.

The neighborhood white boys all had the same general expectation as to how things might play out for them during the next seventy or eighty years: we would love God, get jobs like our dads, marry nice Catholic girls. And live in Jackson Heights—or maybe even, if we were lucky, Forest Hills or Kew Gardens—and have houses full of kids who would go to St. Joan of Arc school as we did and would fight in the alleyways and streets and knock each other's blocks off, mostly for fun, as we also did.

———

"Stupid. Asshole. Shithead."

The Italian kid, an eleven- or twelve-year-old with slicked-back black hair who lives across the street, throws a rock that lands with a crash near my feet. The crew of kids I play with, eight-, nine-, and ten-year-olds, run away, laughing.

"Who's a stupid asshole?" I say.

I'm skinny but I'm not running away.

(Even at nine, I'm not big on retreat.)

Beat me. So what?

Boom, smack.

The Italian kid lands a punch on my left shoulder. Another on my upper arm.

My little brother, Steven, and a crowd of kids edge closer to watch the dark-haired Italian slam his hand into my skinny chest again and again. Probably they wonder why on earth a scrawny little kid would frantically thrash around on the ground with someone twice his size rather than shrug, say something like "Forget it, will ya?" and walk off. Instead, and with all the fury in my little nine-year-old heart, I pound my fists against the kid from across the street. The crazed anger I taste in my mouth when my father beats me at home sparks up my throat when, a moment later, I roll on the asphalt drive toward a closed garage door, into the hard white wood of which he kicks my flailing legs, again and again.

The group watching has grown and now includes at least eight or nine people bigger than the Italian kid and certainly big enough to intervene and stop the whole thing. If they want to, which they don't.

Isn't anyone going to help? The thought crosses my mind as my head smashes against the garage door. I look up at Mick and Paddy and Joe, who live on the block, and Francis, Thomas, and Billy, who I know from school. Jackson Heights is a neighborhood in which you see everyone you know at least three times a day, including all the kids I fight with on the playground. *No,* I think, as the Italian kid kicks me, blinding white fury burning behind my eyes. *No. No one is going to help.*

———

Wonder Bread. I need Wonder Bread. That's what I thought as I picked myself up off the ground when the whole thing was over and the kids, except for my brother, who seemed always to be there then (and also throughout the rest of my life), went off to knock someone else's block off or to have dinner—meatballs or something equally terrific, at least for the Italian kids. (Who remembers, or wants to remember, what the German or Irish kids ate?)

My maternal grandfather, Walter Sowden, drove a Wonder Bread truck and was one of the loveliest men I knew. The only one of my four grandparents who wasn't Irish or Catholic, Walter Sowden grew up in poverty in Greenpoint, Brooklyn; my mom says he married into an Irish Catholic family because he wanted a place in a more vi-brant culture. Whether he found it or not, I don't know, but I do know that my grandmother, Mary Fitzgibbon Sowden, a devout Catholic, went to church every day of her life and prayed that her Lutheran husband would convert. He never did, but they had what looked like a truly bonded, wonderful marriage, and there was always a cupboard full of Wonder Bread in their two-bedroom apartment, which was walking distance from the house and also the alleyway where the Italian kid shoved my skull into the garage door.

"Want some bread and jelly?" That's all Grandpa Walter ever said to me. He never once asked how I'd gotten bruised or why my knees were skinned.

Fight. Eat Wonder Bread. Go out, fight again. That's it—one of my favorite childhood routines. During those years in Jackson Heights, I think I ate more Wonder Bread than anyone in the world.

"Bye, Grandpa," I'd say after I finished my bread and stood up, ready to go back into the street. "Be good, Eddie," Grandpa Sowden would say as he walked me to the door. And then, Steven right be-hind me, I'd head outside, looking for another fight or, better yet, the same fight, with the same dark-haired kid who took me down an hour ago. That's how it always was: if I won a fight, which I rarely did, it was over, we could be friends. But if I lost, as I usually did and as I had to the Italian kid, I'd keep fighting, today and tomorrow and the days after, long past the point where I or anyone else could possibly remember what the beef (assuming there was one) had been in the first place. I'd keep at it forever. There was always more bread.

———

"Corpus Domini nostri Jesu Christi custodiat animam tuam in vitam aeternam." The body of our Lord Jesus Christ, may it preserve your soul unto life everlasting.

I kneel before the altar in St. Joan of Arc church. My mom is there in a fancy dress and my brother, Steven, and my aunt Nonie, who is always with my mother at meals or, when the weather is good, outside on the steps talking with her mom, watching to make sure Steven and I don't get in trouble in the street and certainly in church. The Sowdens and the Hayeses all sit together on a wood pew in the third row—I see them as I face the priest as he puts the Communion wafer in my mouth.

It feels good to be here, in my Sunday clothes, my blue blazer and the white shirt my mom ironed the night before even though it is perma-press and doesn't need pressing. Catholics all over the world take Communion, eat the same wafers, and say the same prayers about taking His body and blood into their own; I know this from catechism class. I don't know a single person besides my grandfather who isn't Catholic, and perhaps it doesn't even occur to me that there is anyone in the world who isn't, but it still makes me feel safe and happy to take Communion and feel connected.

Engraved in the very stones of St. Joan of Arc church, where I took my first Communion and felt connected with Catholics around the world—and with Mick and Paddy and Joe and the other kids I fought in the streets after (and also before) church—are the words *Love Thy Neighbor as Thyself.*

Love Thy Neighbor as Thyself. Okay. I did, I would. I'd love them all—Mick, Paddy, and Joe—even when they beat my balls off in the alley, which they sometimes did immediately following church on Sunday.

Everything I wanted to do was wrong. This I learned at church and also at St. Joan of Arc school, which was across the play lot from church. But as long as I repent, God would forgive me for whatever I did, no matter how bad. I learned a lot about forgiveness at school and about repentance and redemption, which were useful concepts to take with me when I went home to my family each night.

I loved the nuns who taught me about forgiveness and also taught me religious history. The sisters were good-hearted people who, as my mother explained, had made the ultimate sacrifice for God, and even (or especially) to a child, they seemed genuinely dedicated. I felt they really cared about me. The fact that they also smacked me around? I didn't care. I adored nuns. I still do.

The nuns wore habits that made them scary and they didn't like to be questioned much. Sister Cherubim, the lovely woman, taught us about the Inquisition, a subject that struck a real chord with me. (When people or groups of people got hurt, I could relate.) "Why did the Catholics torture all those people? What did the Jews do?" I am nine and I want to know. I keep pushing. "What did they do?" Like most of the other nuns at St. Joan of Arc, Sister Cherubim is particularly unreceptive to political questions. *They got tortured, killed. What did all these people do to provoke this?* I asked again and again.

Eventually Sister Cherubim has had enough. Pulling me into the back room where we hang our coats, she looks me hard in the eye, makes a scary, frosty face, and says, "Keep this up and your soul will suffer eternal damnation," which to a nine-year-old has a very ominous ring to it. I didn't know it then, of course, but Catholicism isn't like Judaism, which instructs you to question everything, all the time; Catholic teachers take more of a shut-up-and-do-what-you're-supposed-to-do approach which, by the way, has its virtues, and which, out of fondness for Sister Cherubim, I quickly adopt, at least temporarily, that day in the coatroom of St. Joan of Arc school.

———

My mother, Jean Sowden Hayes, who grew up in the same neighborhood and went to the same church and the same school, also learned the same basic lessons that I did, though she definitely stuck with the do-what-you're-supposed-to-do way of doing things longer than I ever could.

My mom grew up believing in original sin, and that God was everywhere, and also that, if possible, it was smart to marry someone with a pension. Until she was eighteen, she also believed that Catholic and Democrat were one and the same thing. ("Oh, you *must* go to confession," she later told a neighbor who voted for the Republican and Protestant Richard Nixon instead of the Democrat and

Catholic Jack Kennedy in the 1960 presidential election, and she prayed each night for at least two years thereafter that God would save the neighbor's soul.) My mom shared with the other girls who went to St. Joan of Arc school in blue pleated skirts the general expectation that they would marry at the age of twenty or so and then stay married forever. No one needed to tell my mother or any of the girls she grew up with that nice Catholic girls did not, under any circumstance, tell anyone they had married a drunk, which to my mother's disappointment but probably not to her great surprise (since everyone knew the Irish were prone to drink) she did in 1946, seven years after she met my father at a family dance in the multipurpose room at St. Joan of Arc church.

My father had nice eyes and was supposedly charming. Maybe he got his charm from his father and namesake (and later my namesake), Edward Hayes, who was lively and outgoing and also kind. A bookie and a numbers runner when he was young, Grandpa Hayes had a sales position with an insurance company but lost it during the Depression and moved his family—my grandmother, Margaret Hayes, and my father, then a young child—to Astoria, a neighborhood next to, but socially a notch beneath, Jackson Heights. Like my father, Grandpa Hayes had a terrible drinking problem that probably did not enhance his career options, but he was nice to me. When I was eight or nine and wasn't getting my head knocked around in the alleys or stopping, in between rounds, for sandwiches with the Sowdens, I liked to go to the Hayes house in Astoria. Grandpa Hayes and I watched boxing or wrestling matches together on the little TV in the corner of the living room, where he let me sit on the arm of the couch after he'd put a white handkerchief down. "Here you go, Eddie," he'd say motioning me over to his side, and we'd sit together and watch the fights and drink beer. That's right, both of us.

I tried to stay away from Grandma Hayes, who served as the one and only exception to a rule already forming in my head, that, though they couldn't always protect you, women had privileged access to endless reserves of gentle kindness and great comforts. Grandma Hayes must have been absent (at home with a headache?) the day the women of the world (or at least the women in Jackson Heights) got their keys to this universal reservoir. She was always in a terrible mood and never had a nice thing to say to anyone, and her nasty disposition probably had something to do with my father's eventual predilection for violence and rotten behavior. Sweet as he was, Grandpa Hayes was ruined by drink, which diminished his prospects before killing him outright in the mid-1950s, after a slow, cruel struggle connected with liver failure.

My mom didn't recognize it at first as a problem, but she knew early on that my father was a drinker too. He had too much champagne one night on the honeymoon at the Split Rock Lodge in the Poconos and acted badly. He put my mother down and told her how stupid she was, but she says the possibility that there was a connection between my father's drinking and his subsequent unkindness did not occur to her.

My dad was a good dancer, which impressed my mom. And he had a good education. He had gone to the merchant marine academy, which provided a free education as well as an escape from life with his awful mother. He had a decent job, a middle-management position at the Sperry Corporation, a defense contractor that manufactured submarine parts. My dad's position was roughly analogous to that of the copy-machine guy who comes around to check machines in various office buildings. He went to naval bases around the country and checked out submarines. I don't know if it occurred to my mother that my father's drinking would increase as the years went on—or that his violence, against her and eventually everyone around him, would increase along with it. But if it did, I'm almost certain she wouldn't have, and maybe couldn't have, done anything about it.

———

"What is this foul insult? Is this a joke, Jean?"

I'd come home from school, lessons about forgiveness and human frailty fresh in my nine-year-old mind.

My mom, God bless her, couldn't cook to save her life, a fact that did not escape my father's volatile attention. He'd come home from work, slug down a few martinis from the pewter mug he kept in the freezer, and we'd all sit down to eat.

My mother, ever cheerful, asks Steven and me about school and tells us who she's seen on the way to the store. Everything is fine. Then my father tastes the corned beef or boiled peas.

"Stupid woman! This food will kill us all." He flies into a rage, puts his big, beefy hands under the tabletop, and, spewing insults at my mom, upends the table, sending the dishes flying and scaring us to death. This happens more than a few times.

Often my mother leaves the table and goes upstairs and my dad follows her. Steven and I, hearing awful sounds and not knowing what to do, run outside if it isn't late or dark, or hide behind the couch and wait until it is quiet and we can go upstairs and try to sleep. Next morning, my mother, cheerful as always, lays fresh clothes (blue blazers, white shirts, navy pants that she bought at Macy's) in neat piles at the ends of our beds, gets our breakfast together, and heads off to work. My mother always worked—as a librarian, a shopgirl, and a package wrapper; and for forty-five more years she dutifully filled my father's pewter mug with martinis and placed it in the freezer as he asked and just as dutifully endured his beatings and screaming, then went on with her business, getting up, going to work, trying to protect us when she could.

The Irish don't rat. Bounce them off the wall for a week and they won't tell you a thing. It's in the blood and the body, part of the be-quiet-and-do-what-you're-supposed-to-do approach the sisters so ardently embraced.

She got the worst of it but my mom never told anyone what went on in our house. Not when my father kicked her so hard he damaged her kidney and she called the doctor in pain and told him she had fallen down the stairs and needed help. "Come in," the doctor said. He examined her, gave her medicine for the pain, and called the next day to say, "I don't think you fell down the stairs, Mrs. Hayes. I thought you might want to talk to me, or to someone, about this." She might have wanted to talk to the doctor, or to someone, but she never did. She didn't even tell her father, who must have suspected something was wrong, until decades later, after her mother died.

—

Did my dad see something so awful on the way to Murmansk or Malta or any of the other places he fought during the war, something so awful that he could never recover his better Catholic self? Did he have a genetic predisposition toward depression forceful enough to incite a grown man to smack his young son off a chair while he ate his cereal at breakfast? "I wish it was you who died, you miserable cur," Grandma Hayes told my father over and over again when his sister, Doris, two years older than he, died of lupus at age seventeen. Were the kicks and smacks the miserable but logical conclusion of a genetic chain that began with the awful Margaret Hayes, a woman so nasty that even, with all his schooling in Catholic doctrine regarding redemption and forgiveness, her nine-year-old grandson knew—with as much certainty as he knew that his next plateful of delicious spaghetti and meatballs would be served by an Italian, not an Irish, neighbor—that his mother was an irredeemably nasty woman?

Did genetics, abuse, and the scarring experience of war combine with alcoholic proclivities and general disappointment about work and love and life in a blend toxic enough to render a grown man helpless in the face of its terrible directive to hit and smack and rage? To this day I don't have a clear sense of how to understand my father or the way he treated my mother, my brother, and me. As a nine-year-old I couldn't and didn't articulate the questions.

—

"I could have been a manager. I could have done that. I know the ropes." My dad is at the kitchen table, crying. When he's not raging or drinking, he sometimes cries like this. He takes it very hard when in 1963 the *Thresher*, a nuclear submarine with Sperry parts, sinks in the Atlantic a hundred miles off Cape Cod. The parts weren't in good repair; if he had been a top-level manager at Sperry, the piping would have been in good order and the *Thresher* wouldn't have ended up 8,400 feet below the surface with 129 dead men inside.

It drove my dad nuts that guys who weren't as bright as he was got big promotions and better jobs. The company had plants all over the country and, though they never promoted my dad, they moved him around, beginning when I was seven. It was a way of keeping him on without having to give him a better job, which, in retrospect, wasn't the worst way to deal with an employee who showed up every day and was apparently likable enough but who had a drinking problem that made him a questionable prospect for advancement, not to mention increased responsibility in an industry subject, especially after the *Thresher* disaster, to increasing scrutiny.

The moves from Jackson Heights to Greenville, South Carolina, then, briefly, to Charlottesville, Virginia, and back to Queens followed in jolting succession, as did the beatings with which my father expressed the dislocation and discomfort that resulted from leaving a world of neighbors, friends, and familiar rituals and expectations, and moving to little southern towns full of rat snakes and strangers who knew nothing at all about any of the seven sacraments.

My God, were my brother and I glad to get back to Queens at the end of the awful three-year period in which we moved three times. We lived in Garden Bay Manor, not far from Jackson Heights and all the people I knew and ran around and fought with. My mom was pregnant with my sister, Barbara, when we moved into our new place, a house smaller than, but with the same feel as, the place we lived in with Aunt Nonie. But neither the pregnancy nor my sister's birth changed much for either me or Steven; we liked having a baby around just fine, but we were too much older, too immersed in our kids' lives to be much involved.

St. Francis of Assisi school, which my brother and I now attended, was a lot like St. Joan of Arc down the street, where we once again went to church on Sundays. We were back where we belonged, in a recognizable world, at home.

———

Scheme, hustle, move, and score, the mantra I rely on to this day, took shape shortly after we got back to Queens. My first scheme was aimed at the butcher boy who made deliveries from the alley behind our house.

I'm twelve now and the butcher boy is fifteen and a bully. He liked to beat up the smaller Irish kids in the neighborhood. He beat the balls off all of us. So I got a gang of skinny, freckled kids together, mean little Irish kids whose fathers beat them and who probably went on to become big, mean Irish cops. And we lay in wait in the alley where we knew the butcher boy came with his deliveries each morning. "We'll throw his bike down," I said, "and we'll jump on him and he won't be able to get us." And that's pretty much what happened. When he came down the alley with the packages in a wire basket on his bike, we knocked him and the bike down, jumped on him, got him to the ground, stomped on him, and beat his brains out. *Scheme, hustle, move, and score.* That was it. My first scheme: I picked the crew, planned the strategy, and made the move. There were no more problems with the butcher boy. I could outsmart guys who were stronger than me! This occurred to me for the very first time as I watched the butcher kid limp off with his bike, too battered to ride.

———

The public library in Garden Bay Manor had vinyl chairs with metal legs. Nothing bad ever happens to you in a library. I went to the Garden Bay Manor library several days a week, after school; I liked to sit in the corner, surrounded by shelves, or hide in one of the blond wood cubicles. It was always quiet. I always felt safe there: I never saw my father read a book and I knew it would never in a million years occur to him to look for me, or anything else, in the library.

The librarians, nice Catholic ladies who worked at the front desk, never asked any questions; they were polite and just left me alone. I never took books home—in the summer I never went home either but pretty much lived in the library. I just sat there reading Robert E. Howard's *Conan* books and *Tarzan of the Apes* and other books by Edgar Rice Burroughs, all of which centered on strong, heroic male figures. I read stories about military leaders—Abraham Lincoln, Alexander the Great, George Patton—and history, especially Irish history, which I identified with and loved. For hundreds of years, the Irish fought the British, the most powerful army in the history of the world, and lost, but kept coming back until they finally won their freedom. I had immediate attraction to the romance at the core of books about Michael Collins and to the idea that, though life is hard and full of endless disappointment, there are guys who will do anything for a friend.

I read about the Irish, French, and American revolutions and saw that throughout history unacceptable situations were quite often changed by force. Violence *does* settle problems; the books I read were pretty clear about this. People in power always counsel against violence. But I learned from history—and from my home life—that nonviolence probably won't work. Violence works. The books I read in quiet, safe afternoons at the library reinforced the lessons I learned at home.

The strong exploit the weak. My father was strong and I was weak. His beatings were part of the natural order of things. It made perfect sense in the mind of a precocious twelve-year-old.

My reading perfectly rounded out the tough-guy preschooling I got at church and at home, where I learned to stay alert, to function well under stressful circumstances, to keep my head on straight at all hours of the day and night, and to recover from defeat, all of which was great training for my subsequent life as a big-city lawyer. But the most important thing I learned in the world dominated by my father's sick, drunk conduct was that I could take a beating. I didn't like it. But I could take it. And I could always get up for more.

I had not yet learned, but soon would, that not only can I take a beating—get hurt, knocked down again and again and always get up—but also that *when* I get up, I will get you and *you will be sorry*.

CHAPTER 2

Smithtown, Long Island, pretty much finished my dad off. The cozy suburb, forty miles from New York City, was the closest place he could afford to buy a larger house, a split ranch with bedrooms for each of his kids, which was something that as a 1950s family man, desperate and drunk though he was, he felt compelled to provide.

Smithtown was developed after the war to accommodate soldiers returning from Iwo Jima and the Ardennes and other battle sites, who would have been happy to live *anywhere* on U.S. soil and so didn't mind living in a flat, sterile, disassociated, and, at the time, treeless suburb. It was sleepy and it was lifeless.

Aside from the vets, mostly Irish and Italian, Smithtown's population consisted of people from places like Jackson Heights who had had the strange and baffling experience of running into a black person somewhere in Queens and, as soon as possible thereafter, packed up their families and drove as far as they had to go to get somewhere where they could be with their own people and not have to worry about running into any more black people ever again.

As a consequence, unlike in the busy, lively world of Jackson Heights, where you saw the same people all the time, not just once a week but several times each day, you never saw *anyone* in Smithtown. The streets were quiet except for the occasional station wagon making its way to the supermarket next to a chain of strip malls and car dealerships that looked like they'd been spread with a butter knife over a lot that had once been a potato field and that could be reached only by car. Not that anyone in Smithtown tried to go to the store or anywhere else on foot.

In Smithtown, the neighbors and friends and kids to fight in the alley were replaced by people who kept their distance and, except on their way to work or the market, pretty much stayed inside their $15,000 houses and had their kids play not in the streets but on swings and bikes they kept fenced in their yards. My dad had a rough commute—an hour each way to the Sperry plant in Queens—and the long drive and relative isolation at home accelerated his drinking, which did not improve our lives any.

"Dukie! Who's yer Daddy, Dukie? Who loves you, boy?" My father moved us to Smithtown partly because we could have a yard; that's what upwardly mobile people wanted. My father used ours to raise dogs, two at a time, beagles first and then boxers. Duke, a big brown boxer, was his favorite. *"Dukie. Who loves you, boy?"* He talked to that dog more than he talked to me or Steven. Like most everything else we did or had, Dukie caused big problems, but that was later, a year or so after we moved to Smithtown.

Being far from friends and people she grew up with was tough on my mom, but she pretty much did what she always did—namely, got up, laid our clothes out in neat piles at the foot of our beds each morning, made our breakfast, and went to work. Soon after we moved to Smithtown, my mom started work at Macy's in Bayshore wrapping packages. She worked that job, standing on her feet all day tying parcels with brown paper and string, for something like six dollars an hour, until she was in her late sixties. At that point Macy's decided, maybe to save on insurance costs, to get rid of some of the company's older employees. The store couldn't fire people like my mother who had been there for years, but it could harass them a little and try to get them to leave, which is what it did and which my mother, owing to the strange trajectory my life took, had occasion to mention in the mid-1980s to my then friend John Gotti's tough-guy lawyer, Bruce Cutler, over salmon and pâté at a mutual friend's christening.

"You know, Mrs. Hayes, that wouldn't be right if they did that to you, if they pushed you out after all those years." Cutler talks like a guy who gargles Brillo pads for breakfast.

"If they bother you, you get up, take them to the window, and say to them, 'You see them trucks in that parking lot? If you keep bothering me, there ain't going to be no trucks in that parking lot for a long, long time!' " Cutler tells my mom. "Will you tell them that for me, will you tell them that, Mrs. Hayes?"

My mother turns to me.

"Is that true, Eddie? Is it true? Can he really do that?"

"It's true, Mommy. It's really, really true," I tell her. "He definitely can do that."

And so she does exactly what Bruce Cutler tells her, dropping his name quite prominently, and the harassment ceases instantly and she works until retirement in peace.

That's in the eighties. Back in 1962 my mother is busy moving paintings around on the walls of her new dining room in Smithtown, Long Island, trying to cover up holes my father has left in the plaster slamming her into the wall. He hits her in the face, everywhere, all the time. And he rants and raves and calls her names and says things like, "If it weren't for you, Jean, I could have been a state senator." It is all irrational. It is all drunken. And as my father's drinking increases, which it steadily does after we move to Smithtown, so does the violence. In no time, the house on Oxford Lane, like the other houses we've lived in—in Jackson Heights, Greenville, Charlottesville, Garden Bay Manor—begins to *smell* like terror.

—

"You drove me to this, Jean. *I don't want this, Jean!* You did this. I can't stand that noise anymore."

My father has a knife in his hand. A big, long knife from the drawer next to the sink in the kitchen. My brother is upstairs with a cough. I come down to see why the dogs are barking.

"You? Who asked you to interfere?" my father says when he sees me standing in my pajamas, looking in the kitchen door. "I know how to keep you quiet. I know how to get some peace around here. Come here," he says, holding the knife up over his big, awful, and now trembling face. "I'll show you what I can do."

My father has threatened us and beaten us many, many times. But I can't remember ever seeing a knife in his hand before.

My mother registers a new level of danger. There is a confused, vaguely terrified look on my father's face, as if my mother and not he has the knife in hand and she and not he is yelling and screaming. He watches as my mother marches out of the kitchen, grabbing my arm on her way out.

"Follow me," she says, racing up the stairs. "Get your shoes on," she tells Steven, who is still in bed, sniffling in his pillow. She races into the baby's room, grabs my sister, hustles us all out the back door, and pushes us into the car, locking the door with one hand as she turns the ignition key with the other. We can see my father, still standing in the kitchen with that strange, confused expression, as we drive off toward the Jericho Turnpike and head south. No one says a word.

My mom is a few dollars short at the motel off the turnpike ten miles from our house, but a woman who comes in with her husband, and must feel badly about whatever she imagines has happened to us, gives my mom the money. "Bless you," my mother says, ever the good churchgoing girl. And we go inside and go to sleep as if it were the most normal thing in the world for your mom to pull you out into the night and take you to a motel where you can get a good night's sleep in a big double bed with scratchy sheets.

"I'll be back soon, Eddie," my mom says the next morning. "You and Steven watch the baby." She drives to Oxford Lane, finds my father passed out upstairs, and decides, based on much experience, that it's safe to bring us back. Leaving my father facedown on the bed, she drives back to the motel to get us, but not before reaching her hand into my father's pocket and removing a few bills, which, as she later tells me, is something she continues to do whenever she finds my father passed out (which she reliably does several times a week) for the next eight or nine years.

And, as she also later tells me, at the end of every week, beginning with the morning after the night in the motel off the Jericho Turnpike, she deposits the money she takes from my father's pocket into the private account she eventually uses to pay college tuition for my brother and me. Unable to protect either herself or her children, my mom decided, she says, that she owed us something. During the brief period we lived in Charlottesville she had seen the University of Virginia, its gracious grounds, long lawns with sugar-gum trees, stately domed buildings, and decided, with complete conviction, "This is it, a classy institution: my boys are going here."

The drinking continued after that night in the kitchen and so did the beatings and the rage. We never again saw a knife in my father's hand, but my mother remained alert to what I know she considered the very real possibility he might again threaten or try to kill us. I'm sure she would have taken us somewhere much farther away than the turnpike motel if he had.

———

"Peggy Sharkey, I want to kiss Peggy Sharkey." I go with a crowd of kids to a party after school one afternoon and we play a game that involves each of us awkward white Smithtown High School kids picking somebody to kiss. No one picks me. I pick Peggy Sharkey, who is a year older. *"Peggy Sharkey, I want to kiss Peggy Sharkey."* Forget about that. Peggy Sharkey leaves the room as soon as I say, or maybe as soon as I think to say, her name.

At five foot nine, I weigh 105 pounds: I'm a skinny, absurd kid with not the slightest clue what to do with people other than dodge their punches and try to keep them from beating my balls in. Having spent almost all of the time between my eighth and thirteenth years fighting, I don't have a great sense of how to behave in school, much less how to talk to or otherwise interest Peggy Sharkey or anyone else.

In every high school class, there is a girl who is at least seven inches taller than everyone else. In later life she may be a supermodel, but in high school she is bigger than all the guys. In my Smithtown High School class, the giant is called Sharon Wilson. I invite Sharon to go with me to the junior prom and she accepts. *Scheme, hustle, move, and score.* But now I have a real problem: clueless about how to talk to people, I also have no idea how to dance; what the fuck will I do at a prom?

"Dance with me, Mommy," I say to my mother one day when she gets home from work, and she, who was and is a very good dancer, is (as always) game. We practice the Mashed Potato in the living room, bopping around to the radio; whatever is playing she likes. I practice in my room, without the radio, for hours, and my efforts pay off. Sharon Wilson, apparently surprised by my dancing, is nice to me at the prom and even makes out with me at the end of the night.

—

Surprisingly, given that I am a skinny kid and have little athletic ability, football provides me with the only standout moments of my high school career. I can't catch and I can't throw, but I start on the junior varsity football team as an outside linebacker, a position I get primarily because I manage to evince a solid understanding of the principles of the game, which as I understand them are: watch the guy with the ball and run into him with all your strength, something I am always willing to try, even when it is obvious the physical odds are not in my favor. More than once this carefully studied philosophy of the game brings me unanticipated but great success.

Slosh. Slosh. *Thwack.* On a muddy field in October, the Smithtown eleven are up against Wyandanch High and its team of tough guys, the overwhelming majority of whom are black and very happy to be running around on a wet field knocking over a bunch of white guys again and again. In the final minutes of the game, owing not to athletic superiority but to pure dumb luck, the Smithtown white boys have the edge and, if we can keep Wyandanch from scoring, can win and go home and have a meatloaf or boiled-beef dinner. (The Italian kids on the team will, of course, get real food with actual taste and maybe even a good-looking gravy instead of the brown, runny liquid that looks like it leaked out of an old car.)

The offensive lineman, who's knocked me down about six or seven times and is clearly tired of kicking my ass in the rain, has me down in the mud when I look up and see another black guy running with the ball, in reach of the goal line. I get up. I take off, slosh through the mud, and smack straight into the guy, who slides in the mud and falls to the ground just short of a touchdown. The cheerleaders (including Peggy Sharkey) go nuts. Skinny little Eddie Hayes stopped No. 76, the huge Wyandanch fullback, from scoring!

I have no upper-body strength (no lower-body strength either) and absolutely did not mean to tackle this truck. Find the guy and run into him. That was the strategy. That it actually worked is as surprising to me as it is to the people cheering, so gratifyingly, in the Smithtown spectator stand. (In retrospect, it occurs to me that the inadvertent moment of glory on the football field may have reinforced my general sense about the interesting possibility that I could outsmart those I couldn't overcome with physical force.) My mother and brother aren't at the game. (My father never came.) But man, it feels good to hear people cheering for me.

Other than those few moments on the football field, no one pays much attention to me during the rest of high school. I continue my find-the-guy-with-the-ball-and-run-into-him-hard approach to the game, but the rest of my football career, like the rest of my adolescence, is short on big moments and mostly involves my taking a lot of beatings.

"My fucking son killed my dog. My fucking goddamn son killed my dog."

My dad is pounding his own head up, down, up, down on the kitchen table when I get home from school one day. Duke took off across the lawn, my dad tells me between paroxysms of misery; a truck came up the street, hit the dog, and killed it. I thought I locked the gate to the dog run in the back of the house when I left that morning. My father says, "No, you little motherfucker, you didn't," and stays up all night going out to the backyard again and again, drinking and screaming, "What kind of a fucking maniac kid kills his father's dog?" He keeps us up with the screaming and, starting the next morning, pretty much beats me for three days straight. I don't know if any of the neighbors hear the screaming or not. They didn't say if they did.

No one said anything when my father beat me on the street on my way from school or at the playground in the summertime when school was out. There was absolutely nothing more embarrassing than having my father kick the shit out of me in front of other people, which he increasingly did, maybe because he knew how humiliating it was. Mortified, I did my best to keep clear of him, especially late in the day when he'd had enough time to empty the pewter mug of martinis. But it never occurred to me to complain to my father or anyone else. My job, as I understood things, was to take a beating and, if possible, to keep my mom and brother from having to take one.

There was just one time during my childhood when someone paid attention to me and what was going on in my house. It was during my last year in high school. A famous sociologist, Edgar Z. Friedenberg, the author of *The Vanishing Adolescent* and *Coming of Age in America*, came to Smithtown to do research; he interviewed me, almost by accident: I was one of many kids randomly selected to talk to him about home life and schoolwork.

"Did they send you to me specially?" says Friedenberg, leaning forward on an orange plastic chair in the Smithtown High School guidance counselor's office, after I answer a few of his questions.

Friedenberg is a dumpy guy with stains on his tie and stuff all over his shirt but he is very nice, very decent, and asks intelligent questions about what is happening in my life.

He looks genuinely shocked when I tell him there probably hasn't been a day in my life when I wasn't in danger of getting seriously hurt at home.

"Does anyone know about this?"

"No," I tell him. "I never told anyone before. No one ever asked."

"Why don't you tell someone?" he says.

"I am not going to tell anybody," I say.

Friedenberg is sympathetic though he doesn't have any advice for me. What advice could he give? My father isn't going to *kill* me. He is much more desperate than I am. By the end of high school I already have a sense of how abject and powerless a man must be to hurt his own children.

"I'm sorry. I really am," says Friedenberg. He looks genuinely sorry and it's not the dirty tie. "It sounds terrible, it really does. You're going to have to do the best you can with it, that's all."

This had a big effect on me. Years later I wrote Dr. Friedenberg a letter thanking him for the kindness he had shown me years before. He let me know I still had a shot at an okay life and that's all I wanted.

———

I'm fifteen years old when I see the Help Wanted sign in the window of the Old Tavern, a family restaurant in Smithtown where you can sit at a table with a red-and-white-check oilcloth on top and enjoy steak and potatoes or lasagna and an iceberg lettuce salad for a decent price. (My family never went out for dinner and I can only imagine what might have happened if we had gone and a waitress brought the wrong thing or looked at my dad the wrong way.) The place looks okay. *What the fuck*, I think, and I walk in and, taking a wild shot, tell Dottie Payne, the attractive forty-something-year-old woman who, as I later find out, owns the place, that I want to work.

Dottie Payne tells me she needs a dishwasher. "It's hard work," she says. "Fine," I tell her, "I'll do it."

Talking to people, meeting girls, and having friends: these were dubious propositions for an awkward, skinny kid who'd grown up in a house where most conversation ended in beatings. But sheer physical exertion, standing in the back in dirty steam by the sink in the greasy, hot (especially in the summer) Old Tavern kitchen, scrubbing lasagna baked into the bottom of pots until my sweat runs down the drain with the soap and the sauce and the grease—this is something I can do. No problem. I work every weekend, every holiday, every Christmas.

The fact that Dottie Payne has a lovely daughter makes the prospect of washing Dottie's dishes that much more appealing. I badly want to fool around with Dottie's daughter. But I never do. I just work hard.

Like the library, work gets me out of the house, plus work provides a little money. I go somewhere, do something physical, and people are happy with me! Nobody hurts me *and* they give me money! Work is an incredible discovery. I am a great, hard worker.

The guys scrubbing sauce out of pans in the Old Tavern kitchen are all black, except for me. This is in the early 1960s, before Spanish guys started working in kitchens in Suffolk County and all across America. It's my first experience with black people (the very people the Smithtown neighbors came to Smithtown to avoid), and the guys I work with are completely crazy, always cursing—"Dumb nigger motherfucker, you're a dead dumb nigger, man"—always threatening one another with knives. After working at the Old Tavern for a few seasons, I thought there was a law somewhere that if a black person was going to talk to another black person he had to have a knife in his hand.

Guys in Queens talk about how lazy niggers are and how they never work. But I nearly kill myself, sweating bullets in the greasy, hot Old Tavern kitchen and those black guys in there with me work twice as hard. Did I have any rapport with those guys? No. I didn't have much rapport with anybody. But the guys back there screaming and scrubbing and sweating had an effect on my relationship with black people that has lasted my whole life. They worked hard, really hard, and so long as they did, I didn't care if they called me names and threatened to beat my white balls off.

The guys in Dottie's kitchen helped me understand who I was. When they yelled "Nigger," they didn't mean me. I am a neighborhood white boy, and I'm starting to get a sense of what this means. Disadvantaged, maybe, by my skinny bones and social ineptitude, I nonetheless have a place in the world, in the culture of neighborhood white boys. Urban, Catholic, Irish, and Italian, neighborhood white boys grow up with working-class sensibilities and a general, almost congenial acceptance of the fact that, though they may know—and even be—guys who do well as brokers or lawyers, they won't have a lot of control of their lives and will instead answer to the politicians and big bosses who really call the shots.

If the Old Tavern dishwashers helped me understand who I was, the books I used to read in the library but now read at the oak wood desk my mom got for me at the Holy Comforter spring sale helped give me a clearer picture of who I *wanted* to be.

Having grown up in a house where I was incapable not only of protecting myself from my father's violence and rage but also of protecting my mother and brother, I wanted to find a way or a place in which I could feel capable, protected, and strong.

I'd taken my share of punches and expected, and was ready for, more. But I read a lot about Michael Collins and Conan and Abraham Lincoln and the other strong figures who took their knocks but didn't get beaten. I wanted to be someone like them, someone whom people paid attention to and treated like something other than a piece of garbage kicked back and forth across the street.

Gangsters use the expression *getting called out*. When someone needs protection, he *calls out* to you and, if you know what's good for you, you'll be there. Without knowing the phrase, or even that the phrase existed (much less that I would have eventual occasion to know quite a bit about gangsters and their ways), I knew as Smith-town graduation approached that I wanted to be a guy who would be there if you called and would stand up when the time came, as I desperately hoped it would.

———

I get up one morning in the spring of my senior year and go into the little kitchen with the small round table and three chairs in the center. My father is there, drunk already, beating my brother, who is sixteen and then, as now, quieter and more serious than I am. A bowl of cereal is mashed on the floor near the chair closest to the cor-ner. My father has my brother between the chair and the corner and is pounding him with his giant fists, knocking him onto the wet floor. This cannot continue.

"Leave him alone," I tell my father.

I move between them and face my father.

We are about the same height. I'm smaller but I haven't spent the better part of three decades drinking and I'm in better fighting form.

He looks me in the eye.

"Leave him alone," I say again.

Had I become a man my father might fear or even respect? He is too drunk to know.

He keeps swinging at my brother. I move closer, put my arm up to block the blow.

My father grabs me. I push him back.

"Keep your motherfucking hands to yourself," I tell him. "It's over. That part of our lives is over." And it is.

CHAPTER 3

"Mommy, Mommy, why are you crying?"

I'm home after school in the spring of my senior year. My mom is standing in the kitchen, holding her head in her hand. She isn't on the floor, where I'd found her a few times before. I put my books down.

"What is it, Mommy?"

"You heard from the University of Virginia."

She chokes back tears.

"Don't feel bad, Mommy. I'll get in *somewhere*."

"No. No. No," she whimpers. "You got in!"

"Mommy," I say, "then why are you crying?"

"I'm so happy, Eddie! I'm so happy."

I don't think I have ever seen my mother as happy as she was that day when the acceptance letter came from Charlottesville.

———

My dad drives. My brother, my sister, and I are in the back. My mom sits in the front of the blue DeSoto, beaming, as we drive up

University Avenue onto the grounds, past the immense rolling lawn bordered on each side by grand ash trees and at the end by a columned rotunda modeled after the Pantheon and meant to serve as the center of what Thomas Jefferson, the university's founder, imagined would be a lively "academical" village. Pretty flowers—lilies, marigolds, Virginia bluebells—bloom all over the place. Boys, most from southern prep schools, who've grown up slugging bourbon and hunting and sailing on their vacations, stroll the grounds in loose-fitting khaki pants and tasseled loafers. The whole place is shot through with the smell of flowers and an air of grace and refinement. I feel like I've landed on another planet.

I don't know a single person within hundreds of miles and I don't know a thing about UVA. I don't even know it is an all-boys' school. Until that morning, I've never even seen the place. But the idea had taken hold in my mother's mind, and maybe even in my father's too, that I would come here and that somehow this graceful, elegant institution would serve as the way out of all that they wanted to escape. (Also, Ted Kennedy went to UVA law school, so the place worked for the Irish; I'm sure this entered their thinking.)

Since discussion in my home routinely ended in beatings, it wouldn't have much mattered if we had talked about where I would apply to college, but we never did. UVA was the only place I applied to—I applied early decision and most likely got in on the strength of my standardized test scores, which, though always in the top percentile, were evidence, the school invariably told my mother, that I wasn't "performing up to potential." (I think my mom, who didn't have a clear sense of what "performing up to potential" meant, probably thought it meant working overtime.)

My mother and father walk me into Hancock House, the old brick dorm with the white-columned front where I'd live my first year. I have a tan Lark bag for the few shirts and pants my mom got me at Macy's and no idea what I am getting into. Other than some vague sense of gentility, my mother and father have no concept of where they are either. They are as out of it as I am. We hardly say a word as we walk in. We are all struck, I think, by the same instinctive sense that our Yankee accents will sound screechy and hard and foreign to the fine-looking people around us, all of whom seemed to be greeting one another with bright "y'all"s and "hi ya"s.

"You're a class act, Eddie, real UVA material." That's all my mom says as she hugs me. Then she turns around and gets inside the car to return to Long Island with my brother and sister and dad, who doesn't say a word. She means it, too—despite the obvious fact that a pimply-faced skinny kid from Smithtown with a ridiculous haircut and an accent no one within 150 miles can understand looks as much at home at UVA as on the moon. My clothes don't help: I have pants with zippered pockets, cheap short-sleeved shirts, and pointy black shoes that will stand out in the sea of penny loafers and tassels. *We'll see, Mommy,* I think as I watch my family drive off, leaving me, for the first time in my life, in a nurturing environment. *We'll see.*

I would have been amazed that afternoon to know that in a very short time I would be introduced to a whole new way of dressing, acting, and aspiring. And I would have been shocked to know how quickly I would come to understand that politics could be as effective a way to engage others and command respect as braining someone in an alleyway.

I was about to be put in touch in an amazingly visceral way with the drama of American history, which is the drama of immigrants coming to this country and improving themselves, not just materially but on every level. Quickly it would become clear that so long as I worked hard and displayed particular virtues, among them honor, independence, and a belief in group ideals, I would be accepted here and that this would be true whether I'd descended from southern aristocracy, prepped at an Episcopal school, or come from a bunch of numbers-running Irish bookies in Queens. A little condescension might greet the bookie's grandson, but if he was self-reliant and carried himself with grace and dignity (and got rid of his absurd zipper-pocket pants) he would be accepted; the place was, as its founder intended it to be, fundamentally meritocratic. I was about to become

proof of that. Not on the first day or in the first week in Charlottesville but very soon thereafter.

—

Sigma Phi Epsilon is a beat-up shit hole of a building. There's no
puke or urine in the hall or anything, but the place, another old brick
building supported by impressive white columns, gets trashed routinely and has been trashed routinely for the last ninety-five years.
The boys at SAE, the fraternity three blocks down from Sigma Phi
Epsilon, break the windows out of their identical brick house, with
identical white-columned front, every weekend; on Sunday, there
isn't a window left. Sigma Phi Epsilon isn't as rowdy—some of the
windows are actually in one piece at the end of the weekend.

The SPE brothers are linemen, not wide receivers, not quarter-
backs, not the stars or the big bruisers who run the team and get the
glory but the workingmen who do their jobs and keep the game going. They're cruder and rougher than the boys who join SAE and the
other houses; they come not from prep schools outside Atlanta but
from public schools in Ohio and Pennsylvania. I like them: they remind me of the guys at Smithtown; also it never occurs to me that
college life doesn't have to mean fraternity membership.

I'm at the house on pledge night a few weeks after school starts.
A bunch of guys stand around drinking beer, knocking shoulders. *I do
not have a fucking clue what to do*, I think. *Not a clue*. I recognize some of the
guys from the dorm, some from class.

I have no concept of "doing well at school"; the idea that you are
supposed to stay in your room and study is foreign to me. I mostly sit
in class and watch and never say anything. In fact, other than "How
are ya?" or "Burger, please" in line at the cafeteria, I haven't really
said much anywhere else, either.

Now, to save my life I cannot think of a single thing to say to any
of the guys standing around the keg in the dim light in the dark-
paneled, high-ceilinged living room of the Sigma Phi house. I stand
by the keg. No one pays attention to me.

"Yo! Willie, you kick ass," a guy from my English Literature from 1700–1900 class says to a thick-necked guy standing between me and the keg. "Brother, kick ass yourself," Willie says. I wait for something to happen. Nothing does. I unzip my absurd zipper pocket, put my hand in, and stand there, trying to look casual. I do not know what else to do.

"Ed Hayes. Nice to meet you," I say at last to Willie and his equally thick-necked friend. But my timing is off: the greeting blurts out from nowhere and makes an emergency landing in the center of an exchange I didn't even hear and couldn't understand if I had. My accent does not help. Willie looks at me as if I were a yodeling goatherd, nods, and gets back to whatever it is he was telling his buddy.

That's it. End of conversation. *Not going well,* I think.

I walk around the room looking for something to happen, someone to say something to me, but no one does. It's painfully awkward. What's the scheme? What's the move? I try hard to figure it out as I walk back to my dorm, strains of music mixing with the sounds of rowdy boys raising hell in the autumn night. Not surprisingly, I get word three days later that my pledge has been rejected: I am not invited to join Sigma Phi Epsilon.

———

Joe Fiorvanti stands in the doorway of Hancock House with his angelic-looking blond girlfriend. Fiorvanti, a star football player, lives in my dorm.

I've gone for a walk on the grounds and am on my way back to the dorm. A big guy, maybe six foot eight, looms between the door and the path to Hancock House. He watches me as I walk up the path in my goofy clothes and pointy shoes and starts cursing.

"*Yankee piece of shit. What do you want? Go home, you skinny Yankee asshole.*" He says this in a thick southern drawl I can barely understand.

I have no idea what to say to the guy. He is very, very drunk. Not that I would know what to say or how to talk if he were either sober or Thomas Jefferson himself. I stand there like an idiot, my skinny bones in my silly clothes, drenched in the familiar feeling *Geez, I have no idea what to do.*

"*Fucking Yankee, go home to New Yawk, ya piece of garbage.*"

"Please. Don't curse in front of my girlfriend," says Fiorvanti, who is still on the doorstep with her.

Fiorvanti's father is a hell of a bricklayer in Pennsylvania. If you know where a guy comes from and how he was raised, you can better understand who you are dealing with; I always make it my business to find out what I can about where a guy comes from. A guy whose father lays bricks is not afraid of work, physical work. To my good fortune, Joe Fiorvanti is also not afraid to stand up to a drunk guy who is offending his girlfriend.

"Fuck the Yankee," says the drunk.

"If you don't shut your fucking mouth," says Fiorvanti, "I am going to take your head right off your fucking shoulders. *Capice?*"

The drunk shrugs, staggers off, and that's the end of that. It is also the beginning of my transformation from a Smithtown geek into someone else: Joe Fiorvanti and I become friends, and Fiorvanti, a guy on football scholarship whom all the fraternity brothers like, gives me my first big break at UVA.

"Come with me," Fiorvanti tells me. "Stand there and shut the fuck up. If you talk with that crazy accent people may not like you." It's early spring when Sigma Phi Epsilon has another rush. "You're Sigma Phi Epsilon, Ed. These guys from the North will appreciate you—so long as you don't scare them with that crazy *New Yawk* talk." Fiorvanti has an eighteen-inch neck. He knows how the place works, and I hope that if he tells the brothers to take me, they'll take me. I go with him to the house in the blue blazer I bought at a small store in Charlottesville at Christmas to replace the shiny, tight rock-and-roll-style jacket I had when I arrived, and stand next to him and shake hands with the guys he introduces to me. I keep my mouth shut. I am not surprised but I am still damn glad when I get word, a few days later, that I am in. I'm in. I have a place.

To my immense satisfaction, I find that I can get along with other men, especially men like me, who have primitive but upwardly mobile social sensibilities, which my frat brothers do. They're rough, but they are also what politicians call good material: strong, ready, decent guys whom you can count on and who are easy to move ahead politically because they're smart and accustomed to working hard. As I am about to discover, despite my accent and initial cluelessness, I have a knack for moving ahead politically. Maybe it's genetic, something that my dad and the guys who took their punches at me along the way couldn't beat out of me no matter how hard they tried. Politics is in my blood, and as I am about to find out, I'm good at it.

By the end of my first year, the skinny kid from Smithtown is elected Sigma Phi Epsilon's delegate to the interfraternity council. It's a big deal. Cynics say no good deed goes unpunished. That is not my experience with the fraternity brothers (or anyone else for that matter). Joe Fiorvanti was good to me and so were the boys at Sigma Phi Epsilon, and it wasn't long before I figured out how to move them into positions of power within the school's political organization, which was a good way to ensure that my new friends and brothers got whatever goodies—front-row seats at sports events, free tickets to concerts—were available from the campus treasury.

———

"How could you do this to me? How could you do this to your father? We have no money. We have nothing. What were you thinking?"

A letter arrives from my mom just after spring break, just after I've gotten into Sigma Phi Epsilon. This isn't my mother's tone. I'm sure my father, who my mother has told me is drinking more than ever, had her write to complain about the sports jacket I bought over spring break. I feel awful. The jacket—it's red and brown—isn't even that stylish. I'd brought one jacket with me to Charlottesville and, until I replaced it with the one I wore when I rushed Sigma Phi

Epsilon, I wore it every day. I wanted more clothes. All the guys around me had these great-looking tweed sports coats. I wanted something like that.

During the summer after my first year, I make money working as a ditchdigger during the day and as a busboy at night. Before I return to Charlottesville in August, I go to Brooks Brothers on Madison Avenue in New York to get clothes with my brother, who is starting up at UVA.

"Can I help you, sir?" The salesman is crisp, polished, entirely at home in his starched shirt and a nice tie, both of which are clearly impervious to the ninety-five-degree summer heat. I'm so intimidated I drench myself with sweat and have to leave. I walk around the block twice before I have enough courage to go back and say, "Yes, I need help."

After a brief conversation about my needs and the weights of various fabrics, the salesman briskly, crisply shows me to the tweed coats, khaki pants, and a good pair of shoes. Hardly the hand-tailored Savile Row suits and custom-made English shoes I will learn to appreciate later on, but it is a start.

———

"You'll run, we'll have a good time." I'm trying to get Fiorvanti to run for student office when I get back to UVA with my new khakis and the tasseled loafers like the guys who went to St. Paul's and Groton always wear.

"I have no interest, Ed." Fiorvanti shakes his head slowly on his massive neck.

"C'mon! We'll do things, help our friends. It'll be fun."

Eventually he decides what the hell, and next thing I know I'm marching up and down the halls of Hancock House, knocking on doors, telling guys in seersucker robes or khakis from Eljo's to vote for Joe.

"Why should I support him?" says Bobby Pickett. He's from West

Virginia and I can't understand half of what he says but we like each other, maybe because we're two different kinds of rednecks on the make. "If you do," I tell him, "maybe I can get you set up with a nice dorm room next year." I can actually say this after the end of my first year, when I'm appointed dorm counselor, a prestigious post that comes with a free room (which is important since I don't have money) and also increases my clout and my ability to trade favors.

By the middle of the second year, I'm a walking favor bank. Politics, like work had been years earlier, is a great discovery. And I am as frantic a politician as I had been a street fighter as a kid; in terms of proving myself and getting recognition for standing up to anything, political maneuvering is as effective as—maybe even more effective than—taking on a bunch of guys or a bunch of nuns who could knock me around.

A good politician gets people what they want. You want chopped meat? I'll get you chopped meat. *Just tell me what you want.* This becomes the imperative at the heart of my rapidly developing political sense. I learn fast and my Irish instincts serve me well. My operating principle then, as now, is: I'll do for you today. I'll do for you tomorrow. I'll do for you every goddamn day. But if I ask you to do something for me, you better do it.

I figure out what the guys want and I get it for them. You want girls in your room? No problem. *Just tell me what you want.* You want an endless succession of black musicians doing concerts for a bunch of white guys, I'll get it.

What I want the guys to do for me is pay attention to me, take me seriously, and also vote for me, which they do. In the spring of my second year, I'm reelected to the interfraternity council and also to the University Union, which controls concert scheduling and ticketing.

Eventually, I learn that *Just tell me what you want* is not a bad approach to take with girls. But not while I am in Charlottesville. Here I have no success with girls whatsoever. None. I don't even rate as a failure. The guys go to mixers or are fixed up with girls from Mary

Baldwin or Randolph-Macon College down the road or, if they are substantial guys from prominent Virginia families with Porsches parked in back of the frat house, from Sweet Briar or Hollins College, where the elite girls go. I go along sometimes but never know what to do or what to talk about with the girls who ask me about my classes or what I'm reading.

"Thucydides. *The Federalist Papers,*" I tell Lisa, a pretty girl from Randolph-Macon who asks what I'm reading when I take her to dinner at a hamburger joint at the Corner, in Charlottesville, where there are smart bars and restaurants where students hang out.

"Chaucer, in English class," I continue. Lisa looks at me encouragingly as if to say "Uh-huh, interesting, and . . . ?" I can see she is asking for something but I don't know how to answer. "Chaucer. English class," I repeat, mostly to show her I'm alive, even though I'm incapable of figuring out the basics of how to be with a girl. I wait, speechless, for the waitress to come and take our order. *Soon food will come!* I think. And I can't wait until it does, because eating will give me something to do other than sit here feeling terrible and like a total flop. It would be years before I figure out how to talk to girls; by the time I did, I was a long way from Charlottesville and a long way from Lisa and her nice smile and polite questions.

—

"Whaddya doin' stickin' up for them niggers?" Some of the Sigma Phi Epsilon fellas give me a hard time when I march in support of the UVA janitors, roughly half of whom are black. "These guys are working," I tell Lionel and Tom, two Sigma Phi Epsilon linemen who make fun of me as they pass by. "They *have* to get paid a fair wage."

Lionel and Tom stride off on the lawn, the tassels on their shoes swinging back and forth as they go. I have no particular feelings about race or civil rights but I have strong feelings about work. If you kill yourself working, as these guys do, you should be treated right. I don't like that the university gives the janitors and other grounds workers thirty-two-hour workweeks so it won't have to provide the full benefits that kick in for employees who worked more than thirty-five hours. "I'm a janitor—I worked as one in the summer during high school and was a busboy at night," I tell the jocks who make fun of me later at the frat house. "And what they're doing to these guys isn't right. Fuck you."

The whole country is in a state of complete turmoil in the late sixties, but this is about as much as national politics touched my life at UVA. The nation is blowing up, hundreds of boys about the same age as me and my brothers at Sigma Phi Epsilon are coming home in body bags from Vietnam every month, but here, at least in my world of brothers and favors traded endlessly back and forth, the general attitude about Vietnam is: "War in Vietnam? Really? Fuck that, man! There's a kegger at Delta Kappa Epsilon! Paaaaarty!!!"

Maybe it was because UVA was conservative and militarily inclined and slow to adapt, or maybe it was because I was slow to adapt. But though there were certainly antiwar and civil rights demonstrations at UVA, I don't remember any; whatever demonstrations or expression of justifiable moral outrage against the war took place during those years failed to disrupt or even shape the tenor of college life in Charlottesville in late 1968, when I was entering my third year. I was ambivalent about the war anyway. I knew from reading history and from looking at maps of North Vietnam in geography class that the war was a lost cause. But the military was full of neighborhood white boys, lots of whom had been drafted to fight the war, and, though I had a very high draft number, I was one of them. Besides, as a patriot I felt that if there was a war I was in favor of it. I was an American.

The guys at Sigma Phi Epsilon don't riot about the fact that American soldiers are blowing up mothers and children in bamboo huts in a faraway jungle, but that does not mean they don't riot. Like the rest of the crew at UVA, they favor the bawdy southern-style brawling that is as deeply engrained in the school's tradition as Jefferson's fierce intellectualism and cultural refinement.

"Ooooo-eee." A freshman in trademark UVA costume, starched

button-down oxford shirt and khakis that fall two inches shy of the foot and so reveal the wet, buttery leather tassels on his Brooks Brothers loafers, leaps onto a table, its wood top carved to ribbons with initials and slogans like *DKE sucks* and *PJ is a pussy*, and chugs down a mugful of beer.

"Another, brother!" he calls to a fellow freshman identically outfitted, who stands by and hands up a fresh mug.

"Chug, chug, chug. Do it, Blaine. Do it," a bunch of first-year students gathered around the table chants.

Six steins later, Blaine jumps off the table, smashes a chair into the wall, and starts tearing the place up. The group follows suit, and soon everyone is riotous and crazed and busy trashing the place, which is a problem for me since, as dorm counselor, I'm supposed to keep things under control.

Immediately I think of war, not the one in Vietnam, but the Peloponnesian War, which I read about in Queens and in my first-year history class at UVA.

Just as the Athenian troops are about to invade Sicily, a spy returns from the front, visibly shaken, and tells Alcibiades, who is leading them, "Geez, there really are *a lot* of Sicilians in that army." Sensing the troops are rattled by the report and are losing nerve, Alcibiades stands before them and says, "You know, guys, I want to tell you something. If they lose, they get a new king; if we lose, we're dead. So *don't lose.*"

I know it sounds ridiculous, but as the frat boys take the house apart, I think too of Caesar, who was notoriously promiscuous and, in a dramatic moment in Roman military history, stood before his disquieted troops and tried to calm them by making fun of himself and his hypersexual (including, according to rumor, bisexual) appetites. He did a whole song and dance about the difference between a fruit and a vegetable and what you put where; it worked to calm the troops, who laughed, loosened up, and went out to stick it to whoever wanted to be anything but Roman.

So as the brothers trash the house, I think of Caesar and Alcibiades and the next thing I know, *I'm on the table.*

"You think *you* guys got problems?" I tell the brawlers, some of whom have by this point stained their loafers with beer and vomit. *"You're* raising hell. Jesus Christ! I wish I could raise hell. You think you have it rough? What about me? I'm here from New York. I don't know anybody. And I'm supposed to take charge of you guys. Now, how am I gonna do that? You're a bunch of lunatics!"

I'm hitting my stride, just like Julius Caesar.

"Ooooh, you guys have it soooo tough you have to trash the house! You should try being me! You think you guys got problems because you're away from home and nobody's watching you? What about me? I'm from New York, I don't know a girl for two hundred miles, and I'm supposed to control you and you're acting like a bunch of animals. Calm down or you're going to get in trouble. You're new here, be careful."

I have no idea why, but it works: the guys calm down, stop ripping the ceiling off. I became semifamous for quelling a riot, a lot of the older student leaders take notice, and this helps a lot with my own career as a campus leader. I am a New Yorker, an Irish politician, basically a scheme-hustle-move-and-score guy, always thinking, *What are the moves? How can I advance? What is to be gained here?* It's a type they aren't familiar with at UVA.

———

I'm at my desk, in a gray wool suit, pink shirt, striped tie, and very, very shiny shoes, one evening in the fall of my fourth year at UVA. And I'm listening for a knock at the door.

Eli Banana, one of two so-called ribbon societies at UVA, dates back to 1878 and is an honorary society for hell-raisers, for a select group of boys who brawl with real style and class, many of whom go on to run textile companies in Georgia or big farms in Virginia. UVA's other ribbon society, TILKA, is for leaders, for what New Yorkers call big *machers*; just ten or twelve guys, mostly southerners, get in each year. You don't try out for TILKA Society, you are elected. Society members march by in the night and, in a ritualistic ceremony, "tap" you by knocking on your door and draping you with silken ribbons; all together then, the TILKA Society members and their inductees march across the grounds in procession, a keg held high above their shoulders, ribbons bright in the autumn air.

I had some hooks in at TILKA; I knew lots of guys there; due to the heavy volume of my favor trading by the time I was in my fourth year at UVA, I pretty much knew guys everywhere on the grounds. And I knew I was going to be tapped. That's why I'd gone to Wallach's to buy the gray wool suit and why I was listening intently for the knock on the door, which came shortly before 10:00 p.m., just as I'd been told it would.

My friends told me that some of the TILKA members were horrified by the prospect of taking me in, but my friends let them know that if I *didn't* get in there would be a lot of unhappy fellows around the place.

Whatever they'd said or done, here I was, just three years after my parents dropped me off with the absurd ducktail haircut and the ridiculous zippered pants, marching across the grounds with the school's leaders, living proof of Jefferson's meritocratic ideal. A month later I was elected president of the interfraternity council. Soon thereafter I was named head dorm counselor. Now I was a genuine hotshot. And I found going home particularly unpleasant.

My father's alcoholism started to really peak while I was finishing up at UVA. He left his job, maybe because he couldn't stand the humiliation of watching other guys get promoted. "He doesn't want to work for someone else anymore," my mother told me. They were going to Ottawa, she said. He was going to start up a business selling paint to stores.

It seemed bizarre to me. My father knew one guy from Queens who'd moved to Canada, years before, but other than that, he didn't know anyone there. Why would anyone buy paint from him? Why would he sell paint? How would I know? I was busy maneuvering guys into good dorm rooms, good positions in the student government, and plum, often paid, jobs with the university. I was nobody's idea of a conscientious scholar, but I majored in and genuinely enjoyed government—my Irish-politician genetic heritage asserting itself.

"We're in trouble, Eddie," my mother wrote in letters from Canada that foretold my father's eventual financial ruin. I didn't know what to do and couldn't have helped even if I'd wanted to, which I did not.

———

I'd filled out my application to Columbia Law School when I went to visit my parents in Canada for what would be my last trip home. I had my own room and was a big man on the grounds and had had a taste of how it felt to have respect, to be admired and envied. I wanted more of that.

Ernie Peace, a tough-guy lawyer I remembered at the center of all the action in Jackson Heights, was pretty much all I had in the way of a professional model. He was a cop who'd become a lawyer after studying in night school, and in very short order he'd moved from doing house closings and DUIs to being one of the top criminal lawyers on Long Island. He was an honest, straightforward guy and you'd have to kill him to make him back off from something he felt wasn't right. He wasn't afraid of anything or anybody; you couldn't roll over the guy: you had to pay attention to him. Unlike me, even after my years in Charlottesville, Ernie Peace was a guy who would know what to do when someone, especially his own mother, said, "I'm in trouble." So I'd go home to New York, go to law school, and be like Ernie Peace: that was it for my career planning.

The place my parents had in Ottawa was small. My father had ballooned to close to three hundred pounds and hardly fit in the shabby one-bedroom apartment. It was very depressing and awful. The food sucked and it was freezing and dour beyond description.

I never visited again.

CHAPTER 4

These guys are fucking nuts. My first contact with my law school class-mates leads me to think, *These guys are completely fucking nuts.*

I'm on the subway going home to the small apartment I've rented off Broadway in the West Eighties, after an orientation meeting with older students. Tad Weiss, a student adviser who'd been at the meeting and is about to begin his third year at Columbia, sits next to me on the train.

"Didn't do well in Trust and Estates or Commercial Transactions last year," he says as the train roars through the tunnel. "I guess it's good to know early on that I won't be going far in life."

Won't be going far in life?!

This guy actually thinks his life is over because he got a couple of Bs in law school! *Jesus Christ,* I think. *I'd kill myself if I thought that way at age twenty-three.*

I nearly have a heart attack when I find out that Columbia Law School is full of guys like Tad Weiss, guys who work around the clock and knock themselves out to get better grades so they can get jobs where they can work around the clock and knock themselves out to make partner and better salaries, which they won't have time to spend because they'll be working around the clock.

———

I'm fresh from Charlottesville, looking for excitement, thinking about Ernie Peace and the kind of action that followed him as he swaggered into a room. But by the time our train pulls into the Eighty-sixth Street station after that first orientation meeting, I already have a strong sense that law school doesn't have anything to do with anything exciting.

During the rest of orientation week, guys like Tad tell me and the other first-year students about the big salaries they made at their summer law jobs. Yeah, they say, they had to account for every six minutes of their time, it was a drag, but you get used to it, and the money is great and it's okay in the end. Again I think, *Man, these guys are fucking nuts!* Nobody asked me to account for my time when I worked for five dollars an hour digging ditches or busing dishes. Why the fuck would I go to law school so I could do that? It dawns on me that I really have no concept of what law school is, not to mention what it is that most lawyers do all day long.

I am about to find out that law school is more or less about reading an enormous amount of material, a lot of which can actually be done very quickly in the three or four days before exams. I was not a good law student: I missed a lot of classes, didn't pay much attention when I went, and usually did all the required reading in those last days before exams, which, owing to my ability to focus and remember, I managed to pass.

I learned a lot at Columbia Law School—about smart Jews, gorgeous Dominican women, rough black street toughs, bodybuilding, and clubs full of gangsters and transsexuals. But I regret not having been a better student, as I probably could have learned something about law while I was there, too.

"Hi. How ya doin'?" It's my first week at Columbia and I am walking home when I see a very attractive girl all done up in a red leather coat and high-heeled boots standing on Amsterdam Avenue near the law school at 115th Street. She smiles at me and says, "Real good, thanks." Her skin is dark cocoa brown and she has a beauty mark pasted on the left side of her upper lip. I know about prostitutes, which is what the woman in the leather coat turns out to be, but you didn't see prostitutes on the streets of Smithtown or at UVA and I haven't had anything to do with one before. "Show you a good time for fifteen dollars," she says. Sounds like a fair deal to me. We go to my place and have a miserable experience—mostly because I don't know what to do.

"Here, you take this back," she says afterwards and hands me my money. "It wasn't right."

"Nah," I tell her. "It was more my fault than yours."

"Okay," she says. "But why don't you come and see me sometime?" She writes an East Village address on a gum wrapper.

When I get to her place a few days later, she is on the way out with her pimp, on the run from the police. Everyone is yelling and screaming and I, a skinny-assed twenty-one-year-old neighborhood white boy, walk up and chirp, "Hey! How ya doin'?" The pimp shoots me a mean who-the-fuck-are-you look, grabs my hooker friend's arm, and pulls her into a gray four-door Buick parked on the street. I hear him cursing as they drive off.

Nothing more happens, but it is just the beginning: I am getting the idea that there are an awful lot of different worlds shoved up together in New York, a lot of which are more interesting than what's going on in the law library.

I'm game to take chances and New York is full of them. I've come to Columbia to learn to handle problems for people and I don't see how you can learn how to handle anything if you stay in the library all the time. The library is full of guys bent over books, guys who never looked away from civil procedure texts and thought, *Jesus Christ! Somebody just invented Dominican girls. I've got to check this out!* I, meanwhile, had just discovered God created Jewish, Latin, African, Asian girls, as well as all-American blondes, and I definitely want to find out more. The adventure I had with the hooker I met on Amsterdam and 115th Street gives me the idea it wouldn't be bad to stay on the streets and further my education out there.

—

I wander around Times Square at night. This was not the cleaned-up, Disneyfied Times Square of Mike Bloomberg's New York. In the seventies Times Square was colorful and dirty and dangerous—the way God intended it to be. Streetwalkers and junkies are everywhere. The lights are bright and if you poked around, which I did, on the streets off Broadway in the Forties, there are plenty of transsexual joints, topless bars, after-hours clubs where I spent a lot of time during law school.

Dirty Edna's, a scuzzy hole-in-the-wall off Forty-fourth Street where I go often and listen to Frank Sinatra and the Four Tops on the jukebox, is not strong on people who work for a living. In fact, most of the crowd at Dirty Edna's and at most of the other area joints is made up of lowlife guys who look like they haven't worked in twenty years but somehow have pocketfuls of money and seem mostly just to stand around, waiting to get indicted. The clubs have a raw, primal energy I like. I go in, nod at a girl, usually one dressed in clothes that could get her arrested if she wore them on the street, and dance for hours.

Sometimes I would go to the Gold Rail, a bar near the law school that was popular with jocks and conservative Columbia guys. I wasn't conservative, athletic, or a drinker. Not after what I'd seen at home. But I often went in and had orange juice and talked to the guys there, including a bright, very straight, wholesome guy who had grown up on a farm, had had an idyllic childhood, loved his mother and his hardworking father, who worked for the postal service, and couldn't have been from a family more unlike the Hayeses of Smith-town, Long Island. George Pataki really believed in the virtue of small-town America and the immigrant sensibility; *my* vision of the immigrant mentality involved the bathroom at Donahue's pub, where a bunch of guys set up the IRA and figured out how to firebomb their enemies, but I told Pataki about my dad and how alcohol messed up his life, and he listened and I liked him. I thought there was a real bond between us. We forged a real friendship in the Gold Rail and kept talking throughout my years in law school.

But women remain the main event throughout my law school career. "You won't even talk to me," says Amy, an attractive woman I met soon after starting at Columbia and badly wanted to go to bed with. *What the fuck would I talk to you about?* I think. *You're a girl.*

It takes a while—my childhood gave me a skewed view of intimacy that took time to overcome—but gradually I find I can get along with women, especially ones who, like the guys at Sigma Phi Epsilon, shared a primal, rough-edged ambition similar to my own.

I couldn't, for example, talk to Cathy Dexter, the athletic blonde I went around with at the start of law school, but I could relate to her. An ambitious, hardworking woman from an Irish working-class family in Waltham, Massachusetts, she was going to graduate school in business administration and, like me, was definitely on the way up.

No way Cathy Dexter was going back to Waltham to live in the kind of working-class neighborhood where she'd grown up. She'd work as hard as was necessary to put money in the bank and some fancy cars in the driveway of the house she'd buy, a house substantially bigger and nicer than the one in which her parents lived.

"Get the fuck away from me," Cathy tells a guy who rushes out from a crowd near Times Square when we're together walking down Forty-third Street one night. The guy grabs her handbag and throws it to another guy waiting near the corner. Cathy, who is on my arm, pulls back. I turn around, see what's happening, and lose Cathy's grasp as I lunge for the guy with her bag. Looking up, I see that she's holding the first guy by the throat, all the while cursing at his accomplice, "Get the fuck back." *Cathy Dexter is a tough broad, my kind of girl,* I think as the guy steps back with a strained, deferential look and hands back her bag. What's a tough, upwardly mobile girl with an all-American cheerleader face and a great body doing with a jerk like me? By the time I hook up with Cathy, I am clearly an aspiring guy and, though I still have about as much sensitivity as a cash register, must seem like a good catch.

Eventually, though, Cathy left me for a nice guy whom she later married. Her departure, which was as amicable as our time together, might well have had something to do with the fact that around the start of my second year of law school I began a series of compulsive involvements with other women.

Dominican women! Jewish women! Black women! For a ready guy who was not holed up in a library all day, New York City in the fall of 1971 was full of spectacular opportunities. And the broad range of experience I started to enjoy with women transformed my life—and my body—in all kinds of unexpected ways.

———

"Eddie, sad news. Mike Fiori is dead." Fiori, a good-looking Italian guy from Smithtown, had gone to Vietnam. My mother is on the phone telling me he's come home in a box. She and my father have moved back to Long Island from their grim Canadian exile. I never talked to Fiori—I didn't really talk to anyone at Smithtown High—but I knew who he was and I felt for the guy. After high school, he'd been nabbed loading television sets off a truck parked outside the electronics store where he worked; given a choice between copping to a crime or going into the service, Fiori decided to enlist in the marines. It's a myth that just black guys went to Vietnam; a lot of the guys who fought and died there were working-class white guys like Mike Fiori who got involved in the same story in Vietnam or elsewhere—viz., they were taken advantage of by bosses of one kind or another, who sent them out to do a job that enriched the bosses while costing the white boys, if not their lives, very often their physical and mental health and their dignity. Fiori wasn't the only white boy I knew who didn't come back from Vietnam. I didn't like the idea of more neighborhood white boys being sent to die there, which is why I'm on the downtown number 1 train in the fall of 1971 on my way to a demonstration against the war in Vietnam.

"One, two, three, four. We don't want your fucking war." A bunch of people, mostly young, a lot with longish hair like mine is now, are chanting in the street when I get downtown. I join the demonstration and march up Lower Broadway. "Ho Ho Ho Chi Minh, NLF is going to win," we chant. We don't get far when a group of construction workers jumps into the street and starts to attack. It does not occur to me to run. People attack, you get beat up—that was my experience. I stay put. Except for some militant Black Panthers and a few white guys who are too slow, almost everyone else gets out of there quick.

A huge construction worker takes a kid by the head and starts smacking him with a helmet. I go to kick the guy in the crotch but he is big as a house and I can't get my foot anywhere near him. He starts swinging, but in a crowd situation it's hard to beat someone unless you can get him down and stomp his head. He's swinging at me and I'm thinking, as I often thought when I was a kid, Okay, Eddie Hayes is going to get kicked up and down the sidewalk again. But some cops step in and break things up. One grabs me. I break loose and head toward the uptown train. Along the way, I run into a guy I know, a hippie who sells drugs and has introduced me to a very funny, very smart Jewish woman named Arlene, who is ten years older than me and very sexy.

Arlene, who has never shown any interest in me before, evidently likes what she hears about me and the demonstration and decides to knock my brains out. After dinner at her big apartment on Riverside Drive, she leans forward and takes my hand, her great, big frizzy Jewish hair falling over her nice olive-complected skin, leads me into her bedroom with a big river view, and half kills me in her big iron bed, which, of course, is just fine with me.

Maybe there is something to this social activism business! I think to myself as

I leave Arlene's big bed with the wonderful soft sheets. *If I can get this every time I take a little beating, I'm ready!*

That evening I make another, slightly more sober resolve—one that changes my life.

Next time I kick some guy in the crotch, I decide, I am going to hurt him.

I start karate a couple of days later. There is a martial arts school on Amsterdam and Ninety-third Street. It's a storefront—no name, no sign—that I pass on my way home from Columbia. As far as I can tell, no white guy has ever entered the place. Everyone there is black or Hispanic. I've only been around guys like this in the kitchens and on the trucks. But these guys are different. A lot of them have strong ideologies, sophisticated, militant politics. Some are thugs or gangsters; some are guys from the street. Without exception they are nice and very polite to me.

The instructor, Gerald Orange, says things like, "Stab your enemy with a car antenna, hit him with a brick—hit him with something! Better yet, if you can, throw the guy out the window and be done!" I learned a lot.

In addition to the hours I spend every day doing karate, I start running and doing hundreds of push-ups a day, I don't like law school any better as I get closer to finishing, and I am doing terribly; all the running and karate is a good escape valve. It works out nicely: my days of physical ineptitude are coming to an end, and as I get in better and better shape, which I quickly do, I have even *better* luck with women.

It doesn't hurt that I start to be really fit in 1972, when the feminist movement is in full swing, which—among matters of consequence to our country and my eventual law practice—means that the Upper West Side of Manhattan is full of thirty-something Jewish (and other) women who are divorcing husbands they have found insufficiently sensitive to their new needs. To my surprise (and delight), a lot of these women find it empowering—and fun!—to sleep with new and much younger guys.

"Hmm. Yes. Health bread. Seven grains," I tell the woman inspecting the kohlrabi in the produce aisle at the health store on Broadway not far from Columbia. "Good with cucumbers," she says. She has a lot of that frizzy Jewish hair that drives me wild. "Call me sometime," she tells me at the register and writes her number on a matchbook. Her name is Eve. She's going through a divorce, she tells me over the dinner she makes for me in her apartment; before dessert (blueberry cobbler) we're in bed. Buy health bread, bump into a woman, leave with her number in my pocket—*boom*, I'm in bed with her! This is the way it goes during those years, again and again: all I had to do was go to the health food store on Broadway and Ninety-ninth Street and stand in the vegetable aisle or by the yogurt case and something would happen.

—

Poll Watchers Wanted: Mississippi Voter Rights Activists Looking for Student Volunteers. A sign printed on 8 x 11 paper and tacked to a bulletin board outside the entrance to the law school catches my eye. I don't give a fuck about Mississippi or rights, and if I had a social conscience I would sell it. But the trip might be exciting, I think (*Something might happen*), and maybe there would be some fringe benefits involved, of the kind I'd enjoyed with Arlene after the antiwar demonstration. I call the number printed on the sign and volunteer.

In November of 1972 I'm a long way from New York and the apartment I now share with my brother, Steven, who is in his second year at Columbia Law. I'm on a hot back road dotted with tar-paper-roofed shacks in what is rightly thought a dangerous and remote area near Meridian, Mississippi, where, in 1964, three young civil rights workers—Andrew Goodman, James Chaney, and Michael Schwerner—had famously been pulled over and shot. My job is to observe voting procedures and make sure everything is fair and proper.

Early Tuesday morning, I'm leaning up against a cinder-block wall in some hot, damp Neshoba County recreational center, watching guys wander in and out of the makeshift polling place. Watching, that's something I'm good at. I've been there just an hour or so when a bunch of rednecked guys I'd seen earlier return to the rec center, saunter over, and line up again and then once again to pull the levers on the gray metal voting machines.

"Hey, whaddya think you're doin', fellas?" I say to two big guys I've watched walk over to the voting machine at least two, maybe three times. My New York voice grates on my own ears with a violence I haven't experienced since my first week in Charlottesville six years earlier. The next thing I know I'm surrounded by sheriffs, big, sweaty-faced southern-style sheriffs with holsters on their thick waists. *Oh, man,* I think as I often have before, *I'm definitely getting killed now.*

One of the sheriffs clears his throat, steps forward, and spits at his shoes. The two guys to his right watch carefully as he nods his big, fat head slightly to the left, signaling me to move toward the door, where I can see a crowd of fifteen to twenty southern gentlemen suddenly gather, all with an apparent interest in beating me to a pulp.

I sweat bullets as the sheriffs muscle me out the door just inches beyond the crowd's punching range. As they do, two black guys, an old, lean, very muscular man and a short, thick, much younger guy, move forward. The stocky guy opens his coat. "Okay," he says to the sheriffs, who take stock of the pistols on both sides of the black guy's belt, "which one of you motherfuckers wants to call me a nigger first?"

Jesus fucking Christ, I think, *I am never getting out of here alive.* The guy with the pistols grabs me, pulls me over, and pushes me inside a beat-up truck against which the old black guy stands with a rifle balanced on the truck hood and pointed at the crowd.

"You drive," says the old guy, nodding to the younger guy with the guns, who is already behind the wheel, and we're out of there at about eighty-five miles an hour on a dusty unpaved road. The kid is unbelievable; he doesn't swerve or brake as we head off, out of the backwoods. *Now I'm having fun,* I think. *This is exciting!*

"Take me with you," I tell the black guys when, after the high-speed adrenaline-pumping ride, they deposit me at the shacklike house in Meridian where I am staying with a host family. "Nah. You stay here, crazy white boy!" the younger guy says and gets back into the truck.

At dinner with my host family, a congenial black man, his wife, and a few unidentifiable relatives, I find out that the guys who hauled my white-boy ass out of the woods had come from Chicago to Mississippi with Charles Evers, the brother of slain NAACP leader Medgar Evers. I think, *You never know who is going to step up and save you when you're up against the wall.*

I went to Mississippi hoping to find adventure and excitement, and maybe even a nice girl who wanted to reward what she'd mistaken for my commitment to others. I returned with a renewed sense that in contemporary life, as in history, the strong exploit the weak and eventually the weak rebel and that, in the struggle for fair treatment, hell often breaks loose and that there may be some goodies involved for those ready to leap into the mess left when things fall apart. I would eventually take on many clients for similar reasons. I think everyone should have a chance, and if I helped protect that chance, there might be adventure or excitement or profit in it for me.

—

Back at Columbia I was working so hard I didn't have much time to think about social justice or chaos. I was working not at law school, of course, but on my outside interests. My schedule was brutal: in addition to the hours I spent at the gym and running and doing karate, I worked several jobs in order to pay tuition and cover my living expenses. On weekends I worked as a law clerk for Simpson, Thacher, a big corporate law firm, and at nights I worked as a bartender at an East Side pub called Paddy Quinn's, which was owned and operated by a couple of hoodlums and was almost always full of criminals and a big assortment of substantial New York guys who subsidized their endeavors. The jobs—and the differences between them—helped clarify what I already knew about myself and made it that much easier to decide what I wanted when I finished law school.

———

"Get Frankie on this. He can take care of it."

Frankie Smith, who managed Paddy Quinn's, is a great safe-cracker. I'm sure he has other criminal skills; he's actually been to jail, for killing a guy in an after-hours club, but he's at Paddy's full-time now, keeping the place in line.

Paddy Quinn's Pub is on Seventy-seventh Street and First Avenue, which happens to be across the street from a building in which a number of hookers seemed to live. The fact that Paddy Quinn, a muscular Irish guy with a bird tattooed on his right arm, hates pimps, is well known among the girls, who come in often, complaining about theirs. Paddy Quinn does not let any pimps into his bar, and Frankie Smith enforces the policy with his muscle. Everyone knows that. Especially the working girls with pimp problems.

The bar at Paddy's is a good vantage point from which to watch different New York worlds—the worlds of call girls, ex-convicts, businessmen, executives, tough guys—intersect. You name it, all kinds of people come in; Joe Namath is there all the time looking for action, which he always finds.

After a while, it occurrs to me that Smith and Quinn, who keep swag—hot jewelry—in the register, are fooling around; there are cops around, too, and after a while I begin to assume at least some of them are corrupt. There is a set of rules outside the rules: this begins to dawn on me as I stand in the dim light behind the oak bar of Paddy Quinn's, looking into a whole new world of New York life.

On Fridays I am at Paddy's until four in the morning. I'm up at 7:30 the next morning on my way to Simpson, Thacher to put in a full day answering phones and arranging library services for junior associates, who work all hours, nights, weekends, all the time.

The senior associates constantly bark disapproval at the junior guys. "No! That's not it. Go back. Get the federal statute. Whatsa matter? They forget to teach you about federal jurisdiction at Yale?" The junior guys, who aren't much older than me, stand there looking miserable and defeated, not to mention pale and out of shape. If I didn't work, I'd starve. But these guys are here because they *want* to be! They spend the nights of their greatest virility here. What for? So they can help one corporation take over another corporation and then go fire their mothers who work down on the shop floor?

In September of my last year at Columbia, when it comes time to decide what kind of a life as a lawyer I want to have, the days at Simpson, Thacher and the nights at Paddy Quinn's help make it clear: I don't want a straight life. I don't want to sit in an airless office and take orders and account for every six minutes of my time. For one thing, I know that if some guy comes in and tells me to come in on Saturday night when I have a date with a knockout girl, that would be a problem. And I might hurt the guy.

There isn't a lot of danger in a big law firm or a lot of passion either, at least until the senior partners get carted off to jail, and my experience—the violence and uncertainty of being at home with a dangerous father—has prepared me for a different kind of life: I am at home in places where things go wrong all the time. I like chaos. I like danger.

In 1974, when I graduate, Bronx County, New York, was full of bodies. Women got shot up on their way to buy milk. Guys cut one another's guts out with carpet knives to get an ounce or two of dope. You could get hurt anywhere, no one was safe, and the most dangerous job in the world was driving a cab or working in a bodega. People were busting one another out of windows and smashing one another up on the streets. The rising murder and violent-crime rates in Bronx County were the subject of national debate, the talk of Swedish tourists—who actually took tour buses up to see the charred ruins of the South Bronx—and later the animating principle behind controversial movies like Daniel Petrie's *Fort Apache, the Bronx*. Jimmy Carter would accurately call the Bronx "the worst slum in America" after he himself took a tour.

Bronx County, New York, was the perfect place to begin my life as a lawyer. And when the district attorney's office—which was full of Jewish lawyers, Irish cops, tough black detectives, all mixed up in rough justice—came to Columbia looking for recruits, I signed right up.

CHAPTER 5

Freddy Bratman sees a known black stickup guy with a dog.

Like all the other cops who work the 41st Precinct, Bratman, who is black, operates with an incredible level of alertness and a constantly heightened sense of danger. Taking no chances, he draws his weapon and chases the skinny felon down Macy Place.

Dog at his heel, the stickup guy runs through the door of a crumbling wreck of a building, into a lobby that stinks of piss and trash, up several flights of stairs that stink of piss and trash and of smoke as well, through a heavy fire door, and onto the roof.

Bratman runs right behind him. As he steps onto the roof, gun drawn, the first thing Bratman sees, before he can even make out the shape of the fleeing man, is the bright flash of pit bull teeth.

"Sic," says the skinny black guy, and lets go of the metal leash.

Boom.

Before he's even thought to do it, Bratman fires four rounds through the animal's head. With the dog dead, Bratman, who has been doing karate (pounding boards, blocks, and people) for so long his hands look like hammers, handcuffs the stickup guy and brings him into custody, but not before taking a moment to beat the guy's balls off with those knobby hammer hands of his.

The neighborhood goes nuts. The following morning dozens of people storm the precinct yelling about brutality and injustice. By day's end, they are throwing things—garbage, rocks, whatever they have—at the building. It's a big, unruly crowd. Bratman and the other cops, who keep baseball bats behind the precinct house to protect themselves on the way out, are on edge.

"Next time, shoot the owner," the police captain tells Bratman, loudly enough so the rest of the cops can hear. "No one gives a fuck if you kill a robber but they get really mad when you shoot a dog."

Shoot people, not dogs. This pretty much sums up the governing mentality in Bronx County, New York, when I report for duty as an assistant district attorney in the fall of 1974.

———

The Bronx County State Supreme Courthouse on the Grand Concourse is a nightmare. There's graffiti on the walls, the toilets don't flush, the sinks are clogged, the place smells, you have to worry about people stealing stuff out of the courtrooms. Gangs fight in the hallways, kids pull knives on one another in the bathrooms, and guys are always being arrested with guns in the courthouse. Stories about cops, dogs, and violent death like the one Bratman tells me during my first week on the job add to the flavor of the place.

As a new assistant district attorney working out of a small office (painted the drab gray green of all institutional workplaces) on the sixth floor of the courthouse, my job is to go into the lower courts, the misdemeanor and criminal courts, and handle whatever comes up. In 1974, roughly a zillion and a half criminal cases come up—low-level crime, drug dealing and possession (usually heroin or pills, sometimes cocaine or marijuana), so many robbery and burglary cases it is hard to keep track of them all, and car theft, over which, for some reason, Puerto Rican kids retain a monopoly.

"Do you want to press charges, ma'am?" I ask an older woman who comes during my first week on the job and tells me an endless story about how her Chevy Impala didn't work but was stolen and now works fine.

A Puerto Rican kid, notorious for stealing cars like the Impala and fixing them up, just got pinched doing the same thing to another car.

"Press charges?"

The lady looks at me like I'm nuts. "I haven't been able to get this goddamned car to work right in two years. This kid steals it. When the police bring it back two months later, the damn thing works better than ever! Press charges? Are you nuts? I want to give the kid money!!"

"Okay, okay," I tell her, "let's forget it."

Welcome to Bronx County Criminal Court.

—

Handling cases involves standing before a judge at a wooden table stacked up with manila folders, looking through each quickly, often in the few minutes before the clerk calls the case detailed inside the folder, and making snap decisions about how much time I can get a guy to take for whatever thieving or dope dealing he's done. How many times has the guy been in before? How tough is the judge? How relentless or smart or susceptible to getting shoved around is defense counsel? These are the kinds of things I ask myself as I flip through the files.

The job also involves constant contact with cops—many of them Irish guys who would rather throw their mothers in front of a moving train than stand up in court and say, "I'm afraid I made a small mistake, Your Honor"—and shlubby defense lawyers imbued with what I've begun to recognize as a distinctly Jewish vivacity and strong moral convictions about the connection between injustice and poverty (along with a clear desire to take every penny they can get their hands on), and DAs, also mostly Jews or ethnic guys like me who aren't cut out for a structured corporate environment and probably would have died in a big law firm.

Action, intensity, and the constant revelation of what was most ragged and raw about human life were (and remain) the defining elements of most of what goes on in Bronx County Criminal Court.

"Ladies and gentlemen, the Bronx is burning," Howard Cosell announces from the broadcast booth at Yankee Stadium in the Bronx during a baseball game in the 1970s. It is. The place is a war zone—drug dealers are at war with the neighbors they rob and terrify and with the cops, who take every opportunity to beat their balls off; blacks and Hispanics are suspicious of the white guys who come in, the social workers looking to give them a hard time, and the cops looking to arrest somebody but most certainly not doing anything that might actually help. If you're white and you see someone black or Hispanic and vaguely threatening in the street, you're a fool to think the guy might not hurt you. Whole neighborhoods are going up in flames; some lose three-quarters of their residents in a span of just ten years. Up in fucking smoke!

If the Bronx is burning—and it is, it is!—Eddie Hayes is burning too. I'm in great shape, running five miles a day, doing hundreds of push-ups. I feel like a commando. I'm ready for anything. *We're losing the war on crime? Yeah? Go fuck yourself. Eddie Hayes is ready. I'm not going to surrender. I am going to go in there and fight to the death.* I'm burning to be at the center of the action, the wild heart of a world full of fear, panic, danger, intensity, vulnerability.

———

No one can get Sabrina Jones to talk. She's a little girl, maybe eleven or twelve years old, in a dirty blue dress. Sabrina was in the stairway in her building and, though the light bulb was out, could clearly see the face of a tall black man as he robbed an older woman whose throat he later slit with a penknife.

Sabrina, the only witness, shakes with fright.

"Sabrina, Sabrina, it's okay, honey," I tell her. "Take your time. Tell us what you saw."

She stares ahead at the drab green wall, doesn't say a word.

"You got to talk," one of two detectives in the room with us tells Sabrina.

She looks at the wall.

The detective glances at his partner; we've been at this for almost an hour. We're getting nowhere.

Then I take over.

"Okay, honey!" I say. "You ever seen a white man walk on his hands?"

"You can't walk on your hands!" It's the first thing out of the kid's mouth all hour.

"Fuck I can't. You wait and see," I say as I fall to the floor, lay my hands flat on the linoleum, and walk up and down the perimeter of the room on my hands. I happen to like walking on my hands, which is not that hard if you're thin and muscular, which I am.

Sabrina laughs. She keeps laughing. I get back on my feet. Sabrina gives me a great big smile.

"You going to come upstairs and testify for me now, honey?"

"Absolutely. Yes. I will," she says, still smiling.

She's a great witness with amazingly precise recall of the man in the hallway, down to his bootleg black Levi's and black zip-up hoodie. The indictment, which the grand jury hands down immediately after she finishes, would not have been possible without Sabrina's testimony.

———

Becoming a good DA has more to do with handling weird situations like this than with anything a law student might have read in criminal law class. Besides, the smart guys, the ones who really like to sink their teeth into nice nuanced legal abstractions, go off to do appellate work, while guys like me—ready guys who show up, pay attention, and act quickly, mostly on instinct—go out onto the front lines and get kids like Sabrina Jones talking and otherwise clean up the blood on the floor. Kipling wrote in The Jungle Book, "The motto of all the mongoose family is, 'Run and find out.'" I'm a mongoose.

Immediately after I begin, I see that there is room to move, room for tough prosecutors to act with a soft side, which is something I sometimes like to do.

I soon take over the prosecution of a bunch of black kids who've been pinched doing a robbery of a grocery store in the South Bronx. The kid who acted as lookout has a prior offense so the prosecutor working on the case before I take over wants to give him more time.

"You know what the prior was for?" a public defender says on my phone about two seconds after I've read through the lookout guy's file.

"Nah."

"He got three years for marijuana ten years ago!"

"What are you talking about? They don't give three years for marijuana!"

"Three years," says the defense lawyer. "He had two ounces. They gave him three years upstate."

"Man! That's messed up. Three years for two ounces. Tell you what," I say to the defense lawyer. "I'll give him the time back. I'll knock three years off the time he's supposed to get now. I'll give that back to him. Tell him to stay out of trouble, will you?"

The guy stays out of trouble. I like it about my job that I see crazy things happen to people—*a teenager does three years for two ounces of pot*—and can actually do something to make them less crazy, less harsh.

———

During those first weeks, I take the subway up to the Grand Concourse wearing a business suit with a white pocket handkerchief. (I save my lavender pants, raw silk cream-colored jacket, and white shoes for the weekends.) I march up the stately steps, walk past the guard, bored as usual after seizing knives, machetes, and sometimes pistols from guys on their way into the building for court appearances, and into my gray-green office to pick up a mountain of manila folders, each stuffed with sorry stories, lunatic facts of lives gone horribly wrong.

The bodega owner who robbed a customer to buy dope for his wife, the Spanish kid who blasted his sister with a .38, the Irish immigrant who became a cop and went nuts and got kicked off the force after he ran over a guy he insisted was a giant caterpillar: there's no protective buffer for these people or for any of the many thousands like them who come through the criminal court system, no way these people can recover from what's done to them.

At the table, I quickly look through the file as the clerk calls each case, see what evidence the cops have cooked up, and figure out how to get rid of the thing. There are so many fucking cases you would be in Bronx County Court until the sun blew up if you brought even a fraction of them to trial. Judging by the number of robbery and burglary cases each day, it's hard to figure out how people can afford to ever leave their houses: they'd go out, come back an hour later, and the whole place would be cleared out. A lot of these guys kill themselves working like dogs at low-wage jobs, finally buy a stereo or TV set, and some schmuck comes in and carries it off the very next day.

Be polite no matter how upset you are; keep that secret: these are key to being a good DA and are easy for me. I spent my whole childhood keeping things secret. I knew how to remain polite, watchful, regardless of how I felt about what was going on around me. I look through those files, figure out how to put stories together in simple, straightforward ways judges and jurors can understand—desperate tales of a poor father of six breaking a car window to steal a radio he can't sell for more than $3.50 on the street, of a woman who whip slaps her sister for no reason and takes her shoes, of kids who stand outside a bodega and rob teenagers for their lunch money. "Your Honor, the kids took the money. But honestly, Judge, they aren't bad kids, they're hungry is all. The state seeks the minimum penalty."

In general my impulse is to tell the truth. If you grow up with a dangerous drunk, you have to learn to acknowledge "This is a dangerous drunk." Look away from what's true and you're going to get hurt.

The immediacy, intensity, and high-stake ramifications of nearly everything that goes on in and around criminal courtrooms give my days as a new DA an unbelievable jumped-up charge.

———

I hear shots outside the window of my prewar apartment on the Upper West Side just off Broadway one evening, soon after I start in the DA's office. There's nothing to see when I look out the window. I race into the hallway, fly down thirteen flights of stairs, rush out the door, and practically fall on a guy lying dead in the street.

There's a cop standing over the body, gun in hand. A lot of people gather around.

My blood pumps.

"Anyone see what happened?" I yell into the crowd.

People on the street start walking away.

"What the fuck are you doing?" I am screaming. "You just saw a guy get shot!"

I grab a woman and her boyfriend and another lady. I hold their wrists tight and won't let go until they tell me what happened.

The dead guy robbed a passerby and started threatening people, they tell me at last. Seeing what was happening, the cop, who was on patrol, ran up and shot the guy in the chest.

You have to be very brave to shoot someone in the chest at close range, which is what you have to do to avoid shooting innocent bystanders. But this cop ran up, put his gun under the guy's left breast, and shot his heart out.

Very exciting, very cool, I think.

The DA assigned to the case (in which the cop was exonerated) eventually became a judge and I'm told he often recounts the story of me running into the street after I heard shots and keeping witnesses from abandoning the crime scene; the judge apparently tells his listeners this is just what a good lawman should do in exigent circumstances. But I didn't run into the crime scene because I had any deep conviction about what good lawmen—or anyone else—should do. I did it because something was happening and I thought it would be fun to check it out. And it was.

——

I like being in the street. I'm much more willing than most prosecutors to go out and investigate cases. Got a Puerto Rican kid stealing cars and fixing them up? Okay, let me see what's what. Got a stickup guy visiting the same six bodegas every Monday? I'm there. Go to the scene. See what you've got. That's how I like to work.

I must be a vivid sight, a clean-cut white boy in a snappy suit and shoes buffed to a high polish walking around scary neighborhoods in which white boys in any outfits are painfully noticeable and genuinely at risk.

The thing that strikes me most when I start going out into different neighborhoods in the South Bronx is that nothing ever smells clean. Nothing is ever clean. There's a sugary sick smell everywhere, in the houses where people sleep on beds without sheets, in the streets, everywhere. People in the Bronx, within spitting distance of the richest city in the richest country on earth, have unbelievably bad diets and mouthfuls of ghetto teeth because they eat sweets all the time and don't go to the dentist. It's just so damn dirty. And slimy. Everything has grease on it, especially the food.

Most everywhere I go I witness the unleashed hysteria of death, crime, murder. Do you know what people look like when they've been stabbed to death? Generally someone who's been fatally stabbed does not have a nice clean wound: there's usually been a lot of slashing and stabbing and slicing—and a desperate struggle that leaves insides tumbling out, stomachs, brains, eyes cut out of faces, heads split open, blood everywhere, faces distorted in agony. Almost always there is a hysterical, traumatized witness or two nearby, as well.

Not often but sometimes the things I see during the day haunt my dreams. I can't sleep and have to take the next day off. A lot of times

I spend the day just walking around somewhere quiet and clean like the Metropolitan Museum of Art.

The homicide detectives I run into at some of the more violent crime scenes help clarify my ideas about tough guys and how they behave. These guys bust down doors with gunmen on the other side, go after armed men in dark hallways, regularly run bravely into blood-chilling, dangerous situations, but they give money to beggars and junkies. They are kind to people. If you can help a guy, help him; if it gets you in trouble now and then, so what? *Not* helping guys will certainly get you in trouble down the line.

That's what I learn from tough Bronx detectives like the big black guy who shot and killed two guys from ten-foot range. One guy he shot six times and hit every time. He was from the backwoods of Alabama, a dead shot with a completely incomprehensible southern black accent. He'd say, "Freeze. Police," and the thugs would turn trying to figure out what the hell he'd just said. Then he'd shoot them. Watching him and other detectives with big guns and long leather coats and hard eyes wielding authority over witnesses gathered in the housing project apartment where two drug dealers had been machine-gunned to death while eating ice cream on folding chairs helped form not just my ideas about tough guys, but also an ambition that was already taking hold during my first months in the district attorney's office: I wanted to work in homicide. That's where the real action was.

Not that there is any shortage of action in regular DA work. It's not just action, though. Desperation, tragedy, and pure lunacy are all part of the mix.

My first week in night court a Spanish guy, his wiry arm bandaged up and his head in a turban, is charged with trying to hold up a pizza place run by Albanians up by Arthur Avenue. Albanians, who have just started coming to the Bronx, are famous for having more guns than any standing Western army, and not just more guns but better guns; pull a .38 on an Albanian guy and you can fucking bet he will have a .45 automatic. That's how the Albanians are with guns; the DA's office is full of ethnic insight like this. And you're a fool if you operate in the court system or anywhere else without a keen sense of ethnic identity.

Next day the bandaged Spanish guy appears before a great Puerto Rican judge named John Carro. Carro looks at the papers that detail the evidence and charges, calls the defense lawyer up to the bench, says something to the defendant in Spanish, and sets an exceedingly high bail.

"Your Honor," I say, "may I ask what you said in Spanish to the defendant?"

"What I said, Mr. Hayes, is that if the defendant is stupid enough to hold up a pizza parlor full of Albanians with a knife, then he should not be allowed out on the streets for a very long time."

Snap! In addition to everything else—the excitement, intensity, visceral impact—Bronx County Court rocks with high comedy.

———

Bad news arrives in the mailbox just two months after I start in the DA's office: I have failed the bar exam. I didn't know when I took the exam that there was an area of law I would genuinely love—courtroom law. Now, because I won't be admitted to the bar, I can't appear in court until I retake—and pass—the exam. (New recruits are allowed into court, on a temporary basis, pending arrival of bar exam results.)

I'm sent to the Complaints Room, the drab (gray green, of course) room on the lower level of the courthouse where people come in off the street with stuff they think the DA should investigate: *The neighbors are stealing the mail. Drug dealers are in the kitchen. Martians are on the roof.* Every fucking thing you can think of.

Complaints seem like a big step down and I'm sorry to be out of the excitement of the criminal court loop but thrilled to find, in no time at all, that the Complaints Room is just as crazy and charged as Supreme Court.

"Meeeeeee fahhder berry en de kaskeet," a guy says hysterically into the phone one day. I can't understand a word he's saying. "Me fahhder no berry en de rite kaskeet."

What? Something about his father and a casket but I can't make out what. "Why don't you come in and we'll talk about it," I tell the guy.

An enormous black guy with a shaved head shows up early the next morning. I didn't know then that West Indians are the hardest-working people on the planet but I was about to find out. West Indians were coming into the Bronx in droves during the seventies and you couldn't possibly understand anything about Bronx neighborhoods, not to mention potential jurors, if you didn't know that a West Indian will work as many jobs and as many hours as you let him. Leave the door open on Sunday and he'll be there working away, saving his money, advancing like there's no tomorrow. (No accident that Colin Powell, the highest-ranking African American in the history of American politics before Condoleezza Rice, is of West Indian descent.)

Not that I learned any of this from the guy who comes in to the Complaints Room saying incomprehensible things about caskets and being a sandhog, which I later find is what they call the guys who build subway tunnels, brute work for sure, but there's dollars in it. Other than the fact that the guy has a lot of money and a Cadillac and bought his father a really nice casket, I can't understand much that comes out of his mouth.

"Berry en de rong kaskeet," he says.

Yeah. Okay. We're having a little impasse here. I don't know what he's talking about.

"Hayes," he says. "Dat's 'n Irish name?"

"Irish, yeah, right," I tell him, and he comes back the following morning with a tough, squat Irish guy with a brogue so thick it's not much easier to understand than the West Indian's bizarre patois, but he too is talking about something that happened with a casket. "Write down the name of the cemetery, the kind of casket, will you?" I tell the Irish guy.

What the hell, I think, I got a bunch of detectives here ready to run around and find out what's what. I'll send them out to the cemetery, make a couple of calls, see if I can figure out what's going on.

Two police detectives visit a burial spot in Queens near Kennedy Airport and a few calls later I find out the cemetery is *reusing* caskets; basically they're selling souped-up models to guys like the sandhog, then, before burial, switching the body to a cheap casket and re- selling the expensive one. The owners of the place get collared and indicted; it turns into a big thing.

Complaints are okay!

———

Six months later, after some rigorous study—a first—I pass the bar and am back in court, more jumped up, more charged and ready for action than before. Now I have some idea what Bronx County Court life is all about. Or do I?

"We could stick them guys up!" A jolly-faced Irish cop smiles at me one of the first times I go to work night court, the arraignment part that's open all night long.

Most of the cops in Bronx County Court go to work, wear their uniforms, eat some donuts, wait for their paychecks. The other 20 percent of the force works hard and does all of the dangerous police work. They are brave, those guys, oh, they are brave!

They run in and rescue poor people nobody gives a fuck about. They wrestle guns from robbers, fight hand to hand rather than shoot at knife-wielding lunatics, dash into burning buildings. Some are psychotic, vicious guys who like to hurt people. But by and large, the cops are people who have a vocation, whose family history pro- pelled them into police work, and who are part of an admirable, close-knit, affectionate group from predominantly Italian or Irish eth- nic backgrounds.

Cops who are stupid or crazy enough to get in trouble and be sus- pended from active duty or who get their guns taken away following an indictment or other dustup often end up working night court like my jolly-faced friend, a former narcotics cop who'd been indicted for sticking up drug dealers.

"Number 34 on the calendar. Indictment 4532. *People v. Collones et al.* Defendant charged with unlawful possession of a firearm." At 3:00 a.m., the court clerk calls the case of Juan C. Collones, a burly His-panic guy with gold block-lettered rings on each of his eight fingers. Collones has been in on at least three prior drug-related charges, which probably has something to do with the judge's decision to set bail at an unusually steep sum.

"Can the defendant make bail?" the clerk asks Mr. Collones, who nods as three cronies step from behind the wooden rail that separates the lawyers' table and the judge's bench from the public seats in the old courtroom. The jolly-faced Irish cop's eyes light up when he sees that one of the guys walks toward the defense lawyer with a leather attaché case in his hand.

"We could definitely stick him the fuck up," the cop whispers to me.

"Are you nuts?" I whisper back. "You don't even have a gun."

"I got a couple in the car," he tells me. "There's probably a hun-dred thousand dollars in there. We go, follow them in my car, and just stick them the fuck up. All you gotta do is stick the gun in the window and say, 'Shut the fuck up.' And boom, take the money."

He's serious!

"Nah, I'm not looking for a second job," I tell him.

He looks at me like I'm nuts.

I bet there were nights he did go out and stick up guys. He prob-ably got on the subway home afterwards with *their* money in *his* pocket.

No one (including me) ever turned in guys like the Irish cop. Maybe the thinking was, *Hell, if you can't stick up drug dealers, who can you stick up?* (Most cops who got caught acting on this simple philosophy got acquitted; who was going to believe a drug dealer anyway?) Maybe it was just that in a world burning up and full of violence in which truly regrettable horrors were regularly visited upon ordinary people, a certain level of background lawlessness is not just presumed but more or less tolerated.

No one in the DA's office—certainly not me—lets everything slide. Not by a long shot.

I've been back in Supreme Court for a few months when I notice I've heard more than once about some crazy fucking kid who has been terrorizing the whole Willis Avenue neighborhood. The kid is nuts, constantly threatening everyone.

After he's been in court half a dozen times for disorderly conduct, menacing, and other relatively minor crimes, I look at him hard and say to him and his defense lawyer, a smart Jewish guy in a shiny suit, "If somebody doesn't kill this kid—and somebody should kill this kid—I'm gonna take care of him." The kid has been locked up four separate times, and released ten days later each time, when I go to the guy's lawyer and say, "It's over. I am going to put this guy away."

"You're picking on him because he's black," the defense lawyer tells me. "It's a totally racist frame-up."

"Fuck that. This is a genuinely scary kid," I retort. "I'm keeping my eye on him. He's finished."

Next time the cops bring the kid in, I see to it he is brought before a very strict judge.

"Your Honor," I say, "in light of the defendant's repeat offenses and the fact that he has repeatedly terrorized an entire neighborhood full of families and children, the state asks for consecutive yearlong terms for each misdemeanor charge."

"The guy's going down," I tell his lawyer. "You might as well plead guilty. Get him to agree to treatment. Or he's going down forever."

Effectively the guy did. He went to jail for more than a year. That was it; no one in the Bronx heard from him again.

There were lots of kids in Bronx County Court who weren't crazy or violent like the kid who was terrorizing the Willis Avenue neighborhood but had just gotten messed up and didn't have families or teachers who could help them out. I knew what it was like to be desperate. As a prosecutor, I often had to decide whether to send kids to jail or to drug treatment, and when I was dealing with someone who had a genuine chance in life, who wasn't crazy or dangerous, I tried to be as softhearted as possible and argued for putting the kid in a treatment program. Part of what was thrilling about my job was that I could—and did—save all kinds of people in trouble.

—

The phone on my gray metal desk rings. A woman is very agitated; she doesn't say anything really, but clearly there is something she wants to talk about. I have some knowledge of this from my mother, who I know wants to but never does talk about her fears and frustrations. The woman on the phone won't even tell me her name or phone number.

"Honey," I tell her, "call back tomorrow. Ask for Eddie. I'll tell you some things."

I know she'll call back. When she does, I tell her about the club I had been to the night before, how I couldn't always get the girls I wanted, how my father beat my mother. Eventually the woman on the phone gets tired of hearing me talk about myself and starts telling me about her boyfriend, who has beaten her and raped her. "He's a cop," she says.

As the son of an alcoholic's wife, I think: *This is not right and somebody's got to help this lady.*

There's a psycho guy in the DA's office who's always doodling pictures of women with huge breasts and animal heads. But he's famous in the office for zealously—and successfully—prosecuting rape cases.

"Look, this woman called," I tell him, repeating what she told me. "I believe her. Is there something we can do?"

"Bring her in," he says.

"I'll be in front of the Supreme Court building on the Grand Concourse at eleven tomorrow morning," I tell the woman when she calls back. "I want you to come and meet me and I will introduce you to the best and the toughest rape prosecutor in the country."

"Ed Hayes," I say, holding out my hand to the slender, pretty white woman in the flowered blouse and cotton skirt who walks up to me outside the courthouse the next morning.

"Louisa," she says.

We shake hands and I take her to meet the chief rape prosecutor; eight months later, psycho though he may be, the guy tries and convicts her boyfriend and sends him to jail.

Whatever I did to help Louisa—and, in the fullness of time, a lot of other women like her—had more to do with watching my mother and tending bar at Paddy Quinn's than with anything I learned or could have learned in law school. I knew from watching as I tended bar at Paddy Quinn's that a man does not stand by and watch a woman take a beating.

As I discovered again and again, Bronx County Criminal Court was full of women getting the hell kicked out of them by boyfriends, bosses, husbands. The law saves and protects, they said in law school. But I learned from Louisa and the others like her in Bronx County that it's not true: the law will not save you, except in theory; in practice, usually one person can save you *if* he feels like it and isn't too tired or busy or just plain out of it. That's it.

Women probably helped me as a lawyer as much as anything I learned at Columbia, in court, or anywhere else. I did a lot of dancing during my early days in the district attorney's office; in fact, when I wasn't working or working out or sleeping I was partying, bopping away, meeting women—African, Dominican, Cuban, Puerto Rican—attracting attention too, as you do not see many white boy prosecutors out at three o'clock in the morning dancing in clubs.

I had little experience with people who'd grown up in Rwanda, Senegal, Santo Domingo, or Havana, but I read books and newspaper stories so I could understand more about who they were and became very attuned to subtleties of ethnic and racial makeup.

Dominicans don't like Haitians, Haitians don't like Puerto Ricans, southern blacks don't like northern blacks, and West Indians don't like anybody. There are thirty-seven different types of Hispanics, and Latin women are the greatest gift God has ever given the world. If

Spanish guys are from the same town, they call one another cousin;
Dominicans have thirty thousand "cousins" because they are all from
the same village. I learned all this and more from the nights dancing
in dark clubs along the West Side Highway and off Broadway in the
Forties and Fifties.

What difference does any of this make in terms of practicing law?
All the difference in the world. If you are African American, you
have an ingrained sense of the capriciousness of power and the ripping feel of injustice. Will this affect the way you behave on a jury?
You bet it will—not all the time but enough of the time to make a
very big difference.

Talk to somebody who says, "I am Jamaican and I have two jobs
and I go to church on Sunday." That's a prosecution juror, pal. Ask
somebody where he's from and he says, "Dominican Republic and I
own a bodega and work fourteen hours a day"—that guy is going to
be putting people in jail. Put a guy on a jury who knows five convicted felons and has had five jobs in the last year and you can bet
he's going to be skeptical when the cop says he put the defendant in
a chokehold only *after* the guy started to "resist arrest."

Ethnic awareness is by far the most reliable key to figuring out
how jurors will behave and probably also the single most important
guide to speaking to and reaching the jurors who make the final decisions about which men and women will walk out of America's
courthouses free for dinner and which ones will walk out the back in
jumpsuits and cuffs. New York, this great so-called melting pot, is
more of a stew pot; you can still pretty much identify each separate
piece of the mix.

Culture clash, something else I experienced through women, was
enlightening. A Jewish girlfriend I had at the time, Judy, took me to
dinner with her family. Her father, who'd been in the fucking Abraham Lincoln Brigade, and her mother argued and yelled the whole
time. I had never seen anything like it.

"Is this part of a religious ritual?" I asked Judy after one of these
meals. "Every night you have dinner and fight and argue." *I never talked
to my parents.*

"We're just talking," Judy says.

Jewish intellectualism—something I'd seen at Columbia and now observed on a daily basis in the DA's office and among the more fervently and ideologically motivated defense lawyers who tried to make a living redressing social wrongs (even though hardly anyone in the Bronx had money to pay them for their efforts)—was a quality I started to admire.

Jews don't accept what's offered to them; they're genetically programmed to think through everything. Of course, they don't stop thinking and some of the ideas are terrible: put four Jews in a room and you have twelve different opinions about everything. If you could somehow combine the Jew's willingness to stand up for what he believes with the Irishman's charm and inclination to go to an adversary's house and blow him the fuck up, that would really be something!

Every day in Bronx County Court the story of New York, the story of huge numbers of Jews and huge numbers of Catholics muscling for position with one another and with the increasing and also shifting immigrant population, is dramatically enacted and reenacted.

The defendants were—and still are—primarily people of color, and in 1974 you rarely saw black people in court who weren't defendants. There were few judges, lawyers, or even court officials of color. The demographics changed—there are more Hispanic defendants now than when I was in the DA's office—but the fundamental dynamic remains the same: upwardly mobile guys dole out justice to people of color, most of whom come from families that for generations have had nothing but that nonetheless press on for advantage; some, despite the odds, will eventually succeed in propelling themselves out of the dirty, bad-smelling streets and will promptly be replaced by new immigrant groups full of people poised to take a good beating in exchange, perhaps, for what seems and sometimes is a solid shot at a better life. A lot of lawyers want to live on a certain refined and almost abstract level, one that's far removed from the daily drama of all this muscling and pushing. I don't. I never want to get too far away from this drama.

As a completely self-concocted guy, I found ethnic distinctions especially interesting, sometimes inspirational. If you are going to prosper and survive in New York, there's a lot to be learned from watching Jews and African Americans, Hispanics, West Indians, Dominicans, and Senegalese. If you want to get ahead, look at what African Americans have done to overcome absurd adversity or at how many jobs the average West Indian worked this week. When you live among a lot of different cultures, you learn that they also have their vices (Irish drinking, for one conspicuous example), and you have to take account of those, as well.

So here, in my mid-twenties, I'm watching, carefully watching West Indian workers, Jewish lawyers, African dancers, and brave Dominicans who will stop at nothing to protect their family business and honor, and I'm protecting Jamaican women from further beatings, and keeping crazed kids from robbing, raping, and terrorizing their neighbors. And I'm also sleeping with exotic women and dancing in clubs and taking late-night calls and heading off to obscure crime scenes and watching very tough, very scary guys lavish pathetic junkies with kindness and money and running into the streets and finding bodies and, and, and . . .

The fun has just begun.

CHAPTER 6

"I want to be in homicide, Kevin. I really want to be in homicide."

Kevin Gilleece, the straight-shooting Irish guy who has been named head of the elite homicide bureau, is shorter than me but very paternal. He puts his arm around me in the green corridor outside Bronx County Supreme Court.

I'm too young and inexperienced to be in homicide. It's the toughest and most consequential prosecutorial work there is. But I'm running, doing push-ups and karate, and staying out all night on weekends; I'm a very *ready* guy, all right?

Gilleece looks at me, gives my shoulder an affectionate squeeze.

"Kid," he says, "I know how to take care of my own."

The next day I'm in homicide.

If Kevin Gilleece told me to cut the throats of the first ten people I saw on the street, there'd be ten dead motherfuckers five minutes later. He's the most decent guy in the world. Whatever he tells me to do, I do. I love him. And I will never forget the break he gave me.

Adrenaline, blood and guts, the cases, the people—I loved everything about homicide. Especially the detectives, many of whom were ex-paratroopers or ex-marines, very fit and, I thought, very glamorous. Guys like Cliff Wright, Jack McCann, Ronnie Marsenison looked tough, as if they knew how to do a day's work, a *hard* day's work. A lot of the detectives knew how to take a beating and how to give one. I learned an enormous amount from these guys and I liked to hang out with them, too.

"Look, guys," I'd say. "It's Friday night, we're out looking at dead people. Let's go look at some girls!"

José and Maxy, detectives I really admired, liked to pull up in front of a club in a black unmarked car, park on the fucking sidewalk, cut the line, and go in without paying. And they wouldn't lock the car. It was a point of pride: no one touches the fucking car, okay? Walking in places with José and Maxy, I really felt like somebody.

Same thing with crime scenes. I'd go in and say, "I'm from homicide. Where's the fucking dead guy?"

All the guys who usually bust your chops in New York City, the bureaucrats and the big shots and everybody else, listen up when you say, "Somebody died here. If I ask you a fucking question, you're gonna answer it."

I'd be in a dark apartment reeking with that sugary smell and the stink of piss and smoke, with the beds without sheets and people with bad teeth and sorry lives full of fear and lucklessness, looking for a body or a weapon or just an idea as to why someone thought to slash the young Hispanic woman twenty-five times on the stairwell where neighbors found her. *I'm not the toughest guy on the block, but I know what to do and I can do it and that makes me a guy you gotta pay attention to,* I'd think as I looked up and down the often terrified faces of whoever was inside when I knocked and said, "Bronx district attorney. Homicide. Open up."

What could be more intense than homicide? Someone's life has been taken and someone is probably going to go to jail for the rest of his life. It's devastating for the witnesses, the family, everybody: all the rawest emotions are in play.

When I was in the lower courts, I sometimes found it hard to get worked up over burglaries, car thefts, or pissant drug sales. It's not good to steal somebody's car or burglarize his house, but most of what you see in the lower courts are desperate people, half of whom are illiterate or suffer from some mental illness and most of whom are lucky to have one parent, forget about two. After a while, it started to feel like the prosecutor's job was just to shovel lots of poor desperate people back and forth to nowhere—from the streets or their awful sad houses into terrible jails and then back again.

But in homicide the crimes were awful and the stakes were always high and it was easy to get worked up, easy to see a messed-up bloody murder victim and think, *I'm stopping at nothing until I find the motherfucker who did this. You killed somebody. I am going to take your life away. You're going to jail forever.* It was easy to feel like this when you saw a mangled little old lady some crazed kid hacked to death with a penknife. I put a lot of people away for the rest of their lives. I got sick sometimes when people I prosecuted were sentenced, but I wanted to get them. Winning life sentences gave me a real sense of power—not the power money brings or the power of belonging to a large organization but the power tough guys have, and gun fighters and brilliant writers, the power to do something by yourself, something that significantly affects the world around you.

———

"We have another little old lady." Kevin Gilleece is calling in the middle of the night. I've been in homicide for little more than a month. Gilleece describes a horrible case. An old woman in Co-op City in the North Bronx had been beaten to death with a board and stabbed. The cops have arrested a guy they think was the lookout. "You gotta go up there," Kevin tells me. "You gotta make this case.

It's an election year, Co-op City has a lot of votes. You gotta do this right." Kevin's boss, Mario Merola, the Bronx district attorney, is an elected official. Doing it right in voter-rich areas means extra votes, increased job security.

Votes or no votes, whatever Kevin tells me to do, I do.

Ten minutes later, I'm on the street in front of my apartment waiting for the police car the office has sent to take me to the crime scene. Jimmy Graham, a detective, is in the apartment when I arrive. Jimmy hates everybody in a nice, furious, nondenominational way: he hates Italians, he hates Swedes, he hates Jews, he hates blacks, Puerto Ricans, and Dominicans. Jimmy doesn't even like Irish women. He's intelligent and a very good detective and I love him, but he isn't making much progress getting anything out of the wiry Latin guy the cops think was the lookout.

"Leave me alone with the guy," I tell Graham. "I want to talk to him."

"Look," I tell the guy after Jimmy leaves, "I don't want to be rude to you, you know what I am. I'm the prosecutor. But I want to talk to you a little bit so we know where we are going. You got a girlfriend?"

"Yeah," he says, "I got a girlfriend."

"I don't mean any disrespect," I tell him, "but did you make love to your girlfriend last night?"

"Yeah," he says, "yeah, I did."

"Well, let me tell you something, pal, that's the last time you get laid in your fucking life! If you don't tell me what I want to know in the next ten minutes, you're going to jail for twenty-five years. Got that? And by that time, your fucking dick ain't going to be worth shit, all right?"

I have no idea where this is coming from, but it keeps coming. "You tell me what I fucking want to know—right now. And what I want to know is, who went in that fucking apartment and killed that little old lady?" Not yelling but looking at the guy and smiling; it scares the shit out of people when you keep smiling at them.

He looks at me.

"If you didn't go in there and didn't kill that fucking woman, then you had better fucking tell me who did."

"What will happen if I tell you?" he says. He's caving.

I tell him that I will let the judge know that he has cooperated and will try to help him as much as I can and that, if I do, things will probably wind up a hell of a lot better for him than if he doesn't talk. "I have you, motherfucker, for felony murder. I got you already. And I have nothing else to do all day long," I tell him, "but bust your balls until they put you away for twenty-five years."

"Okay," he says, "I'll tell you." And he gives me the names of two guys and tells me where to find them, and Jimmy and the other detective get them both and we have no trouble making the case and the guys go to jail for life. I get a good deal for the lookout guy, seven or eight years. I think he really didn't know they were going to kill someone when they broke into that apartment.

When you first go into homicide, once a week you're on call for a twenty-four-hour period. Imagine being a twenty-seven-year-old Irish kid answering the phone at four in the morning, "Homicide!" My idea of heaven.

Early on, I get a call telling me to report to the 41st Precinct House, which, when I arrive, is full of the scariest black guys you've ever seen in your whole fucking life. Not scuzzy scary guys either, but *serious* scary guys, each one of whom has on alligator shoes or a fur coat or a diamond pendant or a hand so full of enormous rings an ordinary mortal would have trouble moving his digits enough to pull the trigger of an automatic weapon. These guys obviously have no such problems.

"Tell me what the fuck happened," I say. And somebody does.

"A social club," says a detective in a gray suit and skinny tie.

Very social, this club, I think, looking around at this collection of hoodlums who have more money on their hands than the detective has in the bank.

"The brothers go in to stick the place up. They go in there, take a few shots at the ceiling, and Otis here"—the guy nods at the scary-looking mustached man next to him—"tells the motherfuckers inside,

'This is a stickup. Don't anyone move. We get your fucking money and your jewelry and we're out of here.' "

"Stick *us* up, motherfucker?!!! *We're* stickup guys." This, I gather, is what the guys inside the social club tell Otis and his crew. "Good luck, motherfuckers!" one of the club guys supposedly says to them just before he takes out his automatic and starts shooting.

Then all holy hell breaks out: everyone in the place is packing, everyone is blasting everybody else. It's an all-out gang war, at the end of which there's blood on every wall in the place, two of the failed stickup guys are dead, and I'm in the precinct house at four in the morning interviewing a bunch of genuinely scary-looking guys, all of whom seem to be named Floyd or Otis or Elijah and none of whom can recollect a single thing about what happened.

Everyone involved has an incredibly long record and has done time at Attica or someplace else upstate where, perhaps, they learned to forget all kinds of things, like who fired on whom and other matters about which prosecutors and cops can be counted on to ask questions. "Nah," the Floyds and the Otises all say, "I dunno *what* happened in there."

I'm looking at these guys in their alligator shoes and their big jewels, thinking, *Holy shit, I'm in the middle of a fucking convention of hoodlums, stickup guys, drug dealers, bookmakers, gamblers, who knows what else. I've never seen anything like it. This is the Wild West, I think. Crazy guys shooting everyone down and walking off.*

That is what happens in the end: everyone goes home. What's the crime? Two stickup guys got shot, that's all; no one remembers anything about it. There are too many shootings involving people who aren't stickup guys to invest precious investigative muscle in figuring out how a bunch of crazed and now amnesiac hoodlums happen to have a couple of their own guys shot up in some godforsaken *social* club you'd have to be seriously nuts to enter in the first place.

I'm a twenty-seven-year-old kid from Smithtown and this could not be more interesting. No, I've never seen anything like any of this before. To be right here, in the middle of this, man, that's something.

One day during my first week back in court I pick up a manila folder that details the case against three kids who went into a bodega with a gun drawn and told the owner to give them all his money. The owner jerked, the kid with the gun panicked and shot him, and he died, slowly. All three kids were indicted on felony murder charges. The one whose file I have in hand (not the shooter) is a Jewish kid who goes to Bronx High School of Science, a diploma from which is a golden ticket out of the abject poverty to which the vast majority of those who pass through the justice system here are doomed forever.

The kid's parents, a healthy-looking lower-middle-class couple, came down to the precinct on the night of the murder. I couldn't tell them their son had been arrested for murder. I couldn't get the words out of my mouth. A sergeant, both of whose kids went to Bronx Science, was on duty that night and came out and told the couple what had happened. They were destroyed. Destroyed. The woman collapsed on the floor. I left the room then thinking, *Holy Christ, how does something like this happen?* The kid has a good life ahead of him, goes on a stickup, he's the lookout, something goes wrong, now he's going to spend what should be his last years of high school in jail. Just being close to experiences like this has a visceral impact that's a lot like a good hard smack in the jaw.

My first St. Patrick's Day celebration as a homicide guy helps seal my sense of ethnic identity. I have never spent time with guys of Irish descent who are not falling-down drunks but instead brave, sometimes to the point of lunacy. In fact, lunatic bravery is something the guys I work with laugh at themselves for.

The Emerald Society has a huge St. Patrick's Day party at a big church on Eleventh Avenue in Manhattan. The place is full of guys like Jimmy Graham—smiling Irish guys, grumpy Irish guys, Irish guys with long hair and earrings—and me. I go to the party with Paddy Hannigan, a very tough and very fit member of the most elite squad of homicide detectives who is married to a Puerto Rican woman. Paddy stops on the way to fill a beggar's cup with money.

"These people got nothing," he says. "No wonder they do terrible things. You have to hurt them sometimes, but really they've got nothing."

By this time, I've realized my father didn't beat me because he was mad at me but because he was mad at himself. It's a harsh, cruel world for a lot of people, but the church on Eleventh Avenue is full of bagpipes and boisterousness and laughter. This, I think to myself, is a tradition that's natural for me and this is a world—unlike the one I knew at law school or even in any of the homes in which I grew up—where I feel comfortable, where I belong.

—

If I did undergraduate tough-guy training during law school at Paddy Quinn's and in the clubs and in the lower criminal courts, I get my postgraduate education work in homicide. Billy Wallace, Jimmy Harkins, Jack McCann, and other of the detectives teach me a lot about what it's like to do whatever has to be done, no matter what the consequences, and to keep cool at all hours of the day or night, no matter what.

"Motherfucker, get up. I'm on Fox Street. We got some bodies. Meet me there."

I have been in homicide for three and a half years and have never heard anyone speak two consecutive sentences without the word *motherfucker* in it. Jerry Leon, a giant black guy with vaguely crossed eyes who has been in a movie called *The Seven-Ups* and is a good detective, is on the phone.

I find Leon on Fox Street, leaning his massive body against the door of his unmarked car. He's got a desperado in custody in the backseat and he's keeping an eye on him. He's parked in front of another car.

About twenty minutes earlier the guy in custody apparently came up to the other car in a great big coat. In a second, the guy swung a shotgun on a leather strap up from under the coat, reached around, pointed at a guy in the driver's seat, and *boom*, blew the guy's head off. His brains are dripping off the roof of the car. What's left up there looks like watermelon rinds: there's no head on the body; it blew smack off. I look at the gore, the smell is terrible, I'm completely speechless. But Jerry Leon calmly looks in with those crazy crossed eyes of his. "Man," he says, "I bet that ruined his whole fucking day." Just as cool as can be.

Lloyd Otis, another detective I liked a lot, had a thing for barmaids and cocktail waitresses and topless dancers and was always in bars late at night. At the time, if you were in a Bronx bar after midnight there was at least a one-in-three chance that somebody was going to come in and stick the place up. It got to be a joke after a while: basically Lloyd Otis couldn't go to the bathroom in a Bronx bar at night without coming out to find someone sticking the place up. A very good shot, Lloyd would come out of the bathroom and shoot the stickup guys.

Lloyd was in the bathroom at a gas station once and came out to find two guys holding up the place. One of the stickup guys had a knife; the other had a gun. Lloyd pulls out his .38. "Police," he said. "Stop." But the guy with the gun jerked toward Lloyd, who of course shot him on the spot; the other guy tried to cut Lloyd with the knife. Lloyd shot but didn't kill him.

"Geez, Lloyd," I say when I hear what happened, "that was terrible."

"You know, Eddie," Lloyd says, "I was staying out of bars. I thought I was going to be okay."

One of the things Jerry Leon, Lloyd Otis, and the other detectives taught me was that often the most impossible and therefore least likely explanation describes what actually happened. So if you are trying to figure why someone did something or where someone is hiding or hid something and have eliminated plausible explanations, examine the implausible. If, for example, you are looking for a drug-crazed guy who hasn't seen his mother since she threw him out of the house when he threatened her with a machete sixteen years ago and who has absolutely sworn to every person he has met since that he would rather swallow cut glass and put needles in his eye than see his mom again and who has been missing since Tuesday, when he whacked his girlfriend to pieces with a machete for no apparent reason, you can bet on it: he's at his mother's now, with the knife in his hand.

Another important thing I learned is that, in terms of solving crime, what people do usually isn't as telling as what they don't do. Look to the guy who doesn't respond when presented with evidence of a terrible crime. Or the guy who evinces no emotion when you tell him his buddies have just described, in detail, how he bashed a livery driver's head in with a club before taking fifty-six dollars from a small black leather pouch on the seat beside the corpse.

There was always drama like this in homicide. It never bothered me to be in crisis situations or in ones where there was lots of violence. That was just like home. But the drama in homicide was different: everybody was in it together. And "everybody" included unlikely characters like Vinnie, an Italian guy who lived with his mother and took care of her, though I'm not sure that's what he wanted to do. He was a great detective, a genuine tough guy, with one of those Italian hawk noses that I always loved. He had a bunch of white patent leather belts and shoes that were ridiculous looking. He was a scary guy with a lot of what was obviously not very repressed hostility.

He calls me once and tells me to meet him at a crime scene, a little house in the South Bronx neighborhood Jimmy Carter once visited and promised to (and then actually did) rebuild. But back then there are wild dogs in the street.

I meet Vinnie and we walk inside the little house together. There is blood everywhere—on the concrete steps leading into the kitchen, on the cheap wood cabinets and on the refrigerator door, in the sink, on the ceiling, in big footprint-shaped splatters on the floor. Somebody did a lot of cutting in here.

The cops have the slasher cuffed in the patrol car by the back door. Vinnie has on white patent leather shoes that match his belt and he looks at the blood, backs up, and says to the guy outside the door, "I ain't walking in there."

"Is the knife in there?" Vinnie asks the guy in the handcuffs, and the guy says, "Yeah, it is."

"Go get the knife," Vinnie tells him.

I look at Vinnie. "Are you fucking nuts? You're sending the perp in to get evidence?"

"I'm not going to get *that* on my shoes," Vinnie says, looking at the blood.

So the guy goes in and comes out with a bunch of knives. "I'm not sure if this is it," he says, handing Vinnie a number of different knives. "Is this it?"

"For Christ's sake, would you go in and look for a knife with fucking blood on it?!" Vinnie tells the guy.

Several minutes pass. Finally I turn to Vinnie and say, "Hey, you know, I think there's a fucking back door." Vinnie calls to the guy and says, "C'mon back here. *Don't leave.* You're staying here with us."

The guy comes out with a knife covered in blood. "That's it!" says Vinnie, all full of triumph.

I'm thinking, *Fucking A.* The blood on that floor is so deep it squishes when the guy walks back and hands us the knife. He stabbed the dead man fifty-six times, but he does just what Vinnie tells him to do. A helpful psycho slasher.

—

After my first year in the DA's office, I had confidence, but I got something else while working in homicide. I don't quite know what I'd call it, maybe a sense of power. Other people could see it. And I was still going out a lot, meeting women in clubs, women who were different from those I'd known before.

The club scene was starting to be a very big deal in New York. My favorite club was a basement place in the West Forties called Le Jardin. It wasn't clean, the bathrooms looked like a place to stack bodies, and it smelled worse. It was like Studio 54, before anyone knew about Studio 54. There were all kinds of people there, gay guys, night people, models, dancers, and one Bronx homicide DA.

I'd go anywhere and I loved meeting people DAs would never meet under ordinary circumstances. I'd bring straight girls to trans-sexual clubs sometimes and often they'd see all this exotic sexuality and get crazed. This was when transgender operations were still very new. I didn't know what was going to happen when I brought someone I'd met in one of those places home with me one night. She was gorgeous and I had seen her in clubs for months. When I took her attractive, tight-fitting dress off, I saw she had the whole deal! She had worked hard and gone through great pain to turn herself from an effeminate guy from Spanish Harlem into a beautiful woman. I was game. I was too ill at ease for it to be a great sexual experience, but what I liked about New York at the time was that you could go out and something was always going to happen, something you couldn't begin to predict.

I was involved with another woman I met in a club, a very beau-tiful, dark Panamanian woman who lived in a luxury Upper East Side apartment and had expensive clothes and an unbelievable col-lection of boots and shoes. It didn't seem like she had a job, as she was always available, mornings, afternoons, middle of the night; she acted as if *no* were a vile word. We went to a movie one night and afterwards she snuggled up and said, "Honey, if you had a lot of money, would you give me expensive gifts?"

"Cylinda, you know if I had a lot of money I would give you in-credibly expensive gifts," I told her. "But if you had money, would you give *me* expensive gifts?"

"Honey," she said, "I have been giving you expensive gifts!"

It hadn't occurred to me she was a hooker. Actually she was gay but made an exception for me. It was kind of a strange thing. But once again, that's the kind of place New York was then: something was always going to happen, you just never knew what.

Working homicide was a big plus with women. With a lot of the girls, there'd be a point where they'd say someone was bothering them or bothering their sister or whoever, and I'd just look at them and say, "Are you crazy? I'm in homicide. I'll take care of it. That's the end of that problem, okay?" And I'd call someone I knew on the force who could handle it, and that was that.

Girls liked the detectives I hung out with and this never hurt me either. Lloyd Wright was a very classy and handsome detective whom I absolutely idolized. A very complicated, tormented, intelligent, and brave guy, he was always the one who kicked the door down at crime scenes and went in before anyone else. He was very cool and he was a killer. Although full of anger, he managed to hide it behind a reserved exterior. He hated other black guys for embarrassing him racially, he hated white guys for giving black guys a hard time, he had a lot of hate, period, but women loved him. I brought him along with me to Manhattan clubs and women went completely nuts over him.

There are lots of perks when you're trying homicide cases. You get free lunches, and you can get friends who are policemen assigned to your cases. I had a friend in homicide who would say, "Listen, I got a girlfriend in the neighborhood where that murder took place. Get me assigned to the case and I'll come in, work like a dog all morning, and then spend afternoons with her." I'd do what I could.

Plus, because homicide trials are so intense, prosecutors usually got a couple of days off when they finished trying each case, which was great for me because I tried so many of them. They used to keep track of who in homicide tried the most cases. I was always number one. I'd try a case, stay out all night for a couple of days, and start up again. And I almost never lost.

I liked to read, and trying a case was a lot like telling a story: you wanted to tell a good tale and you wanted the jury to pay attention. I learned to tell my story simply and clearly. People like TV, so I tried to craft my case the way TV shows are plotted, complete with good guys and bad guys. But I never tried to present anyone as something he wasn't. "Ladies and gentlemen of the jury," I'd say, "this isn't TV. It's real. We take 'em as we find 'em." And people love "evidence"—blood, hair samples, prints; I swear, most people think only criminals have fingerprints!

Strangely, winning big cases often made me sick. Or worse, I would burst out crying. I would have to go someplace where no one could see me, outside the courtroom, sometimes in the bathroom. The truth is, I'd been a crybaby my whole life. I cried a lot as a kid. At school, I remember hiding in closets because I didn't want people to see me cry. No idea what the fuck I was crying about, but I never cried when I got hurt by my father or in the streets. In fact, when I was a kid, laughing was a way to mask pain, and I remember laughing and smiling at the beatings—and everything else—that made me angry. Irish culture is sentimental, and sentiment, in my view, is a virtue: men should cry and there are lots of men I admire who are very emotional and who cry at funerals and things like that. So I didn't think it was odd that I cried at various strange moments. But I started to notice that I cried at times when I should have been happy, when I was victorious at trial, for example, and I thought that was very odd.

It wasn't the crying that got me to a psychiatrist, though. Instead it was my complete inability to talk to women. Yeah, I knew a lot of women and I slept and danced with a lot of them, but I couldn't talk to them. To this day, I can't talk to women that much. What is there to say? I don't find my own feelings that interesting, much less somebody else's.

In my mind, most sensitive people share the sense that they aren't getting what they want. *Well, shut up and go get it*—that's what I've always thought. Clearly, however, there was something wrong with my approach. And after a series of relationships broke up around this point, I went to see a psychiatrist, a woman, on the Upper West Side. I cried during the entire first few sessions. I've since learned that crying is a symptom of depression. And that extreme, inappropriate responses to circumstances are another. But then I had no idea what was wrong or what I was crying about. I just kept crying, from the moment Dr. Abelin asked, "What's wrong?" to the moment she said, "I'm sorry we've run out of time for today."

Thirty years later, I'm still going to therapy, and I'm much better at it than when I started with Dr. Abelin on Central Park West. I have had a lot of great psychiatrists since Dr. Abelin but none had a nicer, more soothing voice. I'm still trying to figure out how to talk to people.

Cecil, a wealthy girlfriend I had at the time who came from a nice Kentucky family (her father was a newspaper publisher) and had gone to a Seven Sisters college, provided me with my first intimate experience of upper-class Protestantism. Cecil was as smart as could be and once ran off to join a circus, which I found very intriguing and attractive. She brought me home to meet her family. I had no idea that upper-class Protestants like to keep their houses cold but apparently they do. The house in Louisville was beautiful and was surrounded by trees God planted on his first day working, but the place was bone cold. After a day, I went to Cecil and said, "Look, I'll pay. Let's get the heat on in here." It was early in my three-decades-plus career as a psychotherapy patient, and neither the conversation with Cecil nor the thermostat advanced much further.

I was at Cecil's apartment in New York when my mom called my brother and left word that I should call her back right away.

"Your father left me," she says when I reach her.

"Mommy, that can't be true. He's Irish Catholic. Irish Catholics don't leave their wives. Jews do," I tell her, "but Irish Catholics aren't supposed to leave."

"No," my mother says. She's crying. "He left me. He took his stuff out. He didn't tell me. He's just gone."

My mom tells me she'd been at work and returned to find the house empty. She checked his closets. Empty. She checked the shelf in the bathroom where he kept his razor. Gone. They had been married for thirty years. Then my father joined AA, where he met a woman who was younger than my mom and with whom he's now run off.

"Well, you won't miss him," I tell her. "He was no good." I mean it.

I never forgave my father. I didn't have anything to do with him after that. I'd been estranged from him before, but after that I stayed permanently estranged. I hardly ever saw him. I talked to him on the phone sometimes. "I'm sorry," he'd say. "It wasn't my fault," he'd quickly add. *Fuck him,* I thought.

I'm a Catholic. I *have* to forgive. But first you have to admit what you've done and ask for forgiveness. My mother did and I loved her for it. But my father never did. Leaving my mother like that was very bad. And he proceeded to give her a hard time about support.

As time went on, I started to give my mom money, but I didn't have much of it back then. After paying my rent and financing long nights in clubs, the DA's salary didn't leave much.

Did I quit the DA's office because I needed money to support my mom? No, I just wanted more money. I loved working homicide, but after four years I saw that, thrilling as it was, homicide work basically involved putting poor people away, and you're always short on cash. If I had wanted to lock up poor people for low wages, I would have been a cop and gotten a gun and tried to prove myself in front of my friends. Also, the image of Ernie Peace—and the action that surrounded him—hadn't left my mind. I began to get the idea that making money and standing up for people was central to what was exciting about Ernie's practice. To really do what he did you needed to be independent, you had to go out on your own. I didn't give a lot of thought to how I would get business or how I'd learn to practice on my own, but I knew I had to try.

They had a party for me when I left the DA's office. It was difficult for me to accept expressions of affection so, though I went to the party, I left the room as soon as I could. Did any of the detectives, the DAs, Kevin Gilleece care when I decided to cross over to the defense side of criminal law? Not at all. It didn't matter to me or to anyone of them. What mattered to me was that there was money out there and action—and for money and action, as for most things, I was ready.

CHAPTER 7

I start making money the minute I go into private practice. In the first two months, I make more than I had during the entire previous year! And most of the business I had came from women I was sleeping with.

I work out of an office, really just a room, at 255 Broadway. I am still going out a lot, but I didn't use drugs, I was always alert, and if you called me I was there—all of which meant I wasn't like most of the people involved in the city's nightlife.

Club owners, call girls, bouncers, party girls and their boyfriends—they all begin calling as soon as I set foot in my room at 255 Broadway. There is a strict law governing New York nightlife: if you are a gorgeous party girl and your boyfriend adores you and pays your rent and buys you wonderful things, then you absolutely must have a brother or nephew who's in endless trouble and is about to get arrested. It's part of the gear.

"Eddie, I got this brother who is a junkie in the Bronx. You gotta go help. He's in trouble!" This is the kind of call that got me started on my way to a big-city legal practice. "Okay, where is he?" I'd say. And one thing leads to another. And then to another.

I knew how to go to court and handle cases and had other helpful attributes, too. I had tried so many cases as a prosecutor that doing so now as a defense lawyer is the easiest thing in the world: all I have to do is create reasonable doubts about what the state (the prosecutors and police) says. Who in their right mind believes the government about anything?

I am alert and can respond to crises quickly, even when roused from sleep. And I learn right away to get money up front from clients who are still worrying, still crying.

"Take it off," I once told a hoodlum who had fingers full of rings and lots of other jewelry. I was afraid he wouldn't pay me and so refused to go into court with him until he handed over the jewelry. (I gave it back to him later, after he brought me cash.)

Aside from the women I knew, I had two strong client bases. I left homicide with good connections and a reputation as a trusted guy who could deliver results. I could go into any Bronx courtroom and make things easy; everyone wanted to cut me a break and I never took advantage. Ernie Peace is a source of business, too; mostly he sends me gangsters and kids who get in trouble in New York.

Ernie is behind my first big payday.

"Ernie tells me you're a very good lawyer." Caesar, a highly decorated helicopter pilot in Vietnam, has been indicted in Newark for transporting stolen oil. He has a prior drug-smuggling conviction and is on probation. I have been in business only a week. "I'm going to jail for a long time if I'm grabbed on this," he tells me. No shit.

"Seventy-five hundred dollars," I tell him. It's the biggest number I can get out of my mouth.

Caesar has it on him, in cash, and he counts it out in hundreds. I have never seen so much money in one place. I have no idea where the Newark federal court is and absolutely no idea what to do with the case.

So I put the cash in my pocket. "I'll take care of it," I tell Caesar. "You'll be fine."

John McNally, a truly great detective, comes with me when I go to see the informant who is the main witness against Caesar. The informant lives in a really bad black Newark neighborhood. Not only are McNally and I the only white people on the informant's block, we are the only white people who have *ever* been on the block.

"John, we aren't going to make it across the street without getting killed. Let's get out of here." I don't want to get out of the car.

McNally has killed guys as a cop. He once walked into a liquor store holdup, pretended he was drunk, and then stuck his pistol in the robber's mouth. He is a detective the way Picasso is a painter: it is what God created him to do. He is always laughing and smiling but he is a fairly scary guy.

"Nah, come on," he tells me.

We go up to the place and knock on the door. The informant opens it a crack, then moves to slam it shut. McNally sticks his foot in the door and keeps talking, his big Irish smile blasting the whole time, and the guy lets us in! I can't believe it.

We're not sitting there for more than ten minutes before John has the guy talking about the various mental institutions he's been in and about the Pennsylvania thefts for which he's been indicted and convicted under a different name, all of which he has neglected to mention to the prosecutors.

"Well, that's something to work with!" I tell John on the way out, and he flashes me that big Irish grin.

"Hey! I bet you didn't know about the mental institutions and the felony record or about boppity, boppity, boppity," I tell the prosecutor as soon as I get him on the phone.

"Well, ah, interesting," says the prosecutor, promising to get right back to me. Next thing I know, he's back on the phone offering probation.

"We'll take it!" I say.

Caesar beats the case, thinks I am a big genius, and moves to Florida, where he gets a job as a helicopter pilot (which to me means he's smuggling drugs there). That's my first big case and it neatly dramatizes the young Ed Hayes in action. I just went around the clock in this fashion.

—

Very early on, I learned something fundamental about the law: if you have money and power, there is a lot of room within the law for play. Everybody knows that the law works differently for people who can afford to bend it, but it is one thing to know this and another to see what it means to the very rich men and the women who love them, at least sort of.

Just after I start on my own, I go to a professional prizefight and then to dinner with friends at One Fifth Avenue, which is then a fancy restaurant. Halfway through the meal, the raucous and charming woman next to me reaches over and sticks her hand in my pants. I am vaguely terrified; nothing like this has ever happened to me. "I'm going home with you," she says. Her name is Annie and I am curious and also a little afraid to argue. Besides, she's not ex-actly giving me much of a choice about whether I take her home or not.

When we get home, I see that Annie has boxing gloves tattooed on her shoulder.

"Why the gloves?" I ask.

"I'm going with a fighter."

Now I'm really terrified. But we get along, and as it turns out, in addition to going with a fighter, Annie is a part-time madam who turns an occasional trick herself. (I am not a trick—I'm a freebie.)

"One of my girls is in trouble! You've got to come over and help me!" Annie is on the phone just a few days after we meet.

As always, you just have to ask and I'm there. In this case, "there" is an enormous Park Avenue apartment where some guy has paid two girls to turn a trick. When I arrive nine detectives are in the hallway giving Annie's friend Patti, a Mexican girl with a shocking body and a terrified expression, a hard time, threatening to lock her up if she doesn't tell them where to find the other girl who has been there and has run out with fistfuls of very expensive jewelry.

When he found out his call girl had lifted his wife's jewelry, the guy who owned the place and the jewels and, apparently, the world, had promptly called not the police but the mayor at home. And the mayor sent the detectives who are giving Patti a working over. The guy's wife will be home in a few days and there is pressure to recover the jewelry before she returns.

I don't exactly know what is going on, but it is clear no one is too interested in Patti, except insofar as she can help find the girl and the missing jewelry.

"Look, Patti, you're going to have to cooperate or you are never going to see the light of day," I tell her when we get outside. She says she has an idea where the girl went, and we tell the detectives, who let Patti go on condition she agrees to meet prosecutors the next day.

I set a fee and tell Patti to be in my office the next morning, which she is, with twenty-five hundred dollars in cash. We go see the prosecutor, an Israeli guy named Sam. Since there haven't been any arrests (once there are some, news stories follow and then, inevitably, scandal, which is what everyone here wants to avoid), I'm betting the guy involved has some very good connections somewhere. I still don't know who he is, but I do know that the prosecutor takes one look at my client—and her unbelievable body—and cannot concentrate to save his life.

He actually tells us to leave. "Come back tomorrow," he says.

"Dress more provocatively," I tell Patti. "And bring me more money."

Patti shows up the next day in a tightly wrapped dress that barely covers her astounding breasts; predating Sharon Stone, she's left her underwear at home and makes sure everyone notices. Prosecutors try but cannot focus because of the way she looks. No one can.

By midday we are out of there and, as we leave, a detective calls to say all the jewelry has been recovered. End of story. I never hear from prosecutors—or anyone else—about any of this again.

I learn a lot from this spectacle, though. Lawyers tend to think legal practice is about law and its enforcement and its application to various exigencies. But most of the time, law is about power. Power in this situation focuses not on the exaction of justice but on the reclamation of riches, which of course works out well for everyone.

Patti calls me the next day to say she wants to take me to dinner.

"Oh yeah?" I say. "Why do you want to do that?"

"Because," she says, "I like you."

Now, this is scary. If I take her to dinner, I'll sleep with her and if I sleep with her, I'll never get paid from any one of these girls again; they'll all want to compensate me in bed instead of paying, and it's going to cause endless problems.

"No, Patti, I'm sorry, I can't do that." I'm very resolved. "Thanks again. No, honey, no."

I have some important advice for any lawyer who is going into business for himself: if you find yourself in similar circumstances, for Christ's sake, sleep with her. Refusing Patti was the stupidest thing I have ever done as a lawyer. You can always get money; someone like Patti comes along once in a lifetime.

The last time I heard from her, Patti was getting twenty thousand dollars a weekend to go to Las Vegas with Japanese businessmen. She was astonishing.

———

Within weeks of my taking care of Patti and Caesar, Paul Goldberger and Larry Dubin, criminal defense lawyers whom I met in court and instantly respected and admired, asked if I'd like to work with them in their office at 401 Broadway. Why not? Dubin is a wizard at cross-examination, especially that of law enforcement officers, most of whom hate paperwork but have to fill out various forms each time they make an arrest. He is so good at using statements made on arrest forms against cops that he probably wouldn't have had any trouble convincing a jury that a blank arrest form definitively and beyond a shadow of all doubt established a conspiracy to kill Kennedy. I learned a lot about cross-examination from Larry Dubin.

I didn't have an office. As my income increased, I became increasingly preoccupied with savings and investments. And also with the idea of buying old houses, fixing them up, and turning a nice profit. As a cost-cutting measure I decided not to bother with an office. I could work in the conference room at Goldberger and Dubin, with a phone; it was a good way to reduce overhead, which, it seemed to me, really killed people.

A secretary seemed unnecessary, too. But the phone, that was essential. I made millions of calls—and made it a point to call every single client every single night, always between eleven and twelve o'clock. The idea was to reach my clients just before they went to sleep so that their last waking thought each evening was: *Eddie Hayes is thinking about me.* People love to know their lawyer is thinking about them.

The women I brought home couldn't figure out what was going on when, no matter what they were doing or planning, I would go off every night between eleven and midnight to make those calls.

The early cases and the late-night calls generated more and more business. Everyone knew someone in trouble, someone whose boyfriend beat them up or who had an interim financial problem or something relatively easy to fix. I knew a lot of attractive, hardworking women who were illiterate and so totally flummoxed by things like medical insurance and housing applications. I could help these people out of lots of relatively minor jams.

And many women I knew from clubs brought in their boyfriends, some of them very substantial, respectable guys who had wives and children but who nonetheless set their girlfriends up in nice apartments and paid the rent and showered them with expensive gifts and jewels. A lot of times I didn't know what these guys were talking about, but whatever it was, I'd say, "No problem. I can take care of that." And I usually did. Which in turn led to more and more business.

Eventually the cases got more complicated. An art dealer, for example, came in to ask for help with a dominatrix I'd seen in clubs who had a passion for art. She was spending large sums of cash on paintings and the dealer might have problems with the IRS.

Obviously, if you're married to a dominatrix, you're not a standard guy, and it turned out his real concern was that the woman's husband might let the authorities know his wife spent hundreds of thousands of dollars in dirty money on paintings that her upscale gallery owner didn't report to the IRS. I worked this out. And in the process I learned a good deal about federal tax procedure and also that the city's sex economy touches more aspects of city life than most people imagine.

—

"I've been arrested. I don't know what to do. I don't have money. I'm broke all the time. Can you help?" A very nice, respectable mom from New Jersey is on the phone one day. The woman has a husband who is pretty useless and she's doing sex shows to pay for her son's tuition. Yes, this is just the sort of thing I can straighten out, fast. I bring her ten-year-old son's report card with me when we go to court in Brooklyn. Usually, on a charge like this, you have to plead to some kind of low-level violation. But a criminal violation really won't help this hardworking mom who's trying to put her kid through school. I show the judge the kid's near-perfect report card. "Your Honor, you gotta throw this out," I tell the judge. "For him," I say, and I point out the nice little kid sitting behind his mom in the courtroom. The judge, an Italian guy who thinks vice is a virtue, gives the lady a break.

"I don't have any money to pay you," the lady tells me on the way out of the courtroom. I tell her not to worry about it. "I have money. I don't need yours." She says, "Well, you can't do that, let me come give you a private show." "No, not that I wouldn't love that," I tell her, "but no, that's fine." "Look, don't insult me," she says. "It's the only thing I have to give you." Uh-oh. This is a *moral* issue.

One of the things I learned is how vulnerable people are. You have a lot of power if you recognize this. The law sometimes protects people who have nowhere else to turn, and sometimes it doesn't. But I could see that I could make things happen for people like the hardworking lady from New Jersey. I could help people. And—the other side of the coin—I could hurt people.

It would be a while before I learned that I could hurt some people in order to help other people—which is really fun!

———

I learned a lot about the mechanics of kept women during those first years in private practice. There were whole buildings in Manhattan full of women whose rent was subsidized by married men who, unless their families were home starving, wouldn't cut back on the women they kept or the costs involved in doing so.

I was fine with these arrangements. You see guys who are fifty-five or something and they're divorcing their fifty-two-year-old wives. What is the sense to that? She's probably been his best friend for his whole life, or at least for enough years to feel like his whole life, so why would he do that? Betray a friend, make your children unhappy, and then go get involved with some woman who probably doesn't like you too much anyway but will definitely have had enough of you when you get to be seventy? Maybe it's latent Catholicism, but I do not think divorce is okay. Sometimes you have to, yes, but there should be strong social disincentives; one thing I look down on Jews for is that they think it's okay to get divorced. My private views aside, I saw that there was a real market in delivering legal services to people who maintained these complicated relationships. In short order—and without a lot of scheming, hustling, or moving—I started to really cash in on the city's sex culture. At one time, I represented high-priced call girls, an after-hours club that featured live sex shows with dwarfs, and a bunch of rich gay guys who trolled transsexual clubs for gay go-go dancers.

My business wasn't entirely sex-related. I had other clients, too.

At one point I represented a family that owned a florist shop. Every month, someone there got pinched for selling pot; each time that happened, it was payday for Eddie Hayes. The family consisted of an Anglo mother and her half-Spanish son, who eventually shot and killed her black boyfriend, who was beating her; after I got him an acquittal, the mother gave me free lasagna for two years, but the murder ended the pot business and, with it, the monthly drug rap.

I wasn't kidding myself: the high life I hungered for when I left the DA's office looked a lot like the low life I'd seen in Bronx County Criminal Court. The big difference was that I was getting rich and my life was changing substantially as a result.

—

Drugs were a problem in the city then and people looked askance at lawyers who represented drug dealers. To me, dealers were just gangsters. Like everybody else. I wouldn't represent child molesters or rapists—I didn't like that—but with drug dealers my feeling was, if you want to use drugs, that's your problem.

Goldberger and Dubin, which had a lot of drug clients, represented a guy named Frank James who was always chainsawing up guys in his basement. Even for a drug dealer, James was a monster. He's doing life in prison now, but he once ran a loose confederation of dealers that included Pistol Pete Spriggs, who got pinched with a couple of pistols, a machine gun, a submachine gun, a kilo of coke, and thirty thousand dollars in cash in Brooklyn. It turned out Frank James didn't feel like paying a big fee to defend his guy.

I had just started out, I was salaried, and I was cheap, so Goldberger and Dubin sent me in to take care of Pistol Pete. I had never been in federal court before—except for the trip to Newark with Caesar—let alone done a federal suppression motion, and had no idea what to do.

The prosecutor lays out the evidence and I start putting the pieces together: it seems Pistol Pete's troubles began when a West Indian guy escaped from the Metropolitan Correctional Center, which is a federal prison near City Hall. An all-out effort to find the escaped convict ended when police showed up at Spriggs's apartment building and showed the superintendent a photograph of the guy. "Oh yeah, he's in his apartment," the super told police, and the feds went in without a warrant and found not a West Indian convict but Pistol Pete Spriggs at home with his gorgeous girlfriend and his automatic weapons.

Things look bad for Spriggs. He's black, he can't read or write, he's before a black conservative Republican judge, and he has a long criminal record, mostly for robberies and stickups. (He's actually done time for holding up a police academy!)

Spriggs is tough, though—he must have done protection work for James, or killing or something. He just sits at the defense table, not saying anything.

His girlfriend, who is a weird but exciting blend of black, Hispanic, and American Indian, has some legal problems, too. It's a mess. I'm trying to do the best I can, but I'm up against seasoned federal prosecutors and I'm totally outmatched. Pete Spriggs is going to jail for hundreds of years, at least.

And then, all of a sudden, I realize Spriggs really loves his girlfriend and she really loves him. And he's not complaining or saying anything like, Why did those rats send me this dopey green lawyer who doesn't know what he's doing? He's not saying a word.

I'm romantic. I look at those two and I say to myself, *Fuck everybody, I'm going to work here.*

I go looking for the super. He's gone, of course, and no one knows where to find him. There's a daughter, too, who also refuses to cooperate. I find her in Queens. She's a very nice girl, young, Spanish, and I'm a terror with this kind of girl. I talk and flirt with her; eventually she takes me to her father and I put him on the stand the following Monday.

"I'm from Paraguay. I don't speak English," he says through an interpreter as soon as he takes the stand. The agents said they spoke to him in English.

"I speak some German, some Guarani—a Paraguayan Indian dialect—and Spanish," he continues, again through an interpreter. "I never talked to those guys in English. I can't speak English and I don't understand it." That's the first thing.

The second thing the superintendent says is: "I had never seen a black person until I was well on in life, because there aren't any black people in the town I come from in Paraguay. I would not be able to pick out a black person in a photograph, Judge, because I really do have trouble telling them apart."

More importantly for Pistol Pete Spriggs, the super tells the judge, "The reason I came here to be close to my daughter is that I am going blind. I can't distinguish hardly anything anymore. That's why I stopped working. So I couldn't possibly have picked out a photo of that guy."

The judge clearly does not like Spriggs and does not want to throw the case out. A month later, however, I get notice that he's granted my motion and suppressed the evidence against Spriggs, leaving prosecutors no choice but to withdraw their charges.

"No," says Spriggs when I tell him he's going home.

"Yes, you are," I tell him. "We got you off."

The Friday after Spriggs's release, his girlfriend stops by my office with a canvas bag. "Pete has no money," she tells me. "All he has is in the bag. He wants to give it to you."

There's a gold watch, not a really good one but gold nonetheless, and some gold rings that are as big as bracelets. Monday morning, I go down to Forty-seventh Street and sell the watch and all the rings, and I take the money—it's a couple grand, which back then wasn't nothing—and I call England.

I had met some tailors from Anderson and Sheppard, the renowned English firm, not long before. They had taken my measurements and shown me some suits but I didn't have the money to pay for them, until now.

"Make up the suits!" I tell the English tailors. "I'm coming over next week to get them!"

I'd started to dress okay at UVA, but to go the next step up, to custom clothing, you have to know what you're doing. I was about to learn.

———

I look nothing at all like a regular Anderson and Sheppard customer when I come into the shop. I pull my money out of my sock. "I've only had this for two days," I tell Norman Halsey, a former paratrooper who now styles some of the best-dressed men in the world. "I want you to do the same thing for me that you've done for other clients. Make me look like a gentleman. When I open my mouth, I'll blow the whole thing, but until then, go ahead, make me look like a gentleman."

As I walk out with new suits—man, did they fit great! One is dark blue herringbone, the other is a pale gray-and-white-striped three-button number with a peaked lapel—Norman says, "Have you ever thought about custom shoes?"

I never had. I didn't know what a custom shoe was.

"I can send you to a man who made Winston Churchill's shoes, who made Humphrey Bogart shoes, a terrific fellow . . ."

Sounds great. Norman sends me out on a train and a bus to a small village and George Cleverley, a retired shoemaker famed for his distinctive "Tuczek toed" shoes. I leave with a five-hundred-dollar pair of custom shoes on order.

When the shoes arrive, I like them so much I decide to go back for more. I'm wild for this stuff. Cleverley makes me the most beautiful cordovan lace-ups. I am so pleased with these people, Cleverley and the tailors. They are genuine artisans, and they have great taste and are accustomed to upwardly mobile men, very few of whom grew up as I did, without a normal range of connections to people who can help explain how life works. I don't know much, but I've learned in homicide that there is no substitute for going to the scene and asking a few questions.

I sit for hours watching these guys stretch fabric, make suits, and do their intricate stitching, and I ask a million questions, which they like. I'm getting good at this. Then I go on a total shoe splurge. I buy shoes as fast as George Cleverley can make them.

It's the start of a whole world of new pleasure, new relationships. After the trips to England, I get to know terrific people like Tibby Weiss, an Orthodox Jew. Tibby comes from a family of Hungarian tailors, guys who know everything about fabric and fit, and has a little place on Delancey Street in New York. Once I go in to see Tibby and see a blue-and-brown-checked fabric, a very odd combination that I nevertheless really like. "I don't know, Tibby," I tell him. "What am I going to do with that?" But I call back four months later to tell Tibby I want the fabric. "Too late," Tibby tells me. "It's gone." I feel terrible. But Tibby too calls back, all excited, two months later. "I found the fabric! Nobody knows what to do with it!" he says, and I send a guy down with the money right away and I have the suit made. I really love this suit—you don't often find brown and blue checks. I love Tibby. And I love his son, who's a lawyer and likes clothes too. I love going down to his store. I love talking to him about Orthodox Judaism and worsted wools. It's a great part of an urban New York life.

Beckenstein Men's Fabrics makes clothes on Orchard Street. Neal Boyarsky and his son John run the place and I go there, too, and buy lavender gabardine and orange corduroy pants, but mostly I go there so Neal can abuse me. "Eddie, it's too goyish." "Neal, I'm a goy." "Yes, but it's not your kind of goyish."

I have to really study up on this stuff and learn how it works. I find all the best tailors. I have one now in New York—Vincent Nicolosi, who works across the street from my office and can hand sew thousands and thousands of stitches that last forever—and two in London, Steven Hitchcock and Edwin DeBoise. You can't buy that many suits, but it has gotten to the point where these guys are my friends and I can't *not* buy from them.

I have strong feelings about men's clothes, which only a good tailor can fit properly. The softer the clothes look, the more I like them; I don't like pads. Vincent Nicolosi can make a suit that's as soft as a nicely worn shirt crafted by one of my two shirtmakers. No one can make an upper-class English spread collar like Frank Rostron can, which is amusing since he's up from the streets of Manchester. Then there's Shaban, the tallest Pakistani in the world, a Princeton graduate who loves to talk politics while I buy the Italian striped fabric he and his Pakistani friends turn into great shirts. If the Knights of the Round Table could wear velvet doublets, I can wear a blue wide-striped shirt with a blue checked collar that Shaban has beautifully crafted.

Shoes! Anyone can dress well up top; shoes make the man. I still go to George Cleverley's, which is now run by John Carnera, George Glasgow, and Anthony Gaziano, a younger guy who is making me shoes with my initials carved into the heel. I even got Vans shoes from a guy named Gabor.

"Why you charging me so much money?" a kid I've gotten off the hook for drug dealing asks me after that first trip to England.

"See these shoes?" I point down to the cordovan custom slip-ons. "They're custom made. If I lose your case, kid, I got to go back to cheap shoes," I tell him. "And I ain't going back to cheap shoes! And you ain't going to jail!" That was my shoe speech. I had many opportunities to make that speech.

About a year after I went into business for myself, I bought a pair of shoes from John Lobb, a great British shoemaker in London. They were custom-made country shoes, the kind you wear in the English countryside. I put them on and said, "Now I've got to get a house."

In 1984, I bought the house to go with the shoes, I swear to God. It was an old wooden Cape Cod–style house in Bellport, Long Island, on Great South Bay, close to the beach. It wasn't the Hamptons, which was good. I was phobic about drinking at the time and a lot of Hamptons social life revolved around drinking and bars. Bellport was picturesque and quiet, and I started going out there every weekend, whatever the season, to rest up from my hectic city life.

Soon I was making the shoe speech about houses. "See this house?" I'd ask clients when they flinched at my fees, and I'd pull out a picture of the Bellport place. Then I'd ask for a lot more money.

That first Bellport house cost fifty-two thousand dollars and it was nice to have. It meant a lot to me. I spent a year fixing it up and I took a lot of girls out there. And I started thinking about gardening and landscaping, which I liked. I also liked the guys who did that kind of work. As I had with the tailors and the shoemakers, I started going around and asking guys in nurseries millions of questions, about shrubs, bulbs, planting.

These guys in the garden centers in Suffolk County were hard-working Hispanic immigrants, many of them illegal. They worked like animals and really knew how to plant. Usually one of them would call a few days after I'd been in to get some shrubs and to talk to them about flowering plants and the use of cow manure and sea-weed to make the stuff grow, and he'd say something like, "Hey, my cousin Pepe stabbed some guy. Can you get him out of jail?" I'd get the guy out and then I'd get free shrubs for years. Not bad.

I had a very nice garden and I was very proud of how well I could dig. I was crazy for shovels. I had every kind of shovel you've ever seen in your life. I also liked folding knives and pocketknives that you could put in your hand and use as a tool the way tailors work making those crazy little stitches and somehow end up with some uncommonly beautiful creation.

Bellport has a ghetto: the south side of the railroad tracks is all nice little white houses, and the north side of the tracks is a black neighborhood. While I was fixing up my house I got in the habit of hiring poor black teenagers to help me in the garden. It turned into something wonderful as I discovered that the Eddie Hayes rule of life, which is that nobody really gives a fuck about you unless you work like an animal and make yourself useful, was transferable. These kids wanted a chance and they were willing to work if you stayed on them. Enoch, Piggy, Craig, Leon, Anthony, Scrappy— they became a rewarding part of my life. I was a pain in the ass some-times, they got in trouble, their lives were an endless saga of family problems, but they have mostly done well out of the relationship and I love them for their bravery and their physical hardiness. Plus, as time went on they have become like uncles to my son Johnny, whom they put on the landscaping crew where he carries his weight like a man. We all go mountain biking together and he's as good as the best of them—and he looks out for his father.

A year after I bought the Bellport house, I sold it and bought a much bigger one, on the water. I didn't need any incentive to work harder, but if you're someone who does need one, a big mortgage can be very useful. I always needed money during the year it took to renovate the rambling white wood house.

The place is almost finished—I am short just a few contractor's fees—when I get a call from Jerry, a stickup guy who's been pinched in Brooklyn.

"I can't believe you got me out!" he says when I spring him. "I've got about nine previous arrests for robbery."

"You're out, pal, and I'm going to get a shoe shine," I tell him. A guy near the Brooklyn courthouse gives the world's best shoe shines.

I'm sitting there getting a three-dollar shine—this is twenty years ago—and Jerry comes back with a bag and says, "I know it's more than this, but I want to give you something right now to thank you for getting me out of jail," and he hands me the bag, which is full of money. It turns out there's five thousand dollars in cash in there, which is enough to put me ahead on the renovation costs. This is more than a payday: it's a lifesaver. Because I know that once I am ahead, I will stay ahead forever.

It's raining and after I give the shoe-shine guy a big tip, I've got two things on my mind: (1) I can't get a taxi and (2) the shoe shine is going to get fucked up in the rain. I put the money in my pocket and duck into a subway. All right, I may fuck up the shine, but I've got the money and I'm thinking maybe I'll take the afternoon off.

"Give me your money!"

Unbelievable. The next thing I know some big six-foot-five, three-hundred-pound black guy is on the train next to me telling me, "I want your fucking money."

"I don't have any money," I tell him, implausibly. I'm wearing a custom-made suit, a custom overcoat, and a hat. I look like a guy who, as this motherfucker seems to know, has a bag stuffed with cash in his right inside coat pocket.

I have had a lot of aggravation and I'm not giving the guy my money.

For one thing, I tell myself, if I give him the money he'll probably kill me anyway, and if he just messes me up but doesn't kill me the police will come and I'm going to have some trouble explaining why I'm running around with a bag of cash from a gangster.

"Look, I'm not giving you any money," I tell the guy, "but I'll give you a token." I hand him a token and get off the train. I walk, in the rain, to the bank, put the money in, and almost forget what the rain is doing to my shoes. I am in a good mood!

I loved this life. I really did. It was a life I understood, with troubled people and tangled relationships and lots of action, and it paid well. I could understand what you had to do, without knowing everything in the world about the history of English common law.

Maybe it was the shoes, the suits, the houses. Or maybe it was the Irish politician in me. But much as I loved criminal law, my ambitions began to extend beyond criminal practice. I wanted a bigger stage and a broader constituency. Gangsters, drug dealers, troubled women—I was worried my life would be subsumed by criminal practice. I had some good fun, though; that's some fucking life.

And it was about to get richer, crazier, even more fun.

CHAPTER 8

The country would go to the dogs in half an hour if journalists weren't around. Usually these guys speak the truth. Which is why everyone is always unhappy with them.

I know a lot of reporters from the courthouse and I love them. If I'd devoted the same energy to movie stars, who make millions, that I put into newspaper guys who make nothing, I'd be worth fifty million dollars today. But I don't like most movie stars. And I only help people I like.

Also, though newspaper guys didn't make me millions, they sure helped me get to the larger stage I was looking to play on.

My first publishing deal is for a group of homicide detectives who are doing a book with Jimmy Breslin. One of the detectives commits suicide and, as a favor to the widow and his friends, I agree to handle his estate. I didn't know anything at all about estates. There is something you're supposed to do to expedite probate but it would cost the family money, so I go to the clerk and, straightforward guy that I am, look him in the eyes and say, "There has got to be a way around this." It being the Bronx, the clerk, of course, knows the way.

That's it. *What the fuck*, I figured, *everything works the same way as the crime business*. This turned out to be a very good insight to have had at the start of a whole New York life in media and politics.

—

It all begins in the mid-eighties with Mike McAlary, a ballsy reporter with *New York Newsday*. One weekend McAlary is out in Bellport with Mike Daly, another reporter, and they drive by a spec house I'm building. McAlary is a young, very romantic guy and his wife wants to live on Long Island. He comes in the next day and says, "I want to buy your house."

"Michael," I ask, "how much money are you making?"

He says he makes thirty-five grand.

"Michael," I tell him, "there is absolutely no way you can buy this house. It's going for $500,000."

"That's *your* problem, Eddie," he says. "Because not only am I buying this house from you, but you're my lawyer now so you're going to have to figure out a way I can buy this house."

"Michael, you're nuts!" I say as he walks out the door.

McAlary calls the next day from a pay phone in Brooklyn, where some huge riot is going on. Yelling and screaming and sirens tear through the phone.

"Where the fuck are you, Mike?"

McAlary says he's in East New York.

"Michael! Cops won't even go in there anymore."

"Well, I'm here," he says, "and I'm going to get some wood." ("Wood" is what reporters call front-page stories.)

"Don't get killed," I tell him.

Next day McAlary is on the front page of the paper. I think, *This guy's got a future*. I call him up and say, "This is what we're going to do: we're going to switch you from *Newsday*, where you are making $35,000, to another newspaper where you're going to make $65,000; at $65,000, a bank will lend you half the money and I'll lend you the other $250,000. You're going to pay that back to me in three years, with interest. If I can raise your salary in the next three years enough so you can borrow the rest of the money, we're all gorgeous. If not, I'm fucked and you're fucked."

"Seems reasonable to me," McAlary says.

The guy is fucking fearless. He will cover anything, do anything. If he writes that some politician is a jerk and the politician complains, next day he will write another column, saying, "I thought about it overnight. This guy is *really really* a jerk. And his wife and all his friends are jerks, too."

In three years, McAlary's salary goes from $35K to $300K. Of course, he gets the house and lives around the corner from me and we have a ball.

———

When I met McAlary, I had a client, a professional basketball player, who was under investigation for carrying packages. Of drugs. Rudy Giuliani was US attorney and pretty clearly had more of an interest in this guy than was warranted by the facts of the case.

"Look," I tell the lawyers in Rudy's office, "you have no reason to believe this guy is involved in serious drug running, and no reason to chase after him, except that he's a high-profile guy and you think he can lead you to other high-profile guys." Giuliani, who loves high-profile prosecutions, presses forth.

So I call McAlary and tell *him* what is going on. Next day the *Daily News* runs a big story saying the US attorney is picking on my guy and there is no evidence against him. Guess what? That's the end of the investigation. The idea that I, as an individual, can match the power of big institutions by co-opting the power of public opinion is not lost on me.

I start to learn how to try cases not just before twelve individual jurors but before twelve thousand or twelve hundred thousand or however many people get their ideas from reading daily newspapers.

I figure out a lot about the newspaper business, too. As the city's demographics change, so do its readership habits. By the 1980s the three tabloids in town—the *Daily News*, the *New York Post*, and *New York Newsday*—are in a death struggle for a shrinking pool of advertisers and readers. There is ferocious competition for talent. My response, of course, is to cash in. My philosophy is pretty simple: if the guys at the top are going to make a bunch of money, the guys who do all the work—the writers and editors, a lot of whom are now my friends—should profit too.

Jim Dwyer, Gail Collins, Richard Johnson, Mike Daly, Jim Willsey, Joanna Molloy—there were lots of good, hardworking people at the city's papers. McAlary was the first, but in time I represented pretty much all of them. I negotiated deals for them with the papers' owners, most of whom were fucking hoodlums. Robert Maxwell, who bought the *Daily News* in 1991, was a thief, and Abe Hirschfeld, who owned the *Post* for eighteen days in 1993, eventually went to jail for trying to have some guy killed. *Hmm,* I thought to myself. *This is a world in which Eddie Hayes can do business.*

"Just wait," I told gossip columnist Richard Johnson, who was getting a lot of grief from his bosses at the *Daily News*. "You're a great reporter. You're a great columnist. Something will happen." Something did happen. Rupert Murdoch, who had sold the *New York Post* in 1988, bought it back in 1993, and the first person he wanted to hire was Richard Johnson. The night the deal went through, Murdoch sent Ken Chandler, the *Post*'s editor, to my house at ten o'clock to say, "I want to hire Johnson."

Murdoch is Australian and a spiritual descendant of every snatch-and-grab felon who was ever transported to that country; Chandler is a tabloid guy if ever there was one: not only did he never see a story unfit—too unsubstantiated, too sleazy, too covered with dirtbag fingerprints—to print, he also never saw a story too unsubstantiated, sleazy, or biased to put on the front page of whatever low-down, sensationalist tabloid he happened to be working for. And they are both perfect for the newspaper business.

"You *are* going to hire Johnson," I responded to Chandler. "He starts tomorrow morning." And he did. Salary hike? You bet. I wasn't doing my job if I got you only a 50 percent pay raise.

There were times when I represented the editors of the *Post* and the *Daily News* at the same time. Conflict of interest? Catch me if you can! That's how we played. I learned that you couldn't enforce civil contracts in New York City. No court, that is, was going to make somebody work for somebody else just because he'd signed a contract saying he would. The employer could make a case for damages, but you could count on the fact that it would drag on for years and that by the time it was over, the ownership of the paper at issue would have turned over at least three times. So I would just say to a reporter or editor client, "You have a contract? Okay, we'll ignore it."

For a while McAlary seems to switch jobs every twenty minutes. The papers are nuts, hiring people back and forth; the guy who moves most winds up with the most money in his pockets. The *News* is wonderful. The *Post* is wonderful. It works for the top guys and it sure as hell works for my friends and me.

There was a great reporter named John Cotter at one of the tabloids. I help him negotiate a move to the other one, doubling his salary in the process. He calls in ecstasy. What's my fee, he wants to know. I won't take his money. "Don't worry," I tell him. "You can make it up to me." He had a heart attack and died soon after. From happiness, I think.

The tabloids treated women reporters like dogs. Joanna Molloy is one of the best—the funniest, most brilliant—writers in the business. Every time Joanna's contract came up, all hell would break loose: the guys at the top reliably tried to stiff her on salary hikes she'd earned. I love Joanna and would do anything for her, which meant that I gladly made sure whoever was handling contracts at her paper was a client of mine. "Raise her salary to a level equal to what the male reporters get," I'd then tell her boss and my client, "or I'm not representing you anymore."

McAlary called one afternoon and said so-and-so at the *Daily News* was a great sportswriter, could I get her a better deal? I couldn't get hold of McAlary's friend, but without speaking to her I got her a new job, at the *Post*.

I called her up. "You start at the *Post* in two weeks and they are going to pay you significantly more than you are getting now."

"Who," she said, "are you?"

"I'm Eddie Hayes. I'm a friend of Mike McAlary's."

"Yeah," she said. "Well, I don't know Mike McAlary." She knew who Mike was but had never spoken a word to him and said she had no idea where he got the idea she wanted to change jobs. But I got her the job, and she took it. Really, it was a very crazy time.

We did outrageous things. If I needed some guy to get a raise, I'd feed him exclusives for a while, so he'd look good. I knew guys in the police department, in the courts, and in homicide; from the guy in the street to the guy in the suite, I had contacts.

I represented Bill Wallace, who ran the executive office of the police department's detective division, and I was friendly with John Timoney, a big boss in the NYPD, and half the action guys on the city's force, too. I'd hear something from one of them about how the cops were going to nail some substantial guy the next day. I'd say, "Oh, can you do that the day after? We already have a story for tomorrow." They'd wait.

Remember the guy who was kidnapped and held for ransom in a hole in Central Park? The guys investigating the case were clients—and friends—of mine and called to say, "We know where he is—he's in a hole in the park. We're going to get him now."

I get Mike on the phone right way. "They're going to get the guy right now," I tell him.

"I can't come now. I have a story in Queens! Can you tell them to wait?"

"Michael, *he's in a fucking hole!* In Central Park. In the ground. I can't tell them to wait!"

"Well, can you tell them to drive slow?" says McAlary. He's nuts!

He got cancer and died in 1998, but he had some good run: he won a Pulitzer, wrote some good books, and was a terrific reporter.

You know, I think to myself after I've upped the salaries of most of my reporter friends, *there's got to be something else I can do with this.* I'm around the courthouse, around cops and hoodlums and drug dealers, all kinds of action guys. I'll call one of my reporter friends and say, "Hey, did you see the story about those hoodlums busted for paying off cops?" Or the dealers tied up with the mob? Or the crooked movie guys? Or whatever I happened to know something about. It turns out I have a pretty good eye for a story because, next thing I know, not only am I negotiating contracts for big-city reporters but I'm playing a big role in what they write.

This ain't bad! I think. Want to keep something out of the paper? Want to put something in? Turns out the guy who keeps the reporters happy has as much to say about what goes in and what stays out as the guy who's spent all his millions to buy the thing. There are guys who will spend fifty to a hundred million dollars to own a newspaper, but if I represent all the guys who work for the paper, I'm doing better than the owners.

I don't make money off this stuff, but I get a big payback. I say all the time that I don't care about anything but money, but it's not true. There is one thing I really care about: loyalty. I am always loyal to my reporter friends, and they are loyal to me.

For one thing, virtually everyone in the business is basically a neighborhood white boy, although not necessarily Irish or Italian or even male. Even the Jews and the women who work in the business have a basic knock-around white-boy sensibility, the sensibility of the guys I knew in Jackson Heights, who grew up in an insular culture, in a world of limited ambitions; often they had a mean streak that was not at all concealed and a high degree of suspicion of others, but also a deep sense of place and an unshakable loyalty to their friends. Other than the part about limited ambition, I identify with all of this. Not that I wouldn't have fought to the death for these guys anyway, white boys or not. I don't abandon people. As everyone knows, things are really bad when the Irish guy starts pulling out.

McAlary, bless his psychotic soul, was dead when my life fell apart a number of years later. But Michael Daly and Joanna Molloy and Richard Johnson and Gail Collins and lots of other reporter friends remained loyal when I was in trouble and they helped a lot.

Back, though, in the eighties and early nineties we were all busy—
making money, having fun, and, incidentally, making the city better,
too. New York was one of the most badly run places on earth. In the
late eighties, when thousands of people were dying of AIDS, you
couldn't test pregnant women for the disease. How stupid is that?
The city's political scene was—and is still—dominated by a culture
of entitlement, the legacy of the liberal Jews and African Americans
who controlled New York City's Democratic Party. The political
climate changed dramatically, however, in 1993, when Rudy Giuliani, an insular and mean-spirited Italian guy who was hostile to
women, insensitive to others, but also brilliant, brave, and determined to do his duty, the ultimate neighborhood white boy, moved
in. At last, the city's politics began to shift away from those who
produced the unworkable culture of entitlement to a politics dominated by people who were striving, as neighborhood white boys
strive, toward bourgeois domesticity and order.

———

"I got a poor kid here, in some trouble for purse snatching. Can you
help him?" Jimmy McManus, who runs the McManus Democratic
Party Club on Eleventh Avenue in Hell's Kitchen, which members of
his family have run for a hundred years, is asking *me* to do something.

Michael Daly introduced me to McManus. And in the early 1980s
I start hanging around him and the Democratic Party Club, where I
learn a lot more about how power and politics work in the city.

McManus is a very decent guy who really cares about people, and
he and the club—which has great connections with the unions, as
well as with all the city agencies established to handle immigrants
and their zillions of problems—see the Democratic Party as a way
for poor people and working New Yorkers to take some control over
their lives. McManus has real power. He can turn out the vote, pick
judges, get them elected, get good jobs for people, and then make
sure that the people who have those jobs help his friends and friends
of the party. Patronage, the reward for service, is the muscle that

moves the McManus political machine. There are a million favors that need to be done—up and down the avenues, everywhere the city's bureaucracy reaches, into the courts, into the schools, with building inspectors and bureaucrats, everywhere—and McManus is a guy who can really help you out.

There's a front room in the McManus club and a few back rooms. You can't have a political club without back rooms. They don't let you do it. It's in the license: you gotta have back rooms so you can have back-room deals. There isn't much in any of the rooms—a bunch of half-empty coffee cups, cheap tables, mismatched chairs. Anybody who wants Jimmy McManus can find him here, probably in one of the back rooms, every Monday and Thursday night. Guys are drinking, playing cards, taking care of problems, going into the back room to smoke and work things out.

"My electricity doesn't work." "My son needs a job." "I don't know what to do with immigration." People walk in all the time and say stuff like this.

"Come on into my office," I say to the guy who needs help with immigration or electricity or whatever, and then I lead him out to the street. That's where business—my business, anyway—gets done.

I have a simple rule with Jimmy McManus: whatever he tells me to do, I do. Jimmy calls and says, "Some guy has been arrested on a C5924 felony," and I'm on my way down to criminal court, whether I know what a C5924 felony charge is or not, to rescue whoever it is. A lot of times it's a kid who just keeps getting in the same kind of trouble again and again; often I don't get paid for any of this. I'll call Jimmy McManus a month after I've resolved the kid's case, and the kid's mom will answer Jimmy's phone. "Jimmy! I never got paid for this and you get free workers!" I'll say and he'll laugh.

Like any other self-respecting Irish guy, I am a natural politician. My basic operating policy now, as it was back in the alley behind Aunt Nonie's house in Jackson Heights, at the frat house at UVA, and pretty much everywhere else I've been, is: *Tell me what you want. Tell me how I can get it for you. Don't worry about paying me now. I'm sure you'll make it up to me later.* Turns out to be a very workable principle.

Since there's no real difference between my work and my life, my involvement with the city's Democratic machine—like everything else I am doing, including going to clubs, sleeping with women, planting my garden, and running into reporters in the courtroom—turns out to be very good for business, too.

One of the first things you see if you hang out on the West Side with Jimmy McManus and the Democratic Party machine is that Democratic fund-raising is often a cash business. You go to rallies. The candidate asks for contributions. People, many of whom are workers and rank-and-file laborers, give cash. Now the campaign has a lot of cash. What happens next? Just what you would expect: the campaign is eventually investigated and Eddie Hayes gets new business.

Ten minutes after the city elects David Dinkins mayor in 1989, for example, a big investigation into his campaign finance gets under way and Suzanne Duboise, the very attractive upper-middle-class black woman who heads Dinkins's campaign finance committee, is on my phone.

Suzanne is as tough as God makes anybody. Nobody can scare anything out of her. "The DA has his entire force serving subpoenas on me. Will you help me out here, Eddie?" she says, and I do.

The next thing I know, Michael McAlary is on the phone wanting me to leak information about Suzanne, which, of course, I refuse to do. The next day Mike writes a column saying something must be going on if she has Hayes as a lawyer. It also says, "I'm not talking to my lawyer anymore because why would I bother to have a lawyer who won't tell me anything?" McAlary's piece runs on the front page of the *New York Post* and is a terrific advertisement for my business. The investigation goes no place.

—

Thanks to my reporter friends, I am now operating in new spheres, have many interesting new women to sleep with, and am more inclined than ever to view life as an endless political campaign. Why shouldn't everybody be happy and why shouldn't I get everyone what they want? This soon leads logically to the next question: Why shouldn't I get all the votes?

In fact, I *was* getting votes now, in the sense that people saw that I could do things for them and, gradually, more and more substantial people placed more and more trust in me. The politician in me made me a lot of friends and I had a lifelong habit of making friends forever. The relationship I started at this time with Si and Victoria Newhouse was one of these relationships; it was also one that changed my life and significantly expanded my horizons—and reach—in the city.

Si Newhouse is incredibly wealthy; he's got billions. Along with his brother, Donald, he owns and runs Advance Publications, a vast media empire that includes Condé Nast, the richest, glossiest magazine group on earth. There's not much that rattles Si. Controversy doesn't bother him. He *likes* it when people are controversial; it adds a little excitement to his life. Si, who was a big friend of Roy Cohn's when he was younger, likes tough guys.

"What do you know about this labor leader in Baltimore?" Si asks me at the dinner party where I first meet him. I have no idea what the fuck he's talking about. I barely know where Baltimore is. But with all my detective, reporter, and political friends, I am usually no more than two phone calls away from finding out anything I needed to know.

At dinner, Si says he gets to his office early. I call him at five the next morning. He answers his phone, and I tell him all about the labor leader in Baltimore, who has extensive ties to organized crime and is being investigated all over the place. I guess Si is impressed. In time, he asks me to find out and do all kinds of other things for him. Whatever he asks me, I do. That question about the Baltimore labor leader is the beginning of a long and productive relationship with Si, Condé Nast, and many of its employees.

———

It turns out there aren't a lot of people who will deliver whatever a person needs. Especially not a lot of lawyers, most of whom listen and talk but won't actually do what needs to be done. As a kid, I had learned about doing and moving. Most family life is based on an exchange of words; in mine, you had to move, get out of a room, duck, take a beating. No one was sitting around the dinner table in Greenville, South Carolina, or Smithtown, Long Island, saying things like, "Oh, that's a nice tie." It was more like, "Take that tie off, or I'll strangle you with it." You had to move. It was the key to survival. *Scheme, hustle, move, and score.*

I knew, long before I met Si Newhouse, that the difference between people who become extremely powerful and those who don't is often just raw ambition. There are lots of very intelligent, competent people out there who would rather spend time with their families or friends than work the extra three or four hours a day needed to go really far in the world. Not me. I was willing to put in the hours, and so I would do better than most people because I tried harder. I was willing to get hurt more and also to hurt more people in the process. I may not be a good person, but if you give me ten dollars I will deliver the body. The good guys in Raymond Chandler, Ross Macdonald, and all the other private-eye novels I loved as a kid followed one simple rule: *There's something in it for me, there's something in it for you, I'll take care of it.* That I could do.

———

Years later, I get word that Si's wife has phoned three times while I am out at lunch. "Three times," I say to myself. "There's a real problem!"

I call Victoria. "What is going on?" I ask.

"There's a guy stalking Si!" He is showing up outside their house and trying to get into Si's office night and day.

I call a couple of detective friends, tough guys from Brooklyn, guys whom I trust not to hurt anybody but who are good for this kind of thing. "Go stand outside Si's place," I tell the detectives. "If you see anyone creepy there, grab him."

They actually find the guy, who is a loon, a nut, which is a problem; you can't beat up a nut and be sure he'll go away. A semilegiti-mate guy, you beat him up, he doesn't come back. But a nut is a nut; you beat him up, he comes back. I don't know what the fuck to do with this guy, who ends up skipping bail. Now no one can find him.

I call a friend of mine who is the second in command of the detective division. "Billy," I say, "we have got to find this fucking guy. He's gone out of state. Do what you have to do, will ya? Find him."

An hour later the district attorney calls. "Eddie!" he says, "I just had *four* detectives show up on this skipped bail. It's a misdemeanor, for Christ's sake! What are you doing?"

"We've got to find this guy," I tell him. "That's it."

"So who is the detective troop working for?" he asks. "Are they working for you? Or are they working for the city?"

I say, "You've got to find this guy. It's for a friend, a client!"

He says okay, and he sends two detectives out to Chicago, where the stalker nut has made traced calls from a pay phone. A woman detective goes to all the flophouses and SROs within walking distance of the pay phone and actually finds the fucking guy and snatches him and calls in the Chicago police, who extradite him to New York, where he's thrown in the can, on aggravated-harassment charges, for a few weeks.

The day he gets out, I make sure that two guys who look like Genghis Khan's bodyguards are waiting for him outside the jailhouse door. "You're going to be in and out of there for the rest of your life if you keep bothering Si Newhouse," they tell him. This time he gets the message.

The guy leaves and no one hears from him again. He was probably a harmless guy. I didn't know anything about him. I didn't know for certain that he was dangerous, but I was afraid he might be.

My relationship with Condé Nast generated a lot of work: its editors and writers can keep you busy forever with their divorces and real estate deals, their brothers-in-law and nannies and drivers with criminal problems. This isn't particularly profitable financially, but it's enormously profitable for figuring out where the levers of power are located and how New York society really works.

I am living large, still going to clubs, but generally learning all manner of things useful to someone elbowing his way around the city and climbing up the social ladder.

———

Out in Bellport, my garden is blooming. I like flowers. I assume that since *Vogue* editor Anna Wintour, who is renting a little house near my house on Shore Road, is an upper-class English woman, she is probably interested in gardening and I try hard to bond with her over roses. Anna Wintour, however, has absolutely no interest in gardening. We have to find something else to talk about; she is on her way up, just like I am.

In truth, I get to know Anna Wintour because, even though she never eats, she likes to order the kind of food I like to eat, steak mostly. If I can wangle a seat next to her at dinner—at Si New-house's or in Bellport—I can eat *my* dinner and *her* dinner.

The level of work and intensity I live with every day is brutal. I continue with my demanding workouts, late-night schedules, and expanding nightly call list and regularly put in very long hours. Even shopping is a lot of work: it's one thing to go to a store and shop for off-the-rack clothes; it's another to pick out fabric and go to the tailor and learn how tailoring works and consider forty-seven different types of shoulder cuts and linings and study up on how the instep of shoes should be cut. A lot of work, of course, is something I enjoy, but it leaves little time for normal socializing. There comes to be little distinction between my social and my professional lives, especially now that so many things are coming together for me.

All of which is to say that, despite the failure to bond over roses, Anna Wintour soon became a friend and a client. She is someone I like and admire. She is a good mother—though she is physically incompetent. It was ridiculous to see her try to pick up her kids or give them ice cream or something. She just can't—she doesn't drive and she can't cook. Luckily, she has people who do those things for her. And she's a really good dancer.

I liked girls, and girls liked clothes: one absolute rule is that if you help a woman buy a dress it's a lot easier to take it off, and if you can get women into gorgeous shoes it's that much easier to get them out of the shoes later. I used to go shopping with my women friends and I knew a lot about women's clothes. Anna, who dresses beautifully, was someone I could always talk to about that.

She comes from a political family—her father was an editor of a big London newspaper and her sister and her brother are both distinctly on the left—and she pays tuition for half the world. She's generous and good-hearted, even though she has the emotional range of a returned garment or a canceled sale at Bergdorf's. Since I myself am totally self-created, I look hard at other people with an eye to figuring out what created them. Anna, who never went to college but learned the values of the culture in which she grew up, is very much a child of the British upper class, which frowns on emotional display.

Watching people carefully, trying to determine what motivates them—essential skills for the trial lawyer—turned out to be very useful for discovering likable traits in people you might otherwise find impenetrable or unattractive. Just as success with a jury will often hinge on understanding the power of small moves, so too did successful handling of press relations and social interactions with cool upper-class British women like Anna.

I also met another English immigrant at about the same time, Tina Brown. Tina is sort of a police reporter for the media and political upper class. She is a very good investigative reporter with a lush body, and both of those assets have helped her make her way in the United States of America. She's good because she sees when things are connected where other people wouldn't notice. I like the women she has around her—they're smart, they're feminine, and they wear good shoes.

A fairly prominent psychiatrist came to see me after his son was locked up for selling drugs. It was a great mess: the father was terrified, as the kid, an eighteen-year-old student at a very good college, was facing extensive jail time.

There was a rat involved; that was clear to me from the first minute. I found the rat, another college kid, and called the prosecutor to say, "Look, so-and-so has got to be the cooperating individual whose testimony you used to pinch my client. So-and-so is at such-and-such a college. I hope you don't mind, but I am going to send someone up there to interview him. I just want you to know that. I am not trying to scare him. I just want to interview him." The key thing was that the snitch was going to be exposed: two seconds after the prosecutor got off the phone with me, I was going to send an investigator to the kid's college, and two seconds after the investigator arrived on campus and started asking questions, everyone in the whole school would know the kid was a rat, which the kid most definitely would not want. As I thought he would, the prosecutor called back and offered reduced charges against my guy.

The encounter taught me the same thing that Patti Bravo—the knockout girl whose body and lack of undergarments rendered the Manhattan prosecutor speechless five years before—had: you have to know where the points of decision are.

As I was finding out, deft handling of both politics and the media requires that knowledge. The press surrounding Anna Wintour's divorce made her uncomfortable. She called me as a lawyer and, I think, as a friend to say that New York magazine was going to do a big story about the end of her marriage and she was worried.

"First of all," I tell her, "you have to cooperate. You can't be a journalist and not cooperate. Second, you are going to get a beating. If you are the editor of a high-profile magazine and you're having a flagrant affair, you are going to get a beating. That's it. But the important thing is: no one is going to remember or even care about what's in the story, so long as the picture on the cover of the magazine is great." She doesn't want a picture. I prevail on her to get the magazine to let her provide one rather than have her sit for their own photographers. Of course, Vogue comes up with a beautiful picture.

When the New York story runs, Anna calls, yelling and screaming, "You shouldn't have had me do this. It's terrible." I tell her, "It's going to pass. Everyone will remember the picture. No one will remember what the article said." Which is true. *Vogue* is bigger than ever and Anna is happier than ever.

———

My relationships with Si and Anna and other Condé Nast honchos generate more and more work. There are even times when I represent both sides of an in-house conflict; while representing Condé Nast, for example, I negotiate severance agreements for a couple of departing editors; no one is unhappy with the outcome either.

I know how to make things work, and I'm getting good at using the combined force of the press and the law and my energy and ability to focus to get people what they want. In return, people help me get what I want: power, money, recognition, and affection. Not just for me but also for the crew of friends I assemble. I call myself a mouthpiece because that is what I am. The word has a pejorative sense to some people, but to me, it's an honor. I love my work, but I know what I do isn't always pretty. The law is made through the exercise of power. History is full of terrible things that have happened under the umbrella of the law. I try to figure out what happened and then make the best of it, often under unpleasant, even corrupt circumstances. I was raised to believe that sin is part of life. Sin—trouble and heartache—is my business. I am not a saint, and the work I do is often tawdry, sometimes sordid, and occasionally disgusting. I've always liked people who keep things clean—maintenance crews, sanitation workers, the cleaning ladies who work nights in offices. I try to keep things clean. Sometimes I get a little dirty doing it. But I believe that if I say what I think happened and then try to figure out the right thing to do, I will live an honorable life.

Constant work, excitement and risk, and intense involvements with women—these had always been good medicine for me. Each worked against the furious anxiety and depressive intensity I had lived with for as far back as I could remember—all the way back to the days I'd run for cover in the Queens library. I self-medicated with work, women, and physical exertion effectively, and also continu-

My grandparents
on my parents'
wedding day.
From left to
right: Edward
Hayes, Mary
Fitzgibbon
Sowden, Mary
Kelly Hayes,
Walter Sowden.

My mother, Jean Sowden—one of
the best dancers in the Rockaways.

My father and mother on their wedding day in 1946.

My mother, me, my brother, Stephen, and my father in front of the family Ford, circa 1955.

Stephen, my sister, Barbara, and me in Smithtown in 1959. Note my ultrastylish flattop haircut.

My Columbia Law School classmate George Pataki and me by one of those lakes they have upstate.

My wedding day, with the two
most important women in my
life—Susie Gilder Hayes
and my mom.

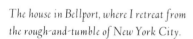

The house in Bellport, where I retreat from
the rough-and-tumble of New York City.

My townhouse/castle in New York. The front door is decorated with a seriously threatening serpent fashioned by master metalworker Wally Vogelsberg. (Courtesy of House & Garden)

Some of the other fruits of my labors.

With my detective buddies, Jimmy Harkins, Billy Wallace, and Jack McCann. Jimmy is bigger, and much more dangerous, than a refrigerator truck.

Manhattan testosterone: Tom Guba (left) bails me out when I'm broke. Note his resemblance to the fictional Mr. Big. Paul Hanley (center), whose grandfather John V. Kenny ran the Hudson County Democratic machine, gets me out of legal scrapes.

The tailors in my life: Vincent Nicolosi
(with Tom Wolfe); Neal and John Boyarsky;
and Edith Singer and Tibby Weiss.

Fred Hughes and Bruce Cutler, godfathers to
my firstborn, in happier days.

Opening Statements,
Matter of Warhol,
November 19, 1993.

Larry Silverstein and Nina and Daniel Libeskind applaud the unveiling of eight World Trade Center Memorial designs. The applause has since died down. (Kathy Willens/AP/Wide World Photos)

Our wonderful kids, Avery Hayes and John Hayes.

My indispensable office crew: Manny Payano, Rajit Sukhu, and Jean Santana; and Eleanor Green and Rae Koshetz.

My Bellport crew—and my second family.

Men in hats: Bruce Cutler and me outside Federal Court in Brooklyn, about to go into battle on behalf of the so-called Mafia cops. (Todd Maisel/New York Daily News)

"Get me Hayes!"

ously, for thirty years. Real friendship, which would provide the greatest comfort of my later life, was something I didn't know much about.

What little I knew, I had learned backwards. In college, I learned something about helping people, which was a good substitute for friendship. I couldn't have intimacy with women—because I couldn't talk to them—but I could have sex, which was a decent enough substitute. And I could show up, which is something. A woman might want me to say something sensitive and insightful. I couldn't do that to save my life, but I'd still be there. And if a woman, or anyone else, asked me to do something, I'd do it. As far as evolved relationships go, this wasn't perfect, but it wasn't so bad either.

But when I started spending real time with my enduring crew of tabloid journalists and media tycoons and high-powered editors and street-smart detectives and big-time powered police brass, I noticed that, holy Jesus, friendships make me happy! This was something my earlier life taught me very little about.

As it all began to come together for me, in the mid-1980s, a lot of people I knew gravitated to Bellport. There were still good buys then and you could get a very reasonably priced, very attractive house, which a lot of my friends did. I persuaded Anna Wintour to buy a place near mine. Then Si came out and bought a big place two blocks from me. Richard Johnson rented an apartment on my property and then eventually bought his own place. McAlary, of course, had the spec house I built and sold to him. I had a whole posse there of people very close to me, which is something that gave me unimaginable pleasure. In a village culture like Ireland, guys like Michael Collins kept their crews close by, wherever they went. A lot of guys keep posses around to serve their interests. I want the people around me to do as well as possible, which they almost always do.

Though my main crew had taken shape, there was about to be some significant expansion. James Truman, for one. I would certainly kill for James, whom I got to know several years after I met Si Newhouse. The editorial director of Condé Nast from 1994 to 2005, he's brilliant and mischievous, and we have a great time talking and confiding and eating terrific food and touring topless clubs, though he makes me nuts sometimes with his incessant interest in spirituality and the meaning of life. I keep telling him there is no "meaning of life." The meaning of life is: *Buy good shoes, go to the gym, have kids, kill your enemies, help your friends.* That's it. You want something else? Sorry, that's it.

Richard Merkin noticed me because my girlfriends were all six feet tall and jet black or five foot three, Hispanic, and in six-inch-heeled shoes. I noticed him because he has a sense of style unlike anyone else's. A painter, illustrator, and brilliant colorist, Merkin wears striped shirts with plaid jackets and likes lavenders and pinks and oranges—interesting colors that look terrific. We introduced ourselves on a sidewalk on upper Broadway. Merkin had on a bright purple coat and I was on the corner with a giant, gorgeous Senegalese woman. We've been friends ever since.

Merkin introduced me to a new spectrum of color in men's clothing and also to Tibby Weiss, the Lower East Side fabric dealer. Both are vital to my life as a lawyer, and a man, in New York. But neither introduction was as life-altering as the one Merkin made in the late seventies when he brought me to dinner to meet his friend Tom Wolfe.

Smart, classically educated, historically minded, thoughtful and loyal to the people around him, and warm and dedicated to his family, including his very good Jewish wife, Sheila, Tom represents everything I admire. He is a respectful, tremendously disciplined man. He works every day. He never loses control of himself, never does anything to excess. He would never blindly follow New York's intellectual elite, or any other elite, for that matter; his only guide is his own carefully considered ideas. Tom Wolfe, the quintessential tough-minded writer, became my closest friend and not only introduced me to the writer's life but imparted a more sophisticated understanding than I ever thought possible of money and power and the way things work in the City of Ambition.

I knew he was a famous writer but I didn't know much else about

Wolfe when Merkin took me out to his house in Southampton one summer Sunday afternoon. I didn't get much chance to talk to him, though.

I had a client then who was a truck driver for the *Times*. He had been a sergeant in Vietnam, where he had held off the Vietcong long enough for his unit to escape an ambush. For that, he had won a Bronze Star with a "V" for valor. But he was a troubled man who went to his parents' house that summer day and told them he was going to kill them. Then he tried to kick their door down. His parents didn't call the police, because the guy had been arrested before and they worried that if he was arrested again, it would be the last they would see of him. So they tracked me down in Southampton and called me. I spent about two hours in Tom Wolfe's kitchen talking on his phone to these people, who were willing to risk their lives to protect their son. I went back and forth with the mother and then the father, sweating blood the whole time trying to figure out how to handle things. Tom stood there by the refrigerator in his kitchen in his shingled house by a lake, watching, listening.

In the end I got the guy's parents to tell him to call me from a pay phone. "Look, pal," I told him, "just sit there. Your mother and your father love you very much, and that's something. Now, don't make a problem. Let your father pick you up and drive you home or to a doctor who can help." And I talked him down. When I got off the phone, I was very tense. It had been a long ordeal.

Tom just watched. My readiness to engage with people and maybe also my ability to explore the depths of all kinds of situations interested Tom. We became close friends instantly. He's the big brother and the father everyone wants to have. Knowing that someone you think is a great man likes you too is an incredible feeling. I adore Tom Wolfe.

Throughout my life, I have always wanted certain kinds of people to respect me. I wanted the homicide detectives to respect me and I wanted some of the gangsters I represented to respect me. Also some of the rough-and-ready women I knew. I really wanted Tom Wolfe to respect me.

Soon after I met him, Wolfe got interested in writing a novel about New York City. He was thinking about setting the book in Bronx County Criminal Court. Would I show him around the place? he wanted to know. Yes, yes, yes, I would.

I took Tom up to the Grand Concourse to meet the detectives. I showed him how the criminal court system worked, how the lawyers won cases, how to use the press in prosecuting cases, and I explained how you got paid, how you had to ask for the money up front when people were still crying, and I showed him what you had to do to get results. It never bothered me to do things other people might find undignified, like getting up in the middle of the night to get some guy out of jail or fight it out in the hall with some guy who didn't want to pay a two-hundred-dollar fee to see his kids again sometime before the Second Coming. I showed him the dingy office I used to work in, with the low ceilings and the dim bulbs, half of which I unscrewed so they wouldn't glare down on the metal desk, and I told him about the status distinctions, a subject to which Tom is very much alive, between ordinary prosecutors and elite homicide DAs, and Wolfe took this, and everything else, in with his usual care and precision.

Tom told me he had a notion about a dark ramp that a bond trader would mistakenly drive his Mercedes off in what would become *The Bonfire of the Vanities*. Was there a place in the Bronx where this could happen? he asked. Yes, there was. In fact, there were a thousand different places in the Bronx where a white man might have accidentally steered his car off an expressway ramp and run into race-related trouble of one kind or another. I had Jack McCann drive Tom around Cross Bronx Expressway ramps at night; they drove around in Jack's Ford until they got to a particular ramp, which for some reason Tom decided seemed right and subsequently immortalized in *Bonfire*.

I introduced Tom to my fellow defense lawyer Bruce Cutler. We went to a Manhattan precinct house with Bruce one night to see a mob client who had shot a guy who was selling stolen suits. When we got to the precinct, we found Cutler's client in a room full of witnesses, all of whom had been secured to a desk with metal chains.

Cutler's client, a big black guy, was sitting quietly in the back of the room, watching TV, completely free.

This was before Cutler started working for John Gotti, but I guess even then there were lots of guys who'd rather not testify against the mob. In fact, it was pretty much assumed that, given half a chance, the witnesses to this particular shooting would be on a plane to the Dominican Republic in half a second, which is why authorities had prudently opted to chain them to that desk. The cops had decided that the perp was unlikely to go anywhere at all. Why would he? Cutler was his lawyer and would take care of him— which is why he was sitting comfortably in the back watching his program when we entered the room.

Dressed as always in a custom cream-colored suit and English spats, Tom coolly took in the strange spectacle. Later he reproduced it, almost to the letter, in the great scene in *Bonfire.*

Associating with Tom Wolfe is a great way to further your education. The guy teaches you something every time you talk to him. Tom was far more supportive of the established order than I was, in general, and more skeptical about the value of chaos and conflict as a means of social change. We disagreed about a lot of things. We had long, heated arguments about El Salvador and Guatemala.

"Look," I'd tell Tom, once again demonstrating my willingness to take on guys much stronger and smarter than me, "there's a very small ruling class down there that has kept order by force of arms, and the people of these countries are entitled to kill them." History is full of guys who've risen up and taken control under these kinds of circumstances. The Magna Carta is basically a statement from the lower classes to the king that says, "Look, pal, you're getting carried away! And we're coming in there with a sword and we'll hack your ass up if you don't straighten out quick."

My view is that there are some people who should be hunted down and killed and people have a perfect right to do the hunting and killing. Fundamentally conservative, Tom had a tough time swallowing this, my central operating principle. But I never had a conversation with Tom from which I didn't emerge wiser and a more careful thinker.

I went with Tom to regular lunches at the Manhattan Institute, a conservative think tank in a sumptuous building on Vanderbilt Avenue next to the Yale Club. It's a place where a lot of powerful bankers and very conservative money guys got together to talk about things like the need for stringent welfare reform and the threat of rent control regulations. I didn't argue with these guys. I'm smart enough to know that sometimes when you are around a lot of guys who are smarter than you are, it's a good idea to shut up and listen.

We bonded instantly on the subject of men's fashion. I admire the English and Celtic traditions; in both a dandy is a tough guy concerned with dress, conscious of his masculinity, and dressed in a manner reflective of fundamental values, chief among these his bravery and willingness to act.

Historically, English gentlemen favor clothing designed to celebrate the warrior tradition of charging. Lord Cardigan, who led the Light Brigade in its famous and monumentally stupid charge, in October 1854, sent his entire regiment to his tailor, who made each man special tight-fitting red pants that both exhibited the soldier's fitness for battle and stayed out of his way as he charged. The men were slaughtered, but they looked good.

Tom dresses in the modern-day style of a British cavalry officer. The wide-waisted suit pants, close-fitted jackets, and spats all have military as well as aesthetic purpose: the waistline exhibits the wearer's fitness for battle and the jacket accentuates how slender and well-proportioned he is; good shoes draw attention to qualities like quick-footedness that suggest speed and readiness for action. Strangely, Tom says one of the most vivid images he has of me involves me running to catch a subway to the Brooklyn County courthouse, where a gangster client was going to be arraigned; for some reason, what stays in Tom's mind is a picture of the soles of my custom shoes flying in the New York afternoon as I dash into the subway. Funny how everything always gets back to shoes.

Richard Merkin clearly taught Tom different lessons about color than those he taught me; Tom likes to wear just two colors at a time, one of which, usually white or cream, is often predominant. When I took him to Vincent Nicolosi, that fabulous tailor with the hands of gold nicely accommodated Tom's style preferences.

An honest analysis of my friendship with Tom Wolfe probably suggests our friendship is not a two-way relationship. Is there any equality to our friendship? Not much. Tom represents everything I admire. He provides a model of what a man can be. In *Bonfire*, though, I was the model—that is, he presented me to the world in the character of the criminal lawyer, Tommy Killian, a guy who wants to get ahead and go along with the fundamental rules but whose attitude, when push comes to shove, is *Go fuck yourself!* That pretty much personifies most of what I believe.

Paul Goldberger's mother's name is Killian, and I asked Tom to name Sherman McCoy's criminal lawyer that because Goldberger taught me so much about being a lawyer. I thought putting Goldberger's maternal family name in there was a way of showing how much I love him. It was Tom's idea to call the Killian character Tommy. "I always wanted to be called Tommy," he told me. " 'Tom' sounds so drudgelike, the name of somebody who's always slogging away."

"I'm dedicating the book to you," Tom told me before *Bonfire* was published. I thought, *Oh, that's great;* I didn't realize the significance at the time. By dedicating his immortal novel to me, and by creating the character that personified my basic beliefs, Tom gave me a place in history. In return, I introduced him to my tailor.

By 1987, when *The Bonfire of the Vanities* became a huge national best seller, heaped with praise from every quarter, things had really come together in my life. I'd made connections between the city's newspapers and the people I knew from the courthouse, police force, political clubs, and social scene. I'd seen how, by bringing these people and these forces together, I could make more money, exert more influence, and live a fuller life.

I brought various aspects of my life together at regular dinners at the Manhattan Café, a manly joint on the Upper East Side across the street from Maxwell's Plum. Cops, politicos, assorted thrill seekers and detectives, journalists like McAlary, Daly, and Wolfe, and guys like Si Newhouse and John Timoney and future New York City police commissioner Bill Bratton all came to talk and eat and have a ball together.

In 1994, Rudolph Giuliani had just put his crusade to improve the quality of city life into high gear by declaring war on the squeegee men who popped out of the dark near the exit ramps off the FDR Drive, swarmed the windshields of frightened white men's cars with long brushes, and then demanded payment for the unasked service.

"I wish you luck," Wolfe tells Bratton, now police commissioner, over steak at the Manhattan Café the night the anti-squeegee program is announced. "But how can you get rid of those guys? They're like fruit flies, swarming around with brushes."

"No. It'll all be over in a few days," Bratton assures him. " 'Fellows,' we tell them the first day, 'you're breaking the law. You'd better leave. Tomorrow we're going to be a little harsher.' And on the third day, we take their mops and their squeegee brushes and we use them to break holes in all their buckets. 'Fellas,' we say, 'we mean business.' There may be a few diehards left," Bratton tells Wolfe, "and those guys we take to jail."

Wolfe, as always, listens and observes carefully. Politely he asks Bratton about the root causes of these things and whether it might, in the interest of getting rid of the squeegee men, be a good idea to try to address root causes.

"It's a good idea to take care of root causes," Bratton says, smiling. "I find, though, that the interruption of individual behavior works well, too."

The interruption of individual behavior works well, too! Tom Wolfe's deep, dark eyes light up. Gold, literary gold! You can't make up things like this; Tom's books are full of the texture of life as lived by a range of different people. Here, right in front of me, he's listening, sifting voices, and finding riches for his expanding collection.

And here I am sitting at a table in what feels like the center of the world, with my crew—Bratton and Wolfe and McAlary and Cutler and the rest of the guys—all of whom have a real say in a lot of what happens in the city, listening, watching, as they enrich one another's lives and eat steak.

Money, weapons, and power—I'm learning that to make your way through New York life you have to have ready access to all three, and suddenly I do. Anything that comes up now, for me or a client or a friend (rarely, of course, is there such a distinction), I can take care of.

Everything in my professional and social life has fallen nicely into place. And one other essential aspect, as well.

CHAPTER 9

Susie Gilder is the tall blonde with big hair and thigh-high leopard boots on the other side of the room. She's impossible to miss. I've heard about Susie Gilder.

Tara Shannon, a model who lives in my building, has been talking about fixing me up with Susie for a long time. And now Toukie Smith, another model, a gorgeous black woman who keeps company with Robert De Niro, is pulling Susie Gilder and her leopard boots and the fringed leather skirt that barely covers her long legs toward me.

The place, a big open loft on Warren Street in Soho, is full of good-looking people involved in art and fashion, a lot of whom are running in and out of the bathroom to do coke. There's a class of people in New York who are not bankers or corporate lawyers and who like to go out at night, people who work hard and play hard, and that's who's here at Toukie's party in 1982.

"I want you to meet this girl," says Toukie.

I'm dressed well, as usual, in a good suit, and I check out this big, healthy blonde in front of me.

"Susie Gilder, you're supposed to be the girl of my dreams," I tell her.

Susie draws slowly on her cigarette.

"Yeah," she says, "I'm probably going to hate you."

Nice icebreaker.

Susie is from California, the part where surfing isn't big. She finished high school after getting out of a juvenile detention home in Stockton, a river port and farm town. Her mom was a supervisor at the Stockton Port and supported Susie and her brother. Susie's father, a drunk but a decorated army officer, abandoned the family when Susie was a child; eventually he was murdered. Then there was a series of stepfathers, all unsatisfactory. In some ways, Susie's had a childhood even harsher than mine.

One of the hardest things in life is not knowing how things work and how to do things right. Parents give a lot of bad advice but, in most cases, at least they tell you *something* they've learned from experience. Susie and I both had to figure everything out for ourselves, and often both of us got things wrong. Susie, for example, always had huge hair, spent a lot of high school with a Harley-Davidson crew in Stockton, and was almost always in trouble.

After the opening salvo, our conversation at Toukie's party turns pleasant and good-natured—though from what I gather, Susie has had a habit of being in the wrong place at the wrong time. I suppose because I'm a criminal lawyer the talk turns to her teenage career on the wrong side of the law.

" 'Feminine flash,' " she tells me. "That's what it said on the side of the black Chevy four on the floor I drove in Stockton." No idea why she's telling me this. I don't like cars. I can think about three things at once, but I can't think about three things at once *and* drive. And the very narrow sculpted shoes I wear are not cut out for pedals. Susie is unassuming, which I like. It's clear she didn't bother too much with school; she had drugs in her pocket when she was frisked after a shoot-out in downtown Stockton, she tells me, and apparently she perjured herself to protect the boyfriend who'd done the shooting.

"I couldn't give him up," she tells me. She's tall, this Gilder girl.

Susie says her biker friends picked her up once after they'd robbed a drugstore, and cops pulled them over and removed a pile of coats from the backseat, where Susie was sitting, and found a stash of stolen pharmaceuticals underneath. "I had no idea!" Susie tells me, smoking away. She is very good-hearted, I can see right away. Maybe a bit naïve, though—at least back then.

"I learned a lot from juvenile hall." Susie gets more attractive by the minute. She starts telling me how she was in for six months and was the only white girl in the place. A day or so after she got in, a group of lesbians came at her and pulled her hair out in clumps; she fought a Mexican girl, too. I gather that Susie held her own with the lesbians and the Mexican girl and that everyone pretty much left her alone after the initial fights.

When she got out of the detention center, Susie was eighteen and had decided she wanted to be a social worker. Moving big handfuls of her lush blond hair around and swaying slightly in a way that works to call attention to her absolutely tiny waist—I swear it's not more than twenty inches—she tells me she realized that she was the only one in the detention center who had come from a real home with real food and a real, caring, hardworking mother, and she got the idea that maybe she could help rehabilitate girls who had less than she did. But mostly she wanted out of Stockton. A month later she moved to San Francisco, got a room in a convent in Haight-Ashbury, and took a job as a telephone operator and another job as hostess in a deli-type restaurant on Union Street.

In two years, she had enough money to rent her own apartment and also to visit Susie Loo, a Chinese girl she had met in San Francisco who had moved to New York. Susie Loo had gotten an appointment with the Eileen Ford modeling agency and Susie went with her for moral support.

"We have our quota of Asian girls," the Eileen Ford director told Susie Loo. "But who are you?" she said, pointing to Susie. They thought she looked Italian. Did Susie want to go to Italy for a shoot? Yes, Susie did. She had her mother go to San Francisco and pack her things and send them, and after a few months in Italy she was on the catwalks of some of the biggest fashion shows in the world. It was a spectacular beginning to her life as a model.

For eight years, she flew all over South America, Asia, and Europe, sometimes doing as many as five shows a day. She lived large, with apartments in Paris and on Sheridan Square in New York, and took care of herself and sometimes supported boyfriends. She learned to speak Italian and had great friendships. She's still friends with a lot of women like Allison Stern and Tara Shannon who were big-haired blond models with her and they stick together. She had a lot of girlfriends who were big, good-looking black models, like Toukie Smith, whom she met through Robert De Niro, who liked big, good-looking black women. Susie had acting ambitions, too, and took classes at the Actors Studio with De Niro and Jessica Lange and Christopher Walken and Al Pacino, and so she had a lot of actor friends as well.

Before Susie leaves Toukie Smith's party, she pulls a 3 x 5 photo out of her wallet of a girl with a big, goofy beehive hairdo. The photo was taken before the Stockton prom, junior year. "Whenever I feel uppity," Susie says, flipping the photo toward me, "I look at this and remind myself how full of shit I am."

We start seeing each other right away.

———

A lot has happened since my days at St. Joan of Arc school, but at all times and under all circumstances I remain a neighborhood white boy, a guy who grew up in a working-class ethnic neighborhood full of people who worked hard, did their jobs, and played by the rules, and I know what the rules are: first and foremost, I am supposed to get married and have children, and then I'm supposed to take my children to church and see that they marry in the one true faith.

Urban areas are full of smart but not always polished guys who go into the legal arena, work at the pointy end of the spear practicing a harsh, unforgiving kind of law, and prosper at that. Then, because they have reasonably good social skills, before they know it they're moving up and getting more and more business because there is always a need for well-behaved (and also well-dressed) garbagemen. That's just what I had become: I was one of New York City's best-dressed garbagemen. I had a lot of criminal cases, some big, some small. You have a problem, you call me, I'm there. I'm used to handling crisis, I'm a very hard worker, and I work around the clock. The idea is to keep the meter running at all times. I invest every penny I make in real estate ventures, starting with a town house my brother and I bought on West Eighty-second Street. I'm making real money, and I'm confident there will be more. I'm ready to settle down and start having kids I can take to church. I call Susie Gilder and ask her to have dinner the day after we meet at Toukie's.

We have dinner at Vandam's restaurant—a dark, edgy place way downtown, in a rising neighborhood called Tribeca. You definitely don't find a hell of a lot of bankers downtown after work hours in 1982. I am probably the only guy there who's ever worked in homicide or anything like that. Susie is upset when I leave her alone at the table for half an hour while I go to the pay phone in the back and make my nightly calls to clients. But we dance a lot after dinner at Hurrah's, a lively, loud club whose owner I used to date. The narrator of Jay McInerney's novel Bright Lights, Big City spends a lot of time (and does a lot of Bolivian marching powder) in a club like Hurrah's—it was the place of the moment.

Then we head down to my client's club where they have sex shows with dwarfs and other diversions. It's a fashionable place, at least with a certain set, and it's hard to get into. Susie is used to hanging around with De Niro and Harvey Keitel, and going to after-hours clubs, so she's fine with it.

We have a good time and form a strong bond. Susie is straightforward and physically impressive, healthy, and hardworking. She has interesting bloodlines; though she didn't make it past high school, she comes from an intellectual family. She speaks perfect Italian. Her father's cousin George Gilder is a distinguished conservative commentator and economic theorist who will become rich and famous as a prophet of the new technology of the nineties; Josh Gilder, another cousin, is a Reagan speechwriter. She would make a fine mother and would produce some fine children. Susie gets mad when I say this. "You think I'm good breeding stock!" she yells. Yes, I do. In fact, Susie is better breeding stock than I am. She's not as crazy as I am.

We do things we both like—going to dinner and clubs, staying out late, meeting people, dancing, and working hard—during the first year after we meet. We take yacht cruises with Robert De Niro and Toukie Smith. We go to the Bahamas once and to the West Indies; the sitting around on the boat is hard for me because I like to move. You read, you swim, you hang around the beach—it's too damned leisurely. These are real master-and-commander-type boats, with all kinds of staff and cooks—you can eat any goddamn thing you want. De Niro is very generous with us. He's a good guy but he doesn't talk. We'd spend a week with him on the boat, and he wouldn't talk for more than an hour the whole time.

De Niro, whose father is an established painter, grew up in the streets of Lower Manhattan decades before it became Soho, and he's still a bit of an Italian street guy. He's honest and direct, if quiet for long stretches at a time, and I like him, unlike some other movie stars I've been meeting. He has a lot of the same communication skills and style I do—my syntax may be broken and I may mispronounce words, but you know what I'm talking about. But I talk a *lot* more.

In addition to having a good time together, Susie and I fight constantly. Fighting with women is new for me. I haven't really gotten close enough to women to fight with them before. Many of my relationships were passionate; most were with women who wanted a greater degree of intimacy than I was capable of. But Susie, who like me, doesn't have the greatest sense of intimacy in the world, has learned to protect herself.

We fight about everything. We fight about where we will stay. Susie's place is on Sheridan Square; my apartment is on West Eighty-second Street—that's where my clothes are, and I want to be near my clothes. If I stay downtown, I have to go uptown in the morning, dress, then come back downtown to the courthouse.

Obviously, I am not going to take all my clothes to Sheridan Square, and I can't possibly commit to a particular wardrobe choice the night before.

Meanwhile, Susie's agent sometimes calls in the morning when we're at my place and says things like, "Come in and bring some heels and your skirt," and Susie says, "Uh-oh. I spent the night with my boyfriend and I don't have the skirt or the shoes with me," and they say, "Who cares? Get here now!" This leads to problems for Susie with work, which leads to more fights.

Most models begin their careers like hockey players, starting early and forgoing formal education. A lot of them don't read. I've spent my whole life reading and I'm passionately interested in books and politics. Susie's lack of interest in reading and politics is another source of constant fighting.

We fight about our families, too, and the question of which one of us emerged in better shape from a troubled childhood. My mother stuck around, even though my father beat her, so that she'd have money to send her kids to college. Susie's mom walked out of the house after *her* husband started hitting, and Susie, who barely finished high school, never even thought about going to college. Susie thinks she did better in the end and I disagree, and we argue a lot about this.

Maybe the fighting is a substitute for talking about feelings— mostly of weakness and vulnerability—that Susie and I both took from our disastrous childhoods. I never felt that there was a single moment in my life when I could afford to be weak. In the age of heavy-duty therapy, people seem to think there is strength in knowing and mastering weakness; God knows I'd had therapy enough for twenty average people by the time I met Susie, but I am convinced that the world does not tolerate weakness. Did Susie and I fight instead of talking? No idea. But the fighting didn't bother either of us. We were good at it.

One thing that works out nicely is that Susie, whose father and a series of stepfathers all cut out on her, has a terrible fear of being abandoned and, as I've said, I *never* abandon people. I go off the reservation from time to time, but I always come back. Call me, and I'm

there. Some of the fights that first year have to do with Susie's jeal-
ousy and abandonment fears, neither of which are helped much by
the fact that she is in her thirties and wants to get married and happens to work in a profession in which, no matter how good-looking
you are, somebody younger and maybe better-looking is always coming up behind you.

After a few months, Susie tells me she is sick of finding other
women's lipstick on my towels. (I think she may have said something
more like, "If you see anybody else, I will fucking kill you.") So we
shake hands and agree not to fool around with other people. I even
leave my custom ginger-colored English suede shoes in her apartment
one night. Susie rightly sees this as a good sign. I call twice that
night to make sure the shoes are all right.

The shoes survive and so do I, and there are more good signs.

—

I have a client in Staten Island who beat his wife to death with a
shovel. At the bail hearing, I tell the judge that my client has prostate problems. "Where is he going to go? His prostate needs some immediate attention," I tell the judge, who also happens to have
prostate problems, and so he agrees to release my client on bail. I'm
concerned when the guy doesn't show up for sentencing; for one
thing, my fee is tied up with the bail money, which we will forfeit
if the client doesn't eventually appear.

I go to the guy's house with a police lieutenant and three detectives. "Be careful," one of the detectives tells his partner, "the guy
might have a gun." I offer to go up to the door and get the guy out,
and the detectives remark on my bravery. Bravery, of course, has
nothing to do with anything. I just want my money.

One of the detectives strongly suggests I wear a bulletproof vest.
I refuse. I am wearing a dark gray suit with a chalk stripe, a beautiful Anderson and Sheppard special, double breasted, with a vest; if
a television camera shows up, the Kevlar vest will ruin the lines of
the suit.

I go to the door, nod at the lieutenant who is hiding behind a bush, and knock hard. No answer. Knock. No answer. One of the detectives rushes up and kicks the door down, and there's my guy hanging in the hallway, dead.

The truth is, I am very taken aback by what I've seen. It's very shocking, very upsetting. So much so that I stop in a lowlife bar on the way back to court, have three shots and a couple of beers even though I can't drink at all, and then stagger into the courtroom. The judge, an old-school, very strict, very elegant black man, looks at me reeling around in the back of the room and says, "Mr. Hayes! Your client, please?"

"Can I approach, Your Honor?" I ask, and stumble up to the bench. "He hanged himself," I tell the judge, who can plainly see that I am not in terrific shape.

"No shit! Now that's fucked up!" he says. The judge actually sees to it that the clerk's office sends me a check when the bail money is eventually processed and returned. I don't want to go home that night. I am badly shaken—it's quite gruesome to see someone in a hallway hanging dead from a rope, his feet dangling down in red corduroy slippers, his neck stretched like a limp giraffe's—and I don't want to be by myself. I'm immensely grateful to be with Susie that night.

———

Lillian Gilder, a former marine sergeant who enlisted the day after Pearl Harbor with her sister, starts giving me orders the minute I walk into her modest one-story house in Stockton. Susie wants me to meet her mom, and in the fall of 1983, we fly to San Francisco for a visit. Lillian Gilder has a neighbor, George Ratamoza, a wonderful Mexican guy, who picks us up and drives us the two or three hours back to Stockton, to the middle-class neighborhood full of winding streets and old trees where Lillian lives. Lillian is nice but can't possibly be bossier. "Put your things there. Sit there. Do this." I have no experience with functioning families and don't know how to react to Susie's mother. I don't particularly like her. I'll take all the orders in the world if I volunteer for something. Otherwise I don't like to be told what to do.

Lillian doesn't particularly like me, either. That's clear from the start. For one thing, I'm hungry from the long trip. After Lillian commands me to put the bags down and wash up, I look for the dining room table and am glad to see a small round oak table, the kind of cheap, undistinguished furniture Protestant families began to pass down fifty years ago, after all the good stuff was taken. I am glad to see it's set, glad to see appealing-looking plates of meat, potatoes, and green beans that Sergeant Gilder commands me to understand are locally grown. Without bothering with much in the way of small talk, I sit at the table, pick up my fork and knife, note that Lillian Gilder is in the kitchen and is not actually serving dinner yet, and so bang the silver, lightly, on the oak tabletop.

From the kitchen, which like the other six rooms in Lillian Gilder's tidy 1950s California bungalow-style house is within earshot of the dining room, I hear Lillian say to her daughter, "Darling, did you get him out of prison?" Susie laughs. Sergeant Gilder resents it that her daughter is on the East Coast with this New York guy. I have a strong *New Yawk* accent, I'm aggressive, I represent gangsters and am in a business many people look askance at, and I'm a pretty flashy guy, none of which is appealing in the least to a big-shouldered Waspy Northern California woman like Lillian Gilder. This adds considerably to the idea that meeting Susie's mom is just a chore I've got to finish, business that's got to be done. Lillian gives me a hard time—it's like going to court. The judge gives you a hard time, so what? It's business.

There is also pleasure in the trip, though. They have great farm stands in Stockton, which I really love. They have these peaches that come to full flavor only for two weeks, a rare peach that's hard to ship and so is hard to find outside Stockton. They have fantastic tomatoes too, great varieties—striped, pink and green, pink and white, and very tasty. It drives Susie nuts that I have to stop at every farm stand in Stockton and ask the farmers how they grow this stuff

and where it comes from and when the tomatoes and peaches are at
their absolute best. I see that Susie is upset about my not getting
along with her mother. But all I can think about is getting some more
of those peaches and crazy-looking tomatoes.

My mother, of course, loves Susie immediately. My mom likes all
the girls I bring home. In fact, my mom pretty much likes everyone,
at least everyone who is fair and decent and seems straightforward
and ready to laugh a little.

—

"I sold my apartment," I tell Susie. I move my clothes and shoes
and growing collection of watches and cufflinks to Sheridan Square.
And though we keep fighting, it's understood—by me, anyway—
that if it works out, we'll get married. Which on May 31, 1986,
four years after we met at Toukie Smith's party, we do.

—

"I do." Susie is spectacularly beautiful in a white dress that our
friend Carolina Herrera has made for her. Monsignor Bernard Ryan
looks at me, a big, happy white boy, in the navy blue double-
breasted suit Vincent Nicolosi has made for me. "And do you, Edward Joseph Hayes, take this woman, Susie Gilder, to be your
lawfully wedded wife?" *Yes, motherfucker. Yes, yes, yes!* "I do."

It is a great day. And a great big wedding. We have three hundred people on the lawn of the house in Bellport. (My mother tells
Susie three months before the wedding that I have to promise not to
make any new friends before the wedding—I've been adding names
to the guest list every day for weeks and she says there isn't any more
room.) All of Bellport and most of New York is here. I couldn't invite any gangsters—which is a shame because they give such good
presents—because there are so many cops here. There are some great-
looking women. Susie's friend Cheryl Tiegs, God bless her, comes
half dressed because she knows I love that. Even the priest has

trouble focusing when Cheryl walks in. Robert De Niro comes and stays, which is extraordinary; in addition to not talking, he rarely stays in one place for more than a few minutes. Harvey Keitel is here. The Greek wholesale florist George Katakas has supplied mountains of lilies—pink and orange and sweet-smelling—that bloom on tables set up all over the lawn. Bagpipers play "Danny Boy," which was actually written by an Englishman and the thrust of which, if you really listen to the words, is, "You are going to have to go out there. There will be loss, injury, and hurt, but you've got to go." It is a nice day, a nice, nice day.

Before the wedding, Reinaldo Herrera, Tom Wolfe, my brother (and best man) Steven, Mike Daly, Michael McAlary, and Bruce Cutler meet at my house. We walk together through the streets of Bellport to the Mary Immaculate Church. It is a proud parade, a triumphant procession.

Father Ryan says Mass. He looks at the congregation and seems almost taken aback by the attractive, high-powered group of people before him. Afterwards everyone walks back to the house and we have a big party on the lawn. Susie and I have worked hard on the house and it is great to have everyone there. We have a big white tent spread out on the lawn near the water and have painted the boathouse at the edge of the grass white; there's disco music inside and traditional Irish music outside. Everyone dances. I dance with my mom; I love my mom, and she loves to dance. She has no idea who Reinaldo Herrera or Harvey Keitel are, but she has a great time dancing with them.

My father comes late. I think he misses the ceremony but he comes back to the house, stays for a brief period, and leaves. Of course I invited him. I feel bad for the guy, he has had such a harsh life. He seems kind of lost. He doesn't know what to say to me. I don't know what to say to him. He hasn't played a role in my life; whatever role he *did* play was bad. What can I say? "Geez, I'm sorry"?

People hand me envelopes all afternoon, and at the end of the day I go in the back with Mike Daly and open the envelopes and count the money inside. "Listen," I ask Mike, "how much do I tip the caterers and the other guys working here?" He gives me a number and I say, "Fuck it, Mike, I've got a lot of cash in my pocket," and give the crew two and a half times the number. I tell Daly, "If I die tomorrow, I want people to speak well of me!"

Susie and I leave the next morning for a honeymoon in England, Scotland, and Ireland. She goes nuts when we get to England, and I have the driver take us straight from the airport to Anderson and Sheppard for some quick try-ons. By then I'm not just a client, I've become the lawyer for the place, and I want to be properly outfitted by them for married life. I have no idea why, when we get to Ireland, Susie keeps saying, "I'm no Catholic. I'm Protestant." It hasn't come up at all before. But she agrees to raise our children as Catholics, and I'm glad. As a child, I learned that life can be harsh but you do what you can, and I want to pass that on, along with some good Catholic forgiveness and a few other choice virtues.

Susie gets pregnant in early 1987. Now there is a beautiful pregnant woman in my bed and we were going to have a family. There is money in the bank and reason to be confident there will be plenty more to support a family. Eddie Hayes, white boy from Jackson Heights, is no longer the skinny neighborhood kid who can easily be pushed around.

—

Had my mother not put a lid on the invitation list for our wedding, I probably would have invited Fred Hughes, an odd, brilliant man who was extremely knowledgeable about art and with whom I got increasingly friendly after Susie and I returned from our honeymoon. Hughes had the air of a courtier, a guy who hangs around the court of a famous person, and the look of a shifty, bird-faced character you might find in a dark café resting in between money-laundering operations.

I have a lot of friends who are gay, but none of them were as sexually mixed up as Fred Hughes, which may explain something about why he got pushed around in the nightclubs where I first ran into

him. He'd get fully drunk, then take on an accent that was a combination of upper-class Englishman and street-corner hustler and proceed to slobber on and scream at people. One night during one of
these performances I stopped the bouncers from throwing him out on
the street. "Leave him alone. He's a friend of mine," I told them as I
half carried him to a cab. "Bear that in mind."

Hughes, who initiated a friendship with me after that, had an unusual personal story. The son of a heavily decorated war hero who
flew in the army air force in World War II, he apparently always
had an ambiguous sexual identity, which was a source of trouble at
home: the senior Hughes, who despised effeminacy, threw him out of
the house at an early age. Fred ended up being raised by a fabulously
rich Houston oil family, the de Menils, who were also great patrons
of the arts. That's how Fred first got involved in the fine-arts world.
He was deeply involved in the planning of the Rothko Chapel, and
in the mid-sixties the de Menils hired him to find rising young artists
to collect, which he did for them in New York.

It was widely known that Hughes began associating with Andy
Warhol shortly after moving to New York in 1967 and had played
a substantial role in shaping Warhol's empire. It was Hughes who
encouraged Warhol to create paintings and drawings available at
different price points so that he could sell to a wider range of con-
sumers. Hughes oversaw all Warhol's business transactions as well.
Many times he accepted compensation in the form of an artwork or
an objet d'art. Warhol would exchange a painting for a Chinese
chest or something like that, and it would be understood that Fred
would get a 20 percent share of the value. How exactly did Fred get
paid? I helped out with problems like that. It was all very fluid and
I didn't charge for my time. For one thing, I had a lot of business and
was doing well; also I liked and respected Fred. He came to Monday-
night dinners at the Manhattan Café with Wolfe and Cutler and
Daly and the rest of the crew and told stories about art and painting—the sweep of his knowledge was amazing. He took me to art
shows and then to the Factory, Andy Warhol's studio. He came to
our apartment and to Bellport. Susie liked him too. But neither of us

could have guessed that this brilliant, odd little man would turn our lives, which had so recently come so wonderfully together, completely upside down.

———

We are in bed in Bellport, in our nice sunny bedroom with six wide windows all facing the water, when the phone rings early on Sunday morning, February 22, 1987. We've been together for three years, married for nine months, and Susie is used to late-night calls from gangsters and other people in trouble. And she is accustomed to my getting out of bed at weird hours and rushing off to get people out of jail or to appear at arraignment. She accompanies me sometimes, which is how she happens to realize that as a criminal lawyer I get people *out* of jail; I guess she thought I was putting them in.

"You've got to be kidding! You're getting these guys out. I have a real problem with that," she tells me when she figures out what's going on.

"What's the fucking problem?" I ask. "One drug dealer kills another drug dealer—what's your problem with that?" She soon settles down on the point.

When the phone rings at six-thirty that morning, I pick it up quickly, as I usually do. Thanks to my father, I know it is crucial to be watchful at all times and also to be able to rouse myself, instantly, from sleep to a state of great alertness. It's a skill that serves me well as a lawyer whose phone often rings at strange hours. The sun is just starting to rise over the water, but my wits are sharp when I answered the phone. Susie barely stirs.

"Eddie, Eddie, it's me. Fred. Andy's dead. You've got to come in."

I look at Susie, sleeping, pregnant. "I can't do it, Fred," I say. "I'm sorry."

"You're my friend. You've got to come," he says through the cream push-button phone on the little bedside table. "There are going to be problems. I need you. You've *got* to come."

"Tell it to my pregnant wife," I say.

"Who's that?" Susie mutters from under the pillows.

"Fred Hughes. Andy Warhol died. Fred wants me to come in."

"Hmmmm. Do you have to?"

The guy is my friend.

"Yeah," I tell her, "I have to."

Much later Tom Wolfe will say that everything that happened next followed from the fact that February 22, 1987, was a Sunday, a day on which Andy Warhol's white-shoe law firm, Paul, Weiss, Rifkind, and Garrison—which drafted his will and does some work for Fred Hughes—is not open for business. Ed Hayes is always open.

An hour later I'm on the Long Island Expressway in a hired car, heading for 57 East Sixty-sixth Street to meet Fred Hughes in the five-story town house where Andy Warhol lived, about to begin what will be the biggest, most protracted, knock-down-and-get-up-and-go-at-it-again fight of my life.

CHAPTER 10

I met Andy Warhol in 1979. I'd noticed a great-looking blond woman, very striking, very exotic. (It turns out later that she once lived with Frank Zappa.) I'd seen her around my neighborhood a few times, and one night I follow her down the block and watch as she walks into a brick building on West Ninety-second Street.

I'm in brightly colored cotton shorts and a T-shirt. It's a hot, steamy New York night, and for no reason aside from the fact that I am always looking for action, I walk to the door, turn the handle, and am not bothered to find it locked: I have a knife in my pocket. I jimmy the lock and walk into a drab green lobby with lots of cheap mirrors. I hear a party going on upstairs and go up to check it out.

I don't know anyone inside this loud room full of thudding music and attractive, strung-out, very sexual-looking people, many of whom seem crazed, drugged, or different in some other fundamental way from the people I knew at UVA or in Jackson Heights, Queens, or anywhere else.

I walk in, someone pinches my ass. I turn around, and it's Andy

Warhol! I know who he is right away. In 1979, Andy Warhol is everywhere. You couldn't *not* recognize him.

"What the fuck are you doing?" I say.

"You wanna be in a magazine?" Warhol says, his pale dead eyes on my face, his hand still on my ass.

"No, I don't want to be in no fucking magazine," I tell him. "Now please take your fucking hand off my ass."

I am ill at ease and much harsher than I mean to be. He takes his hand back and laughs, and I walk down the hall to a crowded, smoky room, where I find the blonde.

"I'm Lorraine," she tells me.

"Ed Hayes," I say. "I've been following you for months."

"Is that right?" she says. "And why is that, Mr. Eddie Hayes?"

"I like the way you look," I tell her, and she laughs.

She's far more surprised to find I'm an assistant district attorney in homicide.

"You gonna lock me up, Mr. Hayes?" she says.

I get the idea this is the first conversation she's ever had with a law enforcement guy who *isn't* trying to arrest her.

"Lorraine, unless you try to kill someone, I don't care what you do. And no, I'm not going to lock you up. Thanks."

Not a bad starter conversation. In fact, our conversation in the smoky living room on West Ninety-second Street is the beginning of a great affair.

I never met Warhol again and could never have imagined on that night in 1979 that Andy Warhol and his strange American genius and unexpected death would play a role in my own life.

———

I have been in some very upscale houses. Not as a kid, but when I was a DA or when I was sleeping with someone with money. But Warhol's town house is astonishing, full of magnificent furniture covered in shagreen sharkskin, unlike any other house I've ever seen.

"Did you pick this out?" I ask Fred, who is there when I arrive.

"Yes," Fred says, nodding at the sharkskin ensemble.

He doesn't seem as bothered as he should be by the fact that his close friend of twenty years has died suddenly at a New York hospital in what turns out to be freak circumstances.

I walk through the house the same way I've walked through hundreds of crime scenes. *Go to the scene. See for yourself.* In homicide and everything else, that's what you've got to do.

I start on the ground floor. There's a comfortable kitchen downstairs, old-fashioned and warm. The Filipino maids, who have nice little rooms on the fifth floor, later tell me that Andy sat here at the head of the big wooden table and ate meat loaf. He loved meat loaf and beef stew. He filled the room with cookie jars, dozens and dozens of the cheap kind you get at flea markets. To Andy Warhola—a skinny kid raised, with two ungainly brothers, in working-class Pittsburgh by their diligent mom, Julia Warhola, after their father worked himself to death in a coal mine—the cookie jars may have supplied the feeling of a wholesome world that seemed far out of reach.

There's great stuff on the walls. I recognize paintings from Picasso's blue period, early American portraits, an Edvard Munch drawing.

We walk up the front stairs, past a clutter of sharkskin-covered furniture, antique sofas, and chair sets in a living room that, like all the other rooms in the house except the kitchen, is so jammed with stuff it's hard to imagine anyone has ever set foot in it.

There are sideboards crammed with dishes and tea sets in the formal dining room. There are statues of dogs and horses, busts of Napoleon, and tables piled with shopping bags full of wrapped packages.

"Holy shit! There are nineteen wooden toilet seats in here," I say, looking inside a closet opposite a bathroom on the first floor.

Fred couldn't be more nonchalant.

"Yeah, he had a thing about wooden toilet seats," he says, and keeps walking up the stairs.

Yeah? Okay. A thing about toilet seats.

We go upstairs to the rooms where Warhol slept and where he evidently also warehoused more of his massive collection of stuff.

More boxes. More packages. Everywhere. Money and jewelry—necklaces, watches, second-rate Rolexes, stuff like that—cover Warhol's white-canopied bed, and there are stacks and stacks of green boxes with silver wigs inside, lined up in orderly rows. I look through the clothes in the closet. They aren't particularly interesting.

There are several attractive dressers in the closet. The dresser tops and the drawers, like the rest of the closet, are stuffed with packages and apparently unopened boxes.

I start going through the packages, randomly tossing some out onto the floor by the bed, when I come across a large wrapped parcel. I pull the paper off and knock a canvas, dark, full of flowers, against the bedroom wall.

"Oh God!" says Fred. "That's a Renoir! It's worth hundreds of thousands of dollars!"

Toilet seats, unwrapped Renoirs, hundreds of thousands of dollars. This is getting interesting.

———

"I've never been up here," Fred tells me on the way up the steps to the next level.

Warhol didn't allow people in certain parts of his house; the room across from the maid's room on the top floor, for example, must have been off-limits.

It's pitch-dark, the windows are so soot caked you can't see out of them; I pull the string on an overhead bulb and, when it lights, Fred's face drops.

"What is it, Fred?"

"*Here* they are!" he gasps.

Dozens and dozens of Warhol paintings, the signature pieces, are all here: the Elizabeth Taylor silk screen, the big Elvis Presley, the Jackie O., the electric chair. Sixty masterpieces rolled up and tossed, apparently randomly, on the uncovered floor. Fred almost faints; there are probably tens of millions of dollars' worth of paintings in here.

———

My mother probably wasn't so different from Julia Warhola—she worked hard and through much of her life made do with little pleasure; connecting with celebrities in movies or the pages of magazines provided a little pizzazz otherwise missing from her life. I'm liking the Andy Warhol I get to know as I walk through his house. Also, I'm a consumer and an upwardly mobile guy, and I very much understand the way buying and having things—cookie jars, custom-made shoes, whatever—can enrich one's life.

Walking through Warhol's house, I get the sense that he was an attractive man, not in appearance but in the life he created, which is now on display in the crowded rooms he has left behind. The things people say about Warhol's being exploitative and voyeuristic don't bother me nor does the large stash of videotapes of attractive young boys with enormous penises, masturbating, that turns up in Andy's room beside the boxes of wigs. So Warhol wasn't comfortable with his homosexuality and couldn't live the erotic life he wanted? His solution to the problem was pretty harmless. He liked porn—like everybody else. So what?

Is it unseemly to walk through a dead man's house, inspecting its contents? Yes, it's unseemly. My whole business is unseemly. In homicide, someone dies, you stand over the body, blood pours out all over everything, you go up to the wife, and say, "Sorry," and start asking gruesome questions. That's unseemly. Life is unseemly! As Raymond Chandler once wrote, "It is not a fragrant world."

———

"Let's see the will," I say as we finish our tour of the town house. Fred pulls an eleven-page document out of his pocket and hands it to me on the steps outside the bedroom. It names Frederick Hughes executor of Andy Warhol's estate.

"You got control," I tell him.

The alternative executor is Vincent Freemont, a completely uneducated but very handsome blond family man who started out sweeping the floors in Andy Warhol's studio during the late sixties and spent the next two decades winning his loyalty. Possibly because Freemont may well have been the only person in Warhol's entourage who didn't have a drinking or a drug problem, he became Warhol's right-hand man. (Oddly enough, according to Warhol's memoir, POP*ism*, Fred Hughes got his start sweeping the floor in the Factory as well.)

Warhol's brothers, John and Paul Warhola, and Fred each get $250,000. The will dictates that the rest of Warhol's estate be used to fund a foundation for the arts.

"Do you have any idea how much it's all worth?" I ask.

"No," he says. "A lot of money."

I have no way of knowing how the precise calculation of "a lot" will be made, but I'm going to learn.

—

"Andy Warhol died this morning." I'm on the phone with my brother minutes after I get the tour of the house on East Sixty-sixth Street.

Steven's firm is Jerry Hall and Mick Jagger's lawyer. Jagger and Warhol had known each other since the early seventies, when Warhol designed a Stones album cover and the Stones' lapping-tongue logo; Warhol went to Stones concerts and birthday parties for Jagger and rented Jagger and the others his Montauk house one summer. For a time he was close to Jagger's then wife, Bianca, who took Warhol with her to the White House to interview Jack Ford—before deciding, sometime in the early eighties, that Warhol was neither charming nor magical but was, in fact, a starstruck vampire. Steven knows a lot about Warhol and his world. Also, I like to have my brother involved in just about everything I do.

"I'll be right there, Eddie," Steven says, and within an hour he's at the house helping me think about possible legal issues and, as litigators do, about what could go wrong.

"Authentication is going to be a big issue," Steven says. "Everyone and his brother is going to be in here claiming to have original works by Andy Warhol. There'll be trademark issues and licensing and copyright questions."

If I were less angry and less interested in fame and public attention—which is to say, if I were a little more like my brother—I would probably know more about things like trademark and licensing issues. But Steven's here and his firm—Manatt, Phillips—specializes in entertainment law and works for sophisticated entertainers, recording artists mostly, including Bruce Springsteen and Paul Simon; he will be invaluable in sorting through the issues connected to the Warhol estate.

Frank Harvey, a lawyer friend who has hundreds of years of experience in estate planning and administration, arrives soon after I phone and tell him I need help.

"The main thing to avoid is conflict," says Harvey. We stand together in Andy Warhol's kitchen—Steven, Frank, and I—while I grill Frank about basic trust and estate law. "Strife between the parties involved will make this a mess. Keeping the parties happy, that's the key to settling an estate."

Avoid conflict, strife between the parties.

No problem. There's plenty of money, there's lots to share, everyone will make out all right. Why, I think, would there be a conflict?

—

The big picture in trust and estate law isn't complicated. I know nothing about the endless nuances, but I'm clear on the basics: you collect the dead guy's assets, count up his stuff, and distribute it (or the cash it generates) according to the terms of the will. That's it. After paying the government its share in estate taxes, of course. The executor and estate lawyers get paid a percentage of the estate.

Confidence or arrogance, call it what you like, I think I know how to handle this case.

When I look at the paintings and drawings and prints inside Andy Warhol's insanely cluttered house, I'm certain that Warhol is one of the great artists of our time. I know from Fred, and the intensive months of conversation he and I have had about art in general and Warhol in particular, that the value of Warhol's work is in decline and subject to debate, and I sense instinctively that the key to settling this right is to get the word out: *Warhol's work is very important and very, very valuable.* I am not unaware that the higher the value of the estate, the greater the fee eventually paid to the estate's executor and counsel.

———

Crowds—of friends, lots of gay guys, neighbors, curiosity seekers, who knows who else—gather outside Warhol's door almost immediately after noon, when CNN broadcasts news of his death. *Go to the scene. Control the scene.* Same thing whether you're in a blood-spattered apartment in the South Bronx that smells of urine and death or here in Andy Warhol's multimillion-dollar town house in the center of the highest per capita income neighborhood in the known world.

I call my detective friends from Warhol's kitchen. I want tough guys here. "I need help," I tell Jack McCann and Ronnie Marsenison, who show up in an unmarked car shortly after noon.

Marsenison, a former homicide detective accustomed to unexpected circumstances, does not look at all surprised when I stuff a wad of hundred-dollar bills into his hands immediately after he arrives at the house. "Go to the hospital and find out what the fuck happened to Andy Warhol," I tell him. Marsenison doesn't miss a beat. "Sure, Eddie," he says, and folds his meaty fist around the bills and heads for the door.

I pull an antique chair and a desk with a sharkskin top out of the clutter in Warhol's living room and place them inside the foyer by the front door. "Sit here," I tell McCann. "Nobody comes into the house. Anybody comes up to the door, they take their hands out of their pockets."

With the growing crowd outside, I am afraid someone might come around and shoot somebody. I'm remembering the notorious shooting of Warhol by the crazed feminist Valerie Solanas in 1968 in the old Factory on Union Square. He attracted crazies, some of them dangerous. "Men, women, dogs, young, old—anyone who wants to talk to anyone here, they take their hands out of their pockets," I tell McCann. I'm not taking any chances.

"Motherfucker, stop," I say to one guy who comes up the steps but refuses to keep his hands in front of him. "Take your hands out of your pockets. Right now. Or I'm going to hurt you."

He takes his hands out.

"What are you getting so upset about?" he says. He's a kid with scruffy hair and tight pants; he probably heard Warhol died and wants to see what's going on, but you never know.

Go to the crime scene. Take control. That's it.

—

Fred understands that settling the Warhol estate right, and also advantageously for him, will require a lot of maneuvering through the mazes of New York's power structure—the newspapers, the courts, the politicians. Fred can handle some of this and he knows I can handle the rest. He wants a lawyer who will be loyal, who will be available at all times, without any wait *ever*, and who absolutely will not fold under pressure, no matter what. He knows I am that guy.

Within a week of Warhol's death, we formalize the terms of an agreement according to which I will serve as sole counsel for the estate of Andy Warhol. Clearly, the estate is going to be complicated, but I have no idea how long it will take to wrap it up; will Fred pay me a flat fee, 2.5 percent of the value of the estate, at closing? Fred agrees. If the estate is valued at about $120 million, as we initially believe that it will be, I'll be entitled to approximately $3 million, of which some will be used to pay Frank Harvey and other experts and lawyers along the way. Not bad for what I imagine will be a few years of work. The fee, as is customary, is payable in thirds: one-third after the will is admitted to probate, one-third after the estate tax return has been filed, and the final third after the estate is finalized. A month or so later, after he realizes that Warhol's work is going to be worth more than we originally thought, Fred asks if I will take a lower fee, 2 percent instead of 2.5 percent of the estate. "Sure," I tell him, and we draft a new agreement. In yet another document, drafted a year later, Fred, in recognition of the fact that I am devoting "substantially all" of my time to estate matters, am "on constant call for estate activities," and have "had to give up [my] law practice in order to advise the estate," again adjusts the fee, slightly upward, to reflect our changed understanding of circumstances.

But the terms of all these agreements matter less than the essence of my bargain with Fred, according to which I will do for him what I have done for so many others: I will help him try his case; I will get the job done, even if it is messy. In return, Fred will give me something I badly want: more money, enhanced status, and what I hope and imagine will be a new kind of life.

———

The fourteen-hour workdays I spend with Fred the week after Warhol's death set the tone for what is going to be nearly ten years of intense, nonstop, around-the-clock high-pressure work.

We're in Fred's office at Warhol's Factory every day from six in the morning until late at night. Once a Con Ed substation, the Factory has been the center of Andy Warhol Enterprises since 1981, when Warhol bought the place for $2 million and moved his crew from an earlier Factory space near Union Square. A massive high-ceilinged place, it looks like a real factory with a few offices, for Fred and Warhol himself, off the side of the main work space. Fred's office is painted red—"Diana Vreeland red," in honor of the *Vogue* editor he adores, he tells me—and decorated with his usual flair and impeccable taste. (There is a full-size portrait of King Frederick of Denmark on one wall.) But the rest of the Factory, like Warhol's house, is crammed with stuff—paintings, drawings, silk screens, most of which are on rolled-up unstretched canvas strewn around Warhol's office and elsewhere throughout the enormous Thirty-third Street space.

Scheme, hustle, move, and score. I've been a planner all my life. I'm ready to strategize. It's what lawyers do—good ones, anyway.

"We need control, we have to get this stuff in order and think about a plan, something like a trial strategy," I tell Fred, who gets to work right away.

With a team of Factory employees, he starts to gather up the canvases so they can be sent off to be stretched and packaged and transported to a guarded warehouse in Queens. The sheer volume of stuff is staggering; it looks like the fall of Rome, someone says after all the paintings, movie reels, furniture, and statues are packed for shipping. Boxes are everywhere.

And the phone never stops ringing. Everyone Warhol knew—from Bianca Jagger to the man who sold him peanut butter at the neighborhood Korean market—comes forward to claim the painting or artwork they say he had "promised" them. Each call gives rise to what seem like dozens of legal problems, and each one mushrooms into a new area of law. There are insurance problems, real estate questions, partnership deals, and, based on what Ronnie Marsenison finds out from nurses present when Warhol died, a possible wrongful-death claim to consider making against New York Hospital. Among the matters we need to attend to first, however, is the matter of Andy Warhol's burial.

———

The funeral—held on February 26, 1987, on the North Side of Pittsburgh, in the working-class neighborhood where Andy Warhola grew up, and where you can still buy five-bedroom houses for

$35,000; and where, I swear to God, you find the biggest, palest white people anywhere in the world—is an entirely working-class affair. Fred and Vincent and I go together and stay at the Pittsburgh Athletic Club, which has a nice gym so that I get a couple of good workouts during the overnight trip.

The people who assemble at the Thomas P. Kunsak Funeral Home mostly sit and smoke and don't say much. Some leave their folding chairs and walk past the open casket where Andy is laid out in black cashmere, with a paisley tie; he is wearing one of his platinum wigs and sunglasses and holds a black prayer book and a red rose in one of his pale dead hands.

Warhol went to church every Sunday and gave food to the poor, which is something Monsignor Peter Tay says in his short eulogy at Holy Ghost Byzantine Catholic Church. After the service, we take a half-hour drive, in a cortege of twenty-five cars, to the Catholic cemetery where Andy will be buried beside his parents, Julia and Andrew Warhola.

"The whole world will remember Andy," Monsignor Tay tells the mourners assembled at the graveside. "Andy had a deep loving trust in God. This man will reach to the steps of the very throne of God," says the monsignor, who never met Warhol. The cemetery workers are getting ready to lower Andy into the ground when his longtime friend Paige Powell runs up and throws a handful of Interview magazines and a bottle of Estée Lauder perfume into the open grave.

I cause some offense at the cemetery. I haven't had a chance to talk to Warhol's brothers, John and Paul Warhola. "Fellas," I say, when I see them there at the grave site, "I'm Ed Hayes. If you want something, tell me. I'll get you what you want." "This is not the right time or place to talk about this," Paul Warhola tells me. He is probably right.

John, who was much closer to Andy than Paul, is really broken up when the cemetery workers slide the casket into place beside the grave. In fact, the crowd that gathers in Pittsburgh—with the notable exceptions of Fred and Vincent, who show no emotion whatsoever—seems far more affected by Andy's death than the

crowd that gathers at St. Patrick's Cathedral in New York to mourn
him a month later.

Swifty Lazar, Paloma Picasso, Raquel Welch, Halston, Calvin
and Kelly Klein, Ian Schrager, Timothy Leary, Bianca Jagger, Viva,
and Ultra Violet file into St. Patrick's to bid Andy Warhol good-bye
on April Fools' Day 1987, along with about two thousand others,
many of them key figures in the worlds of fashion, art, business, and
entertainment. It's not my usual crew, but I've been around artists,
models, late-night people, and the scene isn't entirely unfamiliar.
Fred has taken primary responsibility for the guest list and the
church is packed. Every seat is taken. People stand in the back,
too. White flowers hang—I think Fred has hung them himself—on
every pew.

A flutist plays selections from Mozart. Then Yoko Ono walks to
the dais and talks about Andy and how he touched so many lives.
The art historian John Richardson follows and speaks of Andy's spirituality and commitment to the church. Father Anthony Dalla Villa
reads from the Mass for the Dead: "Lord, Almighty Father, you have
made the cross for us a sign of strength." He continues, "Now that
you have freed our brother Andy Warhol from this mortal life, make
him one with your saints in heaven." *Saints in heaven!?* This is getting
out of hand!

After the service, four hundred mourners go to lunch at Billy
Rose's old Diamond Horseshoe nightclub in the basement of the Century Paramount Hotel, owned by Steve Rubell and Ian Schrager,
who have spray-painted the basement silver in memory of Warhol's
original Factory, on East Forty-seventh Street, which was also
painted silver when it opened in the mid-1960s. It's an elegant affair
but doesn't have the emotional feel the Pittsburgh service did.

—

Fred expresses exactly *no* emotion at the Mass at St. Patrick's,
either. How could he have spent twenty years with Andy Warhol
and have no apparent response to his death? The question has un-

nerved me since the chaotic first moments in the Sixty-sixth Street
town house the morning Warhol died, when I noticed that the Filipino maids, who were crying like babies when I walked in, were
the only ones rattled by his death. ("Don't worry," I tell them.
"You're going to be okay. We'll take care of you." And I do. When
they come forward later, claiming some pictures that they say Andy
gave them and that they have kept under their beds on the fifth floor,
we let them keep some of them, many of which are quite valuable.
Fred and Vincent don't want to do this. "Just give them some fucking pictures," I tell them, and, to their credit, they agree.)

Once the burial and the St. Patrick's service are over, Fred and I
get back to work. Apparently relieved to have the funeral and personal details behind him, Fred zealously applies himself to the business at hand, accounting for the holdings in Warhol's estate and
boosting its value.

———

History matters. Which is why I'm on the top floor of the Surrogate's Court in Lower Manhattan, looking for archived court
records, the day after Warhol's funeral Mass at St. Patrick's.

"I'd like to see the files for the Rothko estate," I tell the anxious
clerk, who in commendable obedience to a mysterious law that gov-
erns the appearance of all law clerks, wears owl-shaped wire-rim
glasses and has at least one visible nervous tic (a slight twitch in the
left eye). He also seems to know everything about everything that has
ever transpired in the New York court system.

The clerk shuffles off to a back room and returns with an enormous
box of papers filed in connection with the estate of Mark Rothko,
the great Abstract Expressionist painter whose unexpected death in
1970 gave rise to a huge scandal. I want to get a feel for what went
wrong.

After I read through reams and reams of documents, I see what
happened: Rothko's executor got caught selling himself a number of
paintings at a significant discount and phonying up the appraisals of

Rothko's work to justify the price he bought them at. The artist's children took the executor to court and made him reimburse the estate for the pilfered assets.

In retrospect, though, it's clear that executing the estate was a phenomenal score for the executor: sure, he got caught selling himself paintings for ridiculously low amounts, but nothing happened except that he had to buy the paintings again for higher sums, but nothing like the prices they would eventually fetch.

There was some side chicanery involved, too: the executor, for example, donated the majority of Rothko's work to a museum, which meant that the ones he retained were the only remaining Rothkos that were on the market and so were worth that much more. But the main action had to do with his having sold himself paintings at discounted sums based on phony appraisals. *This guy totally out-thought everyone! And got away with it!* I think as I read through the documents. *And no one is ever going to let anything like this happen again.*

"Look, Fred," I say when I get back from reading the Rothko file, "they caught this guy, but he got away with murder. It won't happen twice. We have to be straight here. If we work hard, we'll do well. We don't have to fool around."

"We're not doing any of that stuff," Fred says. "You're in charge, Eddie."

Both Fred and I are very conscious of the Rothko estate and what happened to the executor; though, as I now know, Fred viewed the story as an inspirational, not a cautionary, tale.

———

"Some lunatic guy is outside threatening me," Fred says one afternoon after Warhol's funeral when I find him inside the Factory shaking and white as a sheet. "I was there when Andy was shot. You have to take care of this, Eddie." He has a tough time catching his breath.

I will, Fred. I'm taking care of you, I think as I storm outside and find a scuzzy white guy with a weird, slightly out-of-it look in his eye.

"Get the fuck out of here and please don't come back," I tell him. Off he goes down Thirty-third Street.

But the guy keeps coming back. Eventually I have to get some homicide detectives to take him off the street. They push him into a car and ride him all over the fucking city. "Where is your mother, motherfucker?" they ask. The guy, who has no idea who they are or what they're doing, is scared to death. "Brooklyn," he tells the detectives. They drive to the guy's mother's house and pound on her door until she lets them in. "Look, you've got to keep him away," they tell the terrified woman, "for his own good."

That's the last we see of him.

———

Dealing with pissant kids with scary eyes is, of course, far less complicated than most of what Fred and I do in the days ahead.

"Something went wrong," Ronnie Marsenison tells me after talking to workers who had been at New York Hospital the night Warhol died.

Something *definitely* went wrong. You're not supposed to go into a prestigious teaching hospital for routine gall bladder surgery and come out dead! Hospital records show that Min Cho, a Korean private nurse, went on duty at 8:00 p.m. Saturday and checked in on Warhol, who had had the surgery earlier in the day, a number of times during the night. At 4:30 a.m., she noted the patient was pale. At 5:45 a.m., his skin was bluish and his pulse had stopped. She immediately called the cardiac-arrest team. All their efforts to revive him were unsuccessful, and at 6:21 a.m. Andy Warhol was pronounced dead.

"You better find that fucking nurse!" I tell Marsenison, who, through connections he actually has with some Korean general, finds the woman in Florida.

"Go get her," I tell him, and he flies down there right away.

When he meets her, he's really mad because she speaks only broken English and he has to hustle up a priest to translate what she has to tell him. And it turns out, maybe because the private nurse on duty when Andy Warhol died had language problems, that hospital personnel failed to monitor intravenous fluids going into Warhol's body; too much fluid went in and he drowned. We file a multimillion-dollar lawsuit against the hospital, charging carelessness and neglect; in the middle of trial, the hospital settles for a very sizable sum, but that is years away.

Now, among the many things we have to contend with are various issues raised by Warhol's considerable real estate holdings. In addition to the house on East Sixty-sixth Street and the one on Lexington Avenue that he lived in with his mother until she died and that Fred now rents, he owns a nineteen-acre compound in Montauk and a number of rental properties in Lower Manhattan, including one he's leased to the artist Jean-Michel Basquiat, who likes to leave naked women tied to hotel room beds and apparently uses a lot of drugs. The naked women are one thing, I think, and the drugs are another. But the two together—that, I think, could be a problem. Eventually, someone is going to be tied up somewhere and he's going to OD and someone is going to get hurt, and if he's living in Andy's building when that happens, that's gonna be a problem for us. So I show up at Basquiat's place with two detectives who pose as realtors. "Can we check out the place, for an appraisal?" they ask, and the guy (not Basquiat) who answers the door agrees. "Go in there," I tell them, "and see what you find," and they come out with works for heroin and some drugs. Later that day, I phone Basquiat and tell him in no uncertain terms that he has to vacate, and he does, so *that* problem is solved. But really, each aspect of work connected to Warhol and his estate gives rise to a seemingly endless number of issues, most of which are not as strange as this but all of which are complicated.

While we are busy authenticating the nearly seventy-five thousand pieces of art in Warhol's collection and also appraising, securing, and insuring the stuff, we are negotiating with Sotheby's about a series of auctions of his collection planned for the spring. And there

are numerous claims being made against the estate, claims of ownership of Warhol's art, disputes over Warhol's two pension plans for
his employees, income tax issues, every flavor of tangled-up trouble.

We do everything from investigating how it happens that drawings get "lost" in transit from the Museum of Modern Art to settling
disputes over fees due freelance writers who've written pieces for *Interview* magazine, which Warhol started in the seventies. Fred and I
work around the clock, but never, for even a second, do we lose sight
of our essential strategy, to convince the public that Andy Warhol is
a great painter. "Warhol is an important artist. Warhol is of great
value." There aren't enough ways and places we can say this. I know
from my courtroom experience and from the newspaper business and
politics how effective it is to repeat the same concept endlessly, in
as many media as possible. We'll show Warhol as often as we can in
as many venues as we can—in museums, galleries, articles, books.

———

Work on the Warhol estate does not provide an ideal setup for
Susie and my new marriage. For one thing, I am hardly ever home.
But Susie is as driven and determined as I am, and she and I both
know the Warhol case is the opportunity of a lifetime. Which
means that while I work my tail off, Susie cheerfully goes about her
pregnancy business, getting ready for the baby, and doesn't bother
too much about my being gone so much.

Susie calls me at the office one morning.

"Hey, Meatball," she says. "You think you can tear yourself away
for a minute and meet me at the hospital?"

I can't be more present than I am at Lenox Hill Hospital on October 24, 1987, when Avery Gilder Hayes is born. I like hard labor
and I push Susie's legs against her stomach, as the doctor tells me to
do, for three or four hours in the delivery room. Man, is that kid a
beautiful sight when she comes out! I hold Avery Gilder Hayes and
Susie holds her and I hold Susie and—I swear to God—there are a

couple of moments there when, if someone had come in and asked, "Who was Andy Warhol?" I would have had no idea in the world what the person was talking about!

We are still living on Sheridan Square in Susie's one-bedroom apartment when we bring Avery home from the hospital in her tiny English jacket. We have a crib set up in the living room and Susie's old friend Tara Shannon has helped her stencil pink figures around it.

Everyone says having kids completely changes your life and it's true. I attend to diapers and bottles and blankets; every aspect of Avery's little life is fascinating to me.

My mom comes to the christening we have in Bellport, but not my dad. He is too far gone now, obese, ravaged by years of alcoholism, and living out in Long Island with another reformed alcoholic, his girlfriend, whom I have also invited; neither of them shows up for Avery's big day. Bruce Cutler, Michael Daly, and Fred Hughes agree to be Avery's godfathers. (Cutler is the most generous godfather in the history of the world; in time, when Avery decides she wants to be a journalist, Daly becomes her mentor; choosing Fred turns out to have been a mistake.)

Holding my gorgeous baby in her gorgeous christening dress, I think, as I have for some time, about the kind of parent I want to be. As a child, I learned I could not expect to be loved for myself; if someone loved me, it was going to be because of what I did or could do for them. Avery, I vow to myself, can expect love, no matter what. I want her to know that life is harsh and that sometimes you can't control what happens to you but that you do what you can. I will absolutely be more attentive and supportive to Avery than my parents were to me. It sounds corny, but I was always fascinated by history and politics and had learned to love museums; I want to help my kids learn how exciting the life of the mind could be. My dad was sick and drunk and depressed and ineffectual, left to dance at the end of strings manipulated by men more powerful than he was. I want to be a better role model for my children than my father was for me. And one of the things this means—to Susie and to me—is being there, ready to jump at the main chance, whenever it happens to come along.

The Warhol case is that kind of chance. We make arrangements for the super's wife to help with the baby and I get back to work, returning late at night, often to find my beautiful blond daughter curled up asleep with her beautiful big-hearted mother.

———

Fred and I sweat blood and it takes months and months, but after the Sotheby's auction of Andy Warhol's collection in the spring of 1988, it's clear our plan to educate the public about Warhol and elevate the value of his estate has succeeded almost beyond our wildest expectations.

Six thousand people show up at Sotheby's on Saturday, April 23, when the collection goes on view. More than five thousand people are turned away on auction day as the bidding room can hold only a thousand people, all of whom have to establish proof of their seriousness as buyers.

Susie and I sit in a VIP room that overlooks the bidding floor with Fred, Vincent, Factory regular Baby Jane Holzer, Warhol's friend and shopping partner Stuart Pivar, art critic John Richardson, and other members of the art world and watch as Sotheby's sells off Warhol's stuff—Salvador Dalí ear clips, a plastic Fred Flintstone wristwatch, Navajo rugs, Jasper Johns paintings, Indian jewelry, Fiestaware, the cookie jars he kept in his kitchen.

Pivar buys a lot of two cookie jars for $11,500. "Andy always said if you are going to own a cookie jar, you have to have a Silver Mammy," he tells us as he lifts his paddle to the exorbitant heights.

"I want that one," Susie says as the auctioneer moves on to a lot of brightly colored jars.

"I bought that for Andy for fifty cents!" Fred says. "Don't be a fool, Susie. Put your hand down! I'll take you to Canal Street and you can get one of those for five dollars. We'll put a sticker on it—

it'll look better than that thing up there." This is a pretty fair indication of Fred's increasingly fast and loose approach to authentication. The auctioneer puts his gavel down, closing the bids on another
cookie jar lot at $23,100!

The auction goes unbelievably well. Just about every item sells for
far, far more than the Sotheby's experts imagined. Warhol's Rolls-
Royce, which Sotheby's thought would go for $15,000, instead sells
for $77,000, and a piece of jewelry Sotheby's appraisers thought
would go for $2,000 sells for $28,000. ("We're doing pretty good
here," I tell Susie as the gavel goes down on that one.) The cookie
jars Warhol bought at flea markets and street sales for almost
nothing sell for an astronomical total of $247,830.

Sotheby's appraisers had estimated total sales might reach $15
million; at the end of the day, Warhol's rugs and cars and jars and
paintings bring in $25.3 million—$25.3 million and complete vali-
dation of Fred's belief that everything Warhol touched is graced
with genius.

"You're a fucking genius," I tell Fred on the way out. And he is.
We're on a roll.

Andy Warhol: A Retrospective opens at the Museum of Modern Art in
February 1989. Fred and I began negotiating with museum curators
almost the day after Warhol's death. Fred is enormously helpful and
displays his usual unerring taste throughout the many months he spends
helping them select the works that will best represent Warhol's spectacular career.

And on February 1, Leo Castelli, Bianca Jagger, Roy Lichtenstein,
Keith Haring, Claes Oldenburg, Julian Schnabel, Ultra Violet, Baby
Jane Holzer, Dennis Hopper, and hundreds of others crowd together,
craning to see the pen-and-ink shoe drawings that Andy did for
Glamour magazine and other venues in the 1950s, the pioneering Pop
work, the Brillo pads and soup cans from the early sixties, the silk-
screened portraits of Jackie O., Marilyn Monroe, and Elvis Presley,

the disaster series that depicts race riots, electric chairs, and car crashes, and late works, like the Pop pastiche *The Last Supper*.

Overflow crowds line up in the following months to see the show, which critics lavish with serious attention and great praise. "The exhibition underlines Warhol's enormous importance and gift," Michael Brenson writes in the *New York Times*. "Warhol must be considered in the top rank of American painters of the 20th century," Thomas Hoving, the distinguished former director of the Metropolitan Museum, writes, further crediting Warhol with having "changed art history forever." Almost unanimously, critics and reviewers reject the notion that Warhol was a poseur whose glittering surfaces were empty or superficial. Kynaston McShine, who curates the exhibit, writes in the introduction to the catalog: "[The] very celebrity of Warhol's, his sheer inescapable fame, has often disguised the fact that he was one of the most serious, and one of the most important, artists of the twentieth century. He quite simply changed how we all see the world around us."

"And what do you think about the representational versus nonrepresentational abstraction?" asks the very attractive woman seated next to me at the dinner at the museum the night the retrospective opens. What do I think about *representational abstraction*? I don't know the first thing about representational or nonrepresentational abstraction, and I have absolutely no idea what to say to the woman, who couldn't be nicer or more gracious. I make a vague sound and dive into the dinner, feeling, for the very first time since I started work in the weird world of art patrons and collectors, completely in over my head. Dominique de Menil—it turns out the woman attempting to engage me in what might as well be Farsi is a member of the family Fred knows from Texas—is lovely, and I regret failing her so terribly as a dinner companion. But my inability to speak coherently about the aesthetics of contemporary painting aside, the evening— and the exhibit—is an unqualified success.

For years, Warhol phoned his secretary and friend Pat Hackett every morning to give her a blow-by-blow account of his activities the night before. She typed it all out, and it is a fabulously interesting (and in some instances, exceptionally nasty) record of his life and times. Fred and I now hire Lynn Nesbit of ICM to agent the book, and at the end of a spirited auction she sells it for $1.2 million and subsequently raises an additional $1 million in foreign rights. When *The Andy Warhol Diaries* comes out in 1989, it is warmly received by the publishing community and by readers, who snap up more than a hundred thousand copies, making the book a smash best seller that stays on the *Times* list for fifteen weeks and, even more importantly for our purposes, increasing Warhol's significance as a cultural figure.

Fred, who for reasons I don't understand and don't care to learn, despises Pat Hackett and he wastes no time violating the rule against unnecessary conflict by asking me to give her a hard time, which means that Hackett soon hates me and Fred. I nonetheless admire Pat Hackett; she did a great job with Warhol, and *The Andy Warhol Diaries* is a great book.

(Here is how Andy Warhol remembers me from a society doctor's birthday party in the fall of 1980: "And a defense lawyer named Ed Hayes who looked like he was from Laverne and Shirley, like a plant that people invite to parties to wear funny clothes and jump around and make things 'kooky.' Sort of forties clothes, really crewcut, about twenty-nine. He said, 'I can get ya outta anything.' ")

Sales of the *Diaries* and its spectacular publicity splash are solid indications that we are succeeding with our strategy and should work even harder to pump up Warhol's profile.

———

Fred and I now turn our attention to the Andy Warhol Museum, which will be located in Pittsburgh and devoted entirely to Warhol and his work. The idea is to establish a museum that will do what the retrospective did—honor a great American artist—and also stand as a permanent monument to the lasting value of his work. When it opens every kid with a nose ring and lip ring will be there, along with a few surviving Factory stars like Ultra Violet and Billy Name, as well as reporters from major newspapers. Leading art critics will call the museum a fitting memorial to Warhol and his talent.

It may have something to do with the economy, which booms in the late eighties, and it may have something to do with the increased appeal of pop culture for members of the monied demimonde—whatever the reason, the effort to raise Andy Warhol's status and value could not be more successful. By the end of 1989, Warhol's work is selling like crazy and we begin making huge sums of money.

My first payment, a check for $1.2 million, for work on the estate arrives right on schedule. I give a quarter to Frank Harvey, who has been central to every aspect of the legal work I've done, and cover some other expenses with it, but holy shit, this is a lot of money.

—

"It's great," says Fred when he shows me the big wreck of a town house that's for sale on East Eighty-first Street.

Susie and I have planned to use that first check for a down payment on a house, but this one is a mess.

"Fred, you're out of your mind," I tell him.

"In matters of taste," Fred reminds me, "I am always right. You are always wrong."

Fred is, of course, right about *this*. And though it is a wreck and needs major renovations that will take two years to complete, the house—the first tangible item that comes from my work on Warhol—is a terrific windfall in every way. A town house on the Upper East Side of the world's greatest city—you can't do much better than that.

We close on the house at the beginning of 1988. *The Bonfire of the Vanities* is at the top of the best-seller list and the Warhol case is attracting attention that helps cement my new place in city life. I've gotten zillions of calls: are you Tommy Killian? Friends and readers want to know. Yes! I think I am. I'm so busy with Warhol that I turn away business from dozens of people who want me to represent them.

A moment during lunch at the 21 Club on West Fifty-second Street nicely crystallizes a dawning sense of the effect all this may have on my life. Just after I close on the house, I take Frank Harvey and his young receptionist, whose father is a rodeo rider, out to celebrate how well we are doing with Warhol—and everything else. We're at a small table in the front and I'm putting my fork to rest inside a juicy piece of tenderloin when the guy at the table next to us says, in a voice loud enough to slow the pace of my beef to my jowl, "There's a guy in *The Bonfire of the Vanities* modeled on some guy from Queens, a real guy. His name is Hayes, Ed Hayes. He works in the art world now. He's supposed to be a phenomenal lawyer."

A phenomenal lawyer! The phenomenal lawyer is wild with excitement. He always wanted to be one of the fellows, a guy you could count on, a solid member of the white-boy mafia, someone close to the city's nerve center. And here, with a nice plump piece of tenderloin balanced on *his* fork, this guy is telling the white-shoed masses at one of the city's most exclusive lunch spots that Ed Hayes, white boy from Queens, is not only one of the fellows but also *a phenomenal lawyer!* It absolutely does not hurt that the words sounding from the neighboring table seem to have a potent effect on Frank Harvey's pretty young receptionist, who looks at me with fresh interest and— forgive me if I am wrong, rodeo rider receptionist—but also with desire.

Less than two years earlier, on a morning when Fred Hughes and I went to Paul, Weiss to discuss Warhol's will, I had stopped at my office to meet a wiseguy charged with bank fraud. Like many other wiseguys, this one is an endless conniver, always wanting to tamper with something. I have an enormously complicated big-money art-world estate on my mind as I sit down to meet the guy.

"I don't have time for you," I tell him. "I can't represent you anymore. You're going to have to find another lawyer."

I'm getting away from crime and this kind of life, I think, and I'm happy, if deluded, in thinking it.

I have no way of knowing then—or now, as I enjoy lunch at the 21 Club and the rush of my recent success, not to mention the fire in the young blonde's eyes—that the universe of New York's cultural elite, fancy auction houses, and slick corporate lawyers who represent them is even sleazier, more scheming, more conniving, and far more treacherous than anything I've encountered in the crime business.

CHAPTER 11

"You got it!" Fred squeals when he sees the six-foot winged wrought-iron dragon clawing its way out of an iron net on the front door of my town house in the fall of 1989. "You got it! It's good."

"Do whatever seems right," I told Wally Vogelsberg, the brilliant steelworker with a forge in Wycombe, Pennsylvania, who crafted the dragon. "Do what you think seems right for the door."

My wife hates Vogelsberg's dragon. I am not sure about it, so Fred's enthusiasm means a lot to me.

Among the many things he's given me, Fred Hughes taught me about the artistic importance of the strong gesture. And, as he was about a lot of things, Fred was right about the door: it's on all the major New York walking tours today.

From my tailors and shoemakers I know a lot about the pleasure of having a strong connection with men who made things; renovating the house on Eighty-first Street means direct contact not just with Wally Vogelsberg but with Irish craftsmen and every skilled Jamaican coconut head in New York. I know a lot of masons are Irish immigrants and I ask the guys around the New York Athletic Club—

where I go most mornings to bench press and do dead lifts and where many of the guys lifting with me are Irish—if anyone knows a good brickmason.

Sean O'Shaughnessy, a sturdy guy who can lift more than anyone else at the gym, says he's run into a group of first-generation Irish bricklayers that includes a phenomenal mason who was a champion boxer in Ireland. "Name is Tony McLaughlin," says O'Shaughnessy. "Guy can lay a hundred bricks an hour."

"No way you can lay a hundred bricks an hour," I tell McLaughlin when I phone him that evening. "That's too fast. You can't keep that pace up."

Go to the scene. That's what I'd learned to do in homicide, and early the next morning I go down to Twenty-eighth Street in a gray sweat-shirt and sweatpants and stand across the street from the twenty-second-story office building where McLaughlin is working. I stand in my sweats, counting the bricks McLaughlin lays up the front of the building. Man, that motherfucker is fast! I hire him on the spot.

McLaughlin has hordes of Irish immigrants working for him. I can't understand a word out of any of their mouths, and the only guys they will work with are West Indians, whom you also can't under-stand to save your life. But you've never seen a work ethic like a West Indian's—every West Indian I have ever met would work thirty-nine hours a day if he could! It's bizarre to listen to these guys talk their incomprehensible gibberish as they work side by side on my house.

Most days after I finish work with Fred, I stop at Eighty-first Street to check things out. One day I find a big, burly tough guy in the back laying slate. I see that he's having trouble with the slate and also notice that his hands are delicate, soft-looking.

"Geez, Tony," I tell McLaughlin, "that guy doesn't have a brick-layer's hands."

"He used to be a bricklayer," says McLaughlin, "but he's not really been working as one lately."

"Yeah, well, what's he been doing?" I ask.

"Working in banks," says McLaughlin.

"What's he been doing in banks?"

"Well," says McLaughlin, real cool, "sticking 'em up, mostly."

The guy was an IRA gunman, was pinched for bank robbery, did time in Ireland for a few years, and now is in my yard dropping slabs of slate into place in what will be a patio around a small yard where I can garden in the city. McLaughlin's crew is full of former IRA guys. They are very tough and do very good work; they remind me of the homicide detectives.

"Not unless you run a picture of my crew," I tell the editor from *House and Garden* when she calls to say the magazine wants to photograph the house for an upcoming issue. "The magazine doesn't run pictures of workmen," she says. "We can't do that."

"We're gonna do that," I tell her.

"Hayes & Co.," a ten-page feature story written by Tom Wolfe, runs in the October 1990 issue of *House and Garden* and opens with a two-page photo spread of metalworker Wally Vogelsberg, brick mason Tony McLaughlin, two West Indian plasterers whose work looks like porcelain, and architects Turner Brooks and Ross Anderson standing with Susie and two-year-old Avery and me in front of the house. "I would like to think of Eddie Hayes' town house as the start of a new era for craftsmen and tradesmen," Wolfe says in the piece.

We move in the fall of 1989. We don't have a party or anything—we are just home—in a massive 5000-square-foot house with its copper-roofed gardening shed and lion's head roof ornament and cherrywood interior walls. That's it.

———

Trouble with the Warhol case starts at the end of 1989, when Fred gets sick. He'd been diagnosed with multiple sclerosis, a degenerative neurologic disease I would learn a lot about in the days ahead. Often triggered by hard drinking and stress (in each of which Fred indulged heavily), MS weakens muscles; people who have it lose control of their bodies and often their minds.

The disease was dormant in Fred for many years and he went

about his usual business, going to outlandish parties and traveling with friends like Mick Jagger, Sara Giles, and Factory curator Tim Hunt to exotic places. That all ended in summer 1988 when Fred started to have trouble walking and began to rely on an exquisitely expensive cane to get around. His health deteriorated rapidly. And he began to experience wild mood swings.

"This man is mad," says Bridey, a middle-aged Irish nurse with a kind smile whom I hire to care for Fred shortly after he begins to get sick. She has grown children she adores and a husband with whom it would be unwise to trifle. "He throws stuff at people. He hits me with his cane. He rolls around in his wheelchair screaming."

Bridey's report isn't surprising. Fred calls me at the office all day long. "You're not my friend!" he screams into the phone. "You're not helping me."

Several times during the late fall and winter, Fred calls and demands I rush to the town house on the Upper East Side that he's leasing from the Warhol estate, and I do.

"You're such a man! You can do anything! Look at me! You can't help me. No one has done more for you in your life than I have and you can't do anything for me." Fred is in his wheelchair when I arrive in the dark foyer full of Warhol paintings and a Corot landscape and a Julian Schnabel drawing of a distorted fish—all of which Fred loves and has arranged perfectly in this windowless space in a way that makes it seem they were meant to hang together. He shakes and drools. He can't control himself.

His taunts—"You're such a man! You can do anything!"—have a monstrous, familiar ring. "But you can't help me," he shrieks. It's terrible to watch and I start to cry, right here, in the dark foyer filled with Warhols and a Corot and a Schnabel.

A cruel fact is that as Fred gets weaker and weaker after the fall of 1989, I get stronger and stronger. I am at the New York Athletic Club every morning with Alex Porter, a former top wrestler and now a brilliant hedge-fund manager whose eighty-two-year-old mother cut a toe off with a chain saw she was using to clear the family farm where Porter grew up, and John Dougherty, another champion wrestler and another man no army could beat down. "Do squats," Porter tells me. "It'll make you strong." I badly want to have another child, a son, and Porter thinks it's all a matter of squats. Weighing in at 185 lbs, I hump up four sets of twelve 275-pound squats twice a week, lift four days a week and run five days a week before heading to the office or the Warhol Factory.

Increasingly, people come to me, not Fred, with questions about the Warhol estate or about Warhol's work, which drives Fred nuts and fuels his paranoia. Temperamental to begin with, Fred can be well mannered and brilliantly levelheaded one moment and fly into an uncontrollable rage the next.

He is elegantly dressed, composed, and brilliantly focused when we meet in a high-ceilinged, well-appointed room in the Duquesne Club in Pittsburgh with representatives from the Dia Foundation and the Carnegie Institute in the spring of 1990 to make arrangements for the Warhol Museum.

The meeting goes well. Fred has every reason to be proud: he is masterminding the creation of a hugely endowed institution to honor an artist whose work he personally championed and whose value he personally enlarged. But a terrible look comes across Fred's face as we're wrapping up the meeting, shaking hands, bestowing polite back slaps and "well then, good to see you"s all around.

"I must get to the bathroom," Fred whispers in near agony as we step out into the marble hallway. "I must get to the bathroom." I've never seen him so agitated.

"We'll get you there as soon as we can," I tell him.

Fred shakes on his cane.

Soon Fred will be confined to a wheelchair and the house will have to be outfitted with motorized chairs to bring him downstairs, where assistants will carry him out to the car for the ride to the Factory, where they will carry him in. But now, in the Duquesne Club, Fred supports himself on his gorgeously carved cane.

I see Fred's pants darken and I know he will die—of rage or shame—if he finds himself with wet pants in front of the well-tailored Dia and Carnegie swells.

"You're not going to make it, Fred," I say, heaving him over my shoulder.

I squat 275 pounds with Alex Porter and it's not a problem to hump Fred up on my back and then run down the hall to a men's room whose marble walls amplify Fred's raging fury.

"Leave me alone. Don't touch me. You're killing me!" He yells and curses, and then tries to hit me. "You want me dead. You want me dead!"

"I'm trying to fucking help you. I can't leave you here to die. I can't leave you here on the goddamned floor," I tell him. "I'm not doing that."

"I'm not doing that" is something I start to say to Fred with greater and greater frequency.

———

"Eddie, I have a lot of Warhol paintings," he tells me one day. "I want you to sell them overseas, Eddie. They're worth a lot—maybe $50 million. I'll give you 10 percent."

"I'm not going to do that," I tell him.

"They're easy to move," he says. "They're all signed."

"Don't do it, Fred," I tell him.

"Eddie, Eddie, Eddie," he says, "we're not going to get caught!"

"I built my fucking house in Bellport with money from guys who said *they* wouldn't get caught," I tell him. "I'm not doing it."

Fred is my daughter's godfather as well as my friend and I am genuinely confused as to what to do. I have all but lost confidence in his judgment. It doesn't help that, in terms of the estate for which he serves as executor, hundreds of millions of dollars are at stake.

My attitude has always been: if we take care of everyone along the way, no one will be mad if we get rich in the process. My job as lawyer for the estate is to find the value of the estate's assets—the beneficiaries have a right to know what they have and the public has a right to know what it is entitled to in grants. Andy's eleven-page will states that his assets are to be used to fund the Andy Warhol Foundation to promote the visual arts, effectively designating the American public the beneficiary of his holdings, meaning I have a public duty as well as a private motive to battle those who denigrate Andy Warhol, his importance as an artist, and the value of the work he left behind.

The value of the estate is a matter of considerable consequence to Fred, who, as executor, stands to make 2 percent of the entire value of the estate as, per estate law, it is determined by a court of law. Per the terms of my agreement with Fred, I too will be awarded 2 percent of the estate's value, a fee that is slightly higher than usual (often 1.5 percent) but that reflects the fact that, since the fight to convince the public and a court that Warhol is an artist of great significance and value involves considerable risk, I should be entitled to share in any rewards reaped by my efforts.

"Look, Fred, we can make a lot of money. Legitimately. We don't have to fuck around." I tell Fred this from the start. "If we work hard, we'll do well."

Give me a choice between having a bunch of money in the bank or spending an afternoon with a girl in her apartment, and I'm going with the girl, every time. I like money—it's just that some things are actually more important than money. I'm not Mother Teresa, but one thing I believe is that I have to do my job, and if I take on work that involves my promising to take care of people, I'm going to do it— and I'm not going to fuck it up by acting stupid or greedy. Another thing I'm not going to do: if I can help it, I'm not going to break ranks with Fred or anyone else, as it has always been my experience that when one person in a crew breaks and runs, everyone goes down.

I know now quite a bit more about the art world than I knew when I started work on the Warhol estate. I know, for instance, that there are a million ways—legitimate and illegitimate—to make money in the art world and also that Fred and I are not the only ones who are going to walk away with a bundle when the estate settles. The dealers authorized by the estate to sell Warhol's work, the auction house that wins the right to sell off large blocks of the estate's holdings, the accountants who tally up the value of the estate—they'll all line up, as will the agents who represent Warhol works to galleries and the members of the Warhol Foundation who will oversee the selling and the distribution and will also join the receiving line for handouts from museums, galleries, agents, and dealers with whom they do business. Then there are the lawyers—initially David Jewel, an upstanding guy from Donovan, Leisure whom Fred, as he often did, quickly turned on and fired; then a squadron from Carter, Ledyard and a guy named Mark Rennie, a partner at a midsized firm who was eventually disbarred for monkey business involving false accounting on Fred's behalf; and finally big guns at Skadden, Arps, the powerful white-shoe firm that charges more money straightening out the Warhol mess than they eventually charge for defending President Clinton against Paula Jones and all the other big-haired women caught up in the hunting of the president. Let's just say there is a lot of hourly billing being done on the Warhol estate.

The real difference between the art world and the world of Bronx County Criminal Court is that hoodlums in the Bronx have a remedy for their problems: if someone gives you trouble in the Bronx, you don't sue the guy or tie him up in litigation for years, you shoot him. In the art world, you can't shoot guys who give you trouble, but it's just as brutal. Fred knows all the angles.

"The beauty business is entirely corrupt." That's what Fred always said in his more lucid days. "You have to watch everyone every second, or they'll take endless advantage of you."

By the end of 1989, it is, of course, Fred whom I have to watch every second.

———

I don't know it at the time, but Fred has a big problem. There are a large number of unsigned works believed to be authentic Warhols but they will be hard to move unless he can prove they are genuine. Fred stands to make a bundle if he is willing to authenticate these works. I begin to see that Fred is in fact very, *very* willing to do this—in exchange for a piece of the action.

In the spring of 1989, I find out that art dealer Robert Miller, who owns the Robert Miller Gallery on East Fifty-seventh Street, bought a series of Warhol's Superman drawings for $175,000 from an Italian dealer after Fred authenticated one of them. Somehow, as part of the bargain, Fred himself wound up with a drawing from the series.

"Why did you do that, Bob?" I ask Miller, whom I genuinely like, "Why the fuck did you give Fred art in exchange for an authentication?"

"He asked me for it," says Miller.

"Whaddya mean he asked?" I'm getting very worried about Fred.

"You know," Miller adds, "I don't know if he took the drawing for the estate or for himself."

Well, I haven't heard anything about the drawing so I assume it wasn't for the estate.

"Well, they're no good anyway. He authenticated them, but I can't sell them, so you've got to make good on them," Miller says, and he's right.

I get Fred on the phone fast.

"You can't go take drawings for yourself," I tell Fred. "Are you out of your fucking mind?"

Yes. It turns out Fred is absolutely out of his fucking mind.

Using the authority of the estate—and his authority as executor and therefore as authenticator—for personal advantage is improper, and, given what is to be gained, treacherous.

As executor, Fred will be a very rich man when the estate is settled. What does he need money for? He's sick. He's crazy. And crazy for money.

Miller is soon on the phone again, reiterating to me that the drawings aren't legitimate. Worse, since Fred authenticated the drawing, the estate is liable for the 175 grand.

Miller is cool and professional and completely in the right.

"Fuck that," says Fred, "I don't want to pay the guy. I'm mad at him."

Fred's lost it.

I start to worry about what else he's doing and, as I soon discover, there's good reason to worry.

One morning I find him in his red-lacquered office, cool and composed in a dove-gray suit, talking on the phone with a Swiss dealer to whom he sold paintings before Warhol died.

"The electric chair, the small one, yes," Fred says. "Two hundred. Yes."

I know what Fred is doing: he's selling Tomas a small painting of an electric chair.

It is completely lawful to act as agent for an artist who has died so long as the agent acted on the artist's behalf prior to death and so long as he continues to make sales and collect commissions in the same manner he did when the artist was alive. Fred, of course, continues to sell paintings to Tomas after Warhol has died, keeping the 20 to 25 percent commissions for himself. I don't know if Fred is evading taxes on the commissions or socking the money in private Swiss bank accounts and, though I have my suspicions, this isn't the real problem.

The electric chair print isn't in the estate. It's part of Fred's personal collection.

Tomas, the biggest single purchaser of art from the Warhol estate, is also buying Warhols from Fred's personal collection!

Scheme, hustle, move. I am new to the art world but I know a scam when I see one: Tomas is paying a premium for paintings in Fred's collection and, in return, getting a discount on work he buys from the estate.

"You can't do that, Fred," I tell him. "You *cannot* do that. You're going to get caught. There's plenty of legitimate money to be made here. *Don't do that.*"

"Ah, it's okay," Fred says, going back to the papers on his large, meticulously ordered teak desk.

"It is not okay."

I'm terrified. The Rothko estate fiasco is vivid in my mind. The executor there abused his position, purchased paintings from the estate at less than market value, was reprimanded by the court and ordered to pay the difference between the fair-market value of the works he'd purchased and the discounted price for which he'd obtained them. Though the executor came out ahead—the paintings in question vastly appreciated over time—I couldn't imagine a court would again tolerate executorial improprieties in a large artist's estate.

I run downstairs and sit behind a sleek Italian typewriter and—being something of a monkey at a keyboard—hammer out a letter that says, "I hereby agree that I will not sell work from my private collection of works by Andy Warhol as doing so represents a conflict of interest arising from my role as executor of the Warhol estate." Then I insist that Fred sign it. I now believe that Fred's signature on that letter spelled the eventual end of our relationship and the beginning of a very large and expensive mess.

———

Fred's decision to bring in Archibald Gillies to oversee the day-to-day work of setting up the Warhol Foundation as stipulated in Warhol's will does not help.

Gillies tells Fred on their first meeting that he knows nothing about art. No matter. Fred has always been fascinated by old money. And the feel of old money—afternoons on verandas and in paneled libraries with servants rushing about with cool drinks and meals on fine family china—hangs on Gillies like a smell. Gillies doesn't come from real money, but he does come from a good family—his father was an admiral—and he's spent his professional life cozying up to it, managing money for Nelson Rockefeller and John Hay "Jock" Whitney. A Princeton-by-way-of-Choate man, Gillies belongs to a recognizable breed of nonprofit guys who wear funkier shirts than the standard corporate Wasp who has his *own* money in the bank. And after all his years running matters for Rockefellers and Whitneys, Gillies is a consummate foundation man: he knows how to run things, to schedule meetings, to put nice lunches together for board members.

"Nice to meet you, Mr. Hayes," says Gillies, stretching his long arm in my direction when I meet him in Fred's office.

This guy has never broken a sweat in his life, I think as I shake his hand. But I like Gillies okay. He's a decent guy who just wants to be on the team.

As everyone involved knows, or at least as Gillies and Hughes know, his position on the Warhol team is secure so long as he gives Fred—who not only hired him but eventually offers him a seven-year contract that bestows on him a big salary as well as substantial prestige and influence in the art world—what he wants. As Gillies also knows, what Fred wants are the lucrative sales commissions Fred—and Vincent Freemont—earn as the primary agents for Warhol's art.

"He won't do it, and if he does do it sooner or later you're going to get in trouble," I tell Fred when he mentions that, as part of the contract he is going to give him, Gillies will have control over the art in the estate and has promised to award Fred an exclusive contract to sell Warhol's work.

"It's fraud. It's corrupt," I argue. Maybe Gillies can award Fred a contract to sell a portion of the work in the estate, but not without subjecting the arrangement to an outside panel of experts to advise on its terms. And not without first receiving bids from other qualified dealers; there are, after all, dealers better able to distribute the work than Fred. A quid pro quo deal of the kind Fred is talking about smacks of kickback and impropriety.

I know we are going to bring the whole thing down if we start to struggle against one another, which is why I greet the news of Gillies's appointment—and the promises that underpin his position on the board—with great foreboding.

No sooner has Gillies settled into his chair as consultant to the Andy Warhol Foundation than matters start to fall apart in much the way I feared. Within months of hiring Gillies as a consultant,

Fred decides to make him president of the foundation, and Gillies's promise to award him an exclusive sales contract has clearly played a part in his decision to disregard my objections. But Gillies's honeymoon with Fred ends not long after it begins. Six months after he appoints Gillies president, Fred turns against him, as he has turned against Bridey, countless lawyers, and all his friends. Fred and Gillies are soon in battle to oust each other and both are madly angling for control. Gillies, of course, knows nothing about art but a lot about foundations, and he quickly and successfully sets out to shore up his support with the board, two of whose members owe their position—and evidently their allegiance—to him. Gillies now approaches Freemont and tells him that, in exchange for his seat on the board, he is prepared to award Freemont the exclusive sales contract for works in the Warhol estate. It is inappropriate for Gillies to do this; it's treacherous for Freemont to accept, which he does.

Stacked now with Gillies's allies, the board is in position to muscle Fred Hughes out of the picture and, given that Fred continues to get sicker and crazier and to scream more intensely at everyone every day, it is more inclined than ever to do so.

As it has all along, Fred's legal vulnerability leaves the door wide open for his removal. The large number of unsigned Warhol paintings in Fred's personal collection remains a big problem; without signatures, without verification or tax receipts, there is no way for him to prove the paintings are his—and, by the way, maybe they aren't. The upshot is that Fred has a huge number of paintings he can't move; mindful of this, Gillies cuts him a deal: if Fred gives up his place on the board, fires me, and, most importantly, effectively agrees to the foundation's valuation of Warhol's work, the foundation will not only verify ownership of Fred's collection of unsigned paintings but will give him $5 million for his trouble.

Fred should tell patrician-wannabe Archibald Gillies, who is now, ironically and through Fred's own bad judgment, in charge of distributing the legacy of Andy Warhol, an artist of profoundly working-class origins and sensibility, to a mass audience: *I put together massive retrospectives and precedent-setting auctions and concocted from scratch a*

vast cultural institution to honor a major American artist, and I cataloged and ap-
praised, and accounted for, thousands of pieces of artwork and was involved in hun-
dreds of claims made upon the estate from everyone from Bianca Jagger to the
Filipino women who cleaned his house, and I couldn't have done any of this without
Ed Hayes, who was at my beck and call around the clock for a period of years and was
involved in every aspect of this estate, and no, thank you, I can't be bought out. But
he doesn't. Instead, in return for a sweetheart deal with the foundation, Fred agrees to go along with its grossly mismanaged accounting
and, declaring my services inadequate, terminates my connection
with the estate.

"Adequacy of services": the phrase has an oddly sexual connotation
that is especially strong in light of Fred's ongoing obsession with my
virility.

—

Christie's enters the picture at this squalid point, and depths of
corruption are revealed that even I, with my advanced degrees from
Tough Guy School, a regular of the back room of the West Side Democratic Party Club and a lot of other back rooms, could never have
imagined.

In the spring of 1990, the foundation retains Christie's, the es-
teemed art auction house, to conduct a fair-market-value appraisal of
the art in the Warhol estate. Though Fred and I are no longer speaking, we will both be paid a percentage of the total value of the estate and so obviously have a shared stake in a higher valuation.
Gillies and the Warhol Foundation, on the other hand, have an interest in a lowball appraisal. As a nonprofit organization, the foundation will have to give away an average of 5 percent of the value of
the estate *every year*; to do so involves an enormous amount of administrative work, and the more that has to be distributed, the more
work will be required to give it away. In general, higher valuation
would entail greater scrutiny, which Gillies and the foundation,
who are busy currying favor with museums to whom they have sold
paintings at substantial discounts, do not want.

What Fred, who by this time has turned on Gillies as well as on me, and I don't know is that Gillies has had conversations with Christie's and, no doubt in the sober tones in which foundation men communicate serious messages, made it clear that if Christie's comes back with a nice low appraisal—one that's well under the $600 million sum Fred and I have suggested as the fair-market value of the estate—there may be something in it of value for Christie's, namely, exclusive contracts for future sales of works by Andy Warhol. (Ah, gentle reader, does this sound paranoid? Let me tell you now that the promise Gillies made with Christie's respecting these matters was eventually fully documented in a court of law.)

Several months later Martha Baer, the Christie's administrator who oversees the Warhol appraisal, advises me and the foundation that Christie's will predicate its appraisal on the assumption that all the art in the Warhol estate will be sold in one block on one day to one person and that the value of the collection will decline over time.

Nobody buys art that way! I think when I read Baer's letter. *Whoever buys this stuff is going to be buying it on the assumption that it will* appreciate *in value.*

"Who in their right mind would buy a depreciating asset?" I ask Baer when I reach her by phone in her East Side office. "Nobody has ever handled art like this."

"No, no, no, this is how we do it," Baer assures me. "That's how it's *always* done."

We'll see about that, I think.

———

The endless work on the Warhol estate leaves no time for other income-providing work and I am starting to get very strung out. I'm paying experts and appraisers and nothing's coming back, and after years there is no end in sight to the tangle of new issues and new adversaries or the resulting sleeplessness and nausea and daily vomiting. But I get up every morning and run after the vomiting; then, no matter how little I've slept or how much vomiting I've done, I sit down and have a bowl of organic cereal and bananas with Susie and read at least four newspapers—the *Times*, the *Post*, the *Daily News*, the *Wall Street Journal*—and assorted legal papers.

One morning in July 1990, I'm finishing my cereal and thumbing through the *New York Law Journal* when I see a little item about the Robert Mapplethorpe estate. A solo practitioner named Michael Stout, it seems, has been awarded $1 million for his work on the estate; the sum represents an advance on what Stout will get when the estate is disposed of and, according to the *Law Journal*, is based on an estate valuation of $240 million per an appraisal done by Christie's.

By Christie's!

Well, okay, I'm going to need to see that appraisal. I'll be able to tell after a quick look whether Martha Baer is being straight about block sales and other terms on which she says Christie's *always* does appraisals.

"Go down to the Surrogate's Court and ask Marie Lambert to get you a copy of the Mapplethorpe file," I tell one of the young Hispanic kids who work in my office.

Surrogate Marie Lambert is an Italian lady from Brooklyn who is a bosom buddy of Jimmy McManus. She's been around some tough blocks a million times. I've always liked her and she has always had an evident taste for knock-around guys like me.

The Hispanic kid calls a couple hours later. The file is sealed. He can't get it.

I'm on the phone in a shot. "Judge, how are you?" I haven't talked to Lambert since I ran into her many months earlier at the funeral for a crony of Jimmy McManus, who in addition to running the West Side Democratic Party Club works as an undertaker. "Come and see me sometime," says Lambert, and the next morning I'm in her office.

We shoot the shit a bit and then I say, "Judge, I gotta see that Mapplethorpe file. I gotta see that appraisal."

"Nice to see you, Eddie! How are you? Let me see that suit!" says Lambert, squeezing my arm. "You look *good*, Eddie. Nice, strong. You've been to the gym, haven't you?" She says nothing about the file. I leave.

A week later I get a call from her clerk.

"The judge wants to see you," he says. "Why don't you come by and say hello sometime."

All right. I'm not a moron. I stop by the next day.

"Eddie, Eddie! How nice to see you." Lambert looks genuinely pleased. "Sit down, Eddie," she says and excuses herself to go to the ladies' room.

Right in front of me, on a small brown table in front of Lambert's desk, is an open file with a number of documents inside: the Mapplethorpe appraisals!

Christie's, according to the sheaf of papers in front of me, valued Mapplethorpe's estate on the assumption that the sales would be consummated *over time* and that anyone who purchased works from the estate would do so on the assumption that they would *appreciate over time*. Bingo! I slip some of the most relevant papers into the inner pocket of my suit jacket.

"Well, you have a nice holiday, Eddie." Judge Lambert squeezes my left bicep just a little as she comes back in and shows me to the door of her chamber.

"I will, Judge, thank you. Happy holiday to you, too," I tell her on the way out.

Fred, Freemont, Gillies, Gillies's lawyers, and I have a meeting to talk about Christie's appraisal methodology with Martha Baer the following week. The mood is highly strained as we file into the second-floor conference room at the Factory.

"That's not true, is it, Martha?" I ask politely when she finishes explaining yet again that Christie's always sells in one lump block and always predicates sales on the assumption that works bought in large-block sales will depreciate over time. "For one thing," I add, "that cheats the people, the public, out of significant value to which they, as the beneficiaries of the requirement that foundations give 5 percent of their assets to the public each year, are entitled. For another thing, any appraisal based on the assumptions you're making cheats me, which we really don't like."

We keep talking in that fake friendly way people in nice clothing do when they are sitting in nice chairs in self-consciously and overtly civilized settings with lots of expensive paintings on the wall.

"You sure you always do appraisals this way?" I ask in the cool, coiled-cobra-ready-to-strike cross-examination fashion I learned from Larry Dubin and Paul Goldberger.

"Yes, Eddie," says Baer, "that's the way we always do it." She toys gently with her pearl choker.

"And you've never ever done an appraisal any other way?" I ask.

"No, Eddie," says Baer with a half sneer. "Never."

"Really?" I drag the syllables out as slowly as I can. "Because I have right here in my pocket a copy of the Mapplethorpe appraisals." I stop, let that sink in. "Right here," I say, patting my pocket. "And I have a couple of extra copies if any one of you would like to take a look.

"Interestingly," I add, "you'll see that you did the Mapplethorpe appraisals *slightly* differently."

Martha Baer is pale. She gets up and leaves the room. I hear her vomiting in a nearby bathroom. Then she leaves the building and does not come back.

"You motherfuckers!" Neither Gillies nor Fred nor Freemont nor any of the lawyers says anything. "You motherfuckers are getting cute with me. And if there's one thing I don't like, it's anyone getting cute with Mrs. Hayes's oldest son. Gentlemen, if you think you're going to take advantage of me, you're out of your fucking minds."

Gillies and Fred and Freemont and the lawyers get up and leave the room.

———

By the end of 1991, I know that the foundation's accounting is wrong. I'm convinced these guys are going to get caught, and I'm terrified I'm going down with them when they do.

I've been paid $4.85 million for the work I've done on the estate since 1987 and I've paid one-quarter of this to Frank Harvey, who's done a lot of legal work with me, and additional money for overhead

and various experts—art dealers, appraisers, and other lawyers—
who've provided services. According to my agreement with Fred,
I'm entitled to more, to 2 percent of the value of the estate, which
after retaining expert Jeffrey Hoffeld I now think may be worth as
much as $700 million, in which case I'm due an additional $9.15
million. Relying on Christie's lowball appraisal, the foundation says
the estate is worth just $95 million!

Reporters covering the mess can't believe what they're hearing.
Why would Gillies and the foundation argue that Warhol's work—
the foundation's chief asset—is relatively valueless? One obvious reason is that they don't want to pay me more money. The other reason,
though, is that under Gillies the foundation—which is about to run
up a $5 million tab fighting me—has been badly mismanaged and is
fast running out of money. Though it once had $25 million in its ac-
counts, the foundation now has just $6 million in cash and securities.
And though the foundation, under Gillies's leadership, will spend
$7.2 million in administrative costs (including $170,000 worth of
furniture for the foundation's offices) in the fiscal year ending in
April 1994, it will give away just $1.1 million, an embarrassingly
substandard amount; similar groups routinely spend just eleven cents
for every dollar they donate.

Were the foundation to accept my valuation of $700 million, they
would by law have to give away 5 percent of that sum, or $35 mil-
lion a year; it isn't clear that the foundation—which, in addition to
racking up millions in legal fees, has paid out many more millions in
salaries and benefits since Gillies took over— could do that without
going bankrupt.

The possibility that Gillies or the foundation will either accept
my valuation or agree to pay me my fees seems, by June of 1992,
highly unlikely. I couldn't be more strung out. There's no money coming in. Susie's pregnant again. Thanks to Alex Porter and the NYAC
workouts, there's an actual real live penis visible when we go for a
sonogram in the fall of 1992. Squat, as I call him from then on, is due
in February. Susie and I are thrilled about the news, but our joy
doesn't lessen the pressure. So I file a petition in Surrogate's Court

asking for payment of fees due that, as a procedural matter, first ne-
cessitates court determination as to the value of the Warhol estate.

My first instinct when I walked into Andy Warhol's town house
the night he died was to try the case, to show the public that Andy
Warhol was a great, highly valued artist, and finally in 1993, six
and a half years later, I am about to do just that.

———

Judge Eve Preminger's courtroom on the fourth floor of the Surrogate's Court Building on Chambers Street in Lower Manhattan is
full of marble and terra-cotta wainscoting and crystal chandeliers and
fireplaces with marble mantels. It was built in the early 1900s,
when the Democratic Party machine ran the city and the best way to
steal money was to get kickbacks from contractors and architects.
The crooks would get indicted and go to jail for taking kickbacks on
some building project, and then they would get out of jail and go
right back to work on the same building. Every bit of marble and
every piece of terra-cotta inside the Surrogate's Court is there because an Italian contractor and an Irish politician got together and
said, "Let's get a Jew accountant and figure out how to rob the place
blind!"—which, of course, they did. I feel right at home knowing this.

So here I stand on the morning of November 16, 1993, behind a
beautiful carved dark wood table in Judge Preminger's elegantly appointed courtroom until a court clerk arrives and says, "All rise.
The Surrogate of the County of New York, the Honorable Eve
Preminger."

Beautifully dressed, Eve Preminger enters the courtroom through
a heavy wooden door. Before my 2011 petition, as the petition for
fees is called, is assigned to her courtroom, I probably haven't spent
more than an hour in Eve Preminger's company. But the first thing I
do when my petition is assigned to her courtroom is to read up on
her. Born in Austria, educated at Columbia, she is from an illustrious
Hollywood family: her father was a talent agent and her uncle, Otto

Preminger, was a legendary director and an art collector. She is smart, sophisticated, liberal, and she knows about the art and movie businesses. If anyone can recognize "movie accounting," the time-honored Hollywood practice of shuffling debts and assets in such a way that anybody who gets paid a percentage of the profits will find himself out of luck, it is Eve Preminger.

I'm confident as she steps up to the bench and takes her place before a swarm of lawyers and spectators that I will prevail. The value portion of the proceeding, which will go first, is a joke: if it weren't consuming my life and costing me and my family our peace of mind, the idea that the Andy Warhol Foundation is actually going to try to convince Eve Preminger that Warhol's work is of relatively little value might be comical.

"You may be seated," says the clerk.

Susie sits in front beside three of her closest friends, who happen to be three of the best-looking women in America: Diane Dennoyer, CC Rivera, and Sheila Wolfe. CC is why the Protestants conquered the world; if you're ready, she's ready. There are certain women who are sexual goddesses to rock stars or ballplayers, and then there are women who have that appeal for people like Tom Wolfe; Sheila Wolfe, a pillar of proper society who came to be that pillar because she once wore leather printed miniskirts and can compete with anyone in terms of raw feminine power, occupies that second category. Susie and her friends all wear pearls just like the ones Judge Preminger wears. Tom is there for opening statements, and every other day too. Jimmy Harkins, a detective with the body of a beer truck and the mind of Sherlock Holmes, and two of his detective friends—complete savages really, who are assigned to Brooklyn North—are there on opening day too, on the left side of the courtroom. Also two Italian stickup guys, one of whom, "Butchie," whom I once represented, happens to have had a court date that morning at the Criminal Court Building at 100 Centre Street, which is nearby, so he has stopped in to see what's going on. I'm at the counsel table. Bob Jossen, the terrific lawyer I've hired to help me, his brilliant idea man Adam Rowland, Frank Harvey, and my brother are next to me as I stand to give my opening statement.

"All right, Eddie, have your day in court," Jossen told me when I said I wanted to make my own opening statement. "Then sit down and we'll handle it."

"This is not a trial," I tell the court. "It is an appraisal," an appraisal of the value of Andy Warhol's work. I say that after six years of intense work on and absorption in matters concerning Andy Warhol, I am certain that he is an American genius whose work is of tremendous significance—far greater significance than my adversaries suggest—and great value to the American public.

Beth Jacob, the aggressive lead lawyer for Carter, Ledyard, stands and puts forth the position of Archibald Gillies (who does not appear in the courtroom until he is called to the witness stand to answer questions about mismanagement of the foundation and its assets) and the foundation (whose board members also decline to make an appearance during the proceedings): that the court should accept Christie's appraised value for the estate. One and only one person, Jacob tells the court, stands to win or lose anything of real value here: Edward W. Hayes.

Jossen, a brilliant cross-examiner, leaves both Gillies and Martha Baer looking like a platter of sliced-up cold cuts when he's finished with them. He cuts each and every one of their implausible, contradictory claims to shreds, severely if not permanently compromising any credibility they have. Baer leaves the stand in tears.

"Eddie, do I get this right?" says Butchie, who is no brain surgeon but who comes up to me during court recess. "They got something that's worth money and they're supposed to give somebody else something based on what they got? And they're holding it, the money?"

"That's right, Butchie," I tell him.

"And they're not giving a fair count?" Butchie is putting it all together. "Is that right? And they're beating you and beating everyone else they owe?"

"That's it, Butchie," I tell him.

"That's a problem," says Butchie. "That's like you do a job and one guy takes the money with him and he don't cut it up. Whoa! You do that in the street, bro," he says, "you better be a real good swimmer!"

For all their high-priced representation, Christie's and the foundation, who more or less share the view "We are The Art World. We know what we're talking about," really can't swim worth a dime.

———

"Movie accounting," I say again and again in the in-chambers meetings the parties have with Judge Preminger, who seems genuinely aghast at much of what she hears in the courtroom. At one point I suggest the foundation should pay me in art. "Okay," I say, "you offered to settle for $500,000. I'll take drawings equal in value, per your appraised value, to that amount." In response to the foundation's refusal, Judge Preminger notes that the foundation has spent more—two or three times more—pursuing its court battle with me than they might have spent to settle. The judge and the rest of us are wise to the fact that the lawyers, who are getting paid by the hour, don't care.

As the proceedings on my 2011 petition progress, which they do day after day for months, my expensive lawyers and experts—chief among them Jeffrey Hoffeld—analyze thousands of Warhol drawings, paintings, silk screens, and works in other media; on the stand, Hoffeld, a revered art expert and former gallery owner who now appraises art for the IRS, presents sales records for seventy-six paintings and sculptures the estate and the foundation sold, between 1990 and 1993, for over 60 percent more than they had been appraised at by Christie's. To the judge's apparent astonishment and to the overt befuddlement of reporters covering the trial, experts for the foundation testify that, in fact, Warhol was not an important artist at all. (In an article that runs under the headline "Warhol's Backers Argue That Warhol Is Passé," for example, Wall Street Journal reporter Alexandra Peers calls the proceedings "bizarre" and expresses puzzlement over the fact that the foundation that controls Andy Warhol's work and legacy has called veteran art dealer André Emmerich to testify that not only will there be a "period of oblivion" for Warhol but Warhol and his work are likely to become "unfashionable.")

In the middle of this, Mark Rennie, Fred's personal lawyer at the time (it's a highly temporary position), invites me to lunch at the New York Athletic Club one afternoon while the court is in recess. "Fred will give you $2 million to settle," Rennie tells me after I finish a rare steak sandwich. "He's sick. He doesn't want this to go on."

"I'm not taking his money," I tell Rennie. "I know what he's doing here. I'm not going to be part of it. That's it. Thanks for the steak."

I won't take Fred's money. He has his sweetheart deal with the foundation and in my heart I know that Fred stole a lot of the paintings the foundation agreed to validate in that agreement; the whole thing is a cover-up, and if I take the money from Fred, I'm part of it. Besides, he is the worst kind of rat: he shouldn't have betrayed me—for Christ's sake, he is godfather to my daughter—and having done so, can't buy me off.

In considering Fred's offer and also in filing the petition for fees in the first place, I know that stress complicates Fred's illness. My view is that if the continued court proceeding kills Fred, and it very well might, he will have brought it on himself. If Fred is going to die a miserable death—and if every day until that miserable death is filled with agony—well that's what he deserves. Another way of saying this is: there is no settlement; the trial proceeds.

The lawyers continue to bill all through the spring of 1994, a full two years after I first filed the petition for fees, until on April 7 Judge Preminger hands down her opinion.

"Warhol is an artist of international prominence" and "is widely recognized as one of the world's most important and influential artists," Judge Preminger writes in her twenty-five-page opinion; noting that Christie's and the foundation "under-valued" his art, she holds that the value of the collection is $390,979,278—four times the value Christie's suggested in its appraisal—and that the fair-market value of the entire estate, which, in addition to art, includes real estate and securities, is $509,900,000, twice what the foundation contended.

Judge Preminger's decision represents what Paul Alexander, who writes about the trial, calls "an unqualified failure for Christie's and the Foundation, who were in the odd position of having to justify the fact that they had defended a price almost $300 million below the value Preminger put on the estate."

They got creamed.

It's a big, big win for me, but Judge Preminger's opinion in the first of the two-part proceeding doesn't mean I am *actually* going to get paid in the end. God knows, expensive lawyers can tie you up in endless appeals! I'm going broke, and my anxiety and depression and sleeplessness and the digestive mess that comes with it all aren't going to go away anytime soon, especially with the second part of the proceedings on my 2011 petition, the fee-determination portion, set to begin in a month's time.

Which doesn't mean that it doesn't feel good to read the opinion in Bob Jossen's office on the morning of April 7. Or that it doesn't feel better still that night when I kiss my beautiful children, Avery, now seven, and one-year-old Jonathan Francis Xavier Hayes, christened with a name I thought befit a future judge. Then, in a mocha-colored gabardine suit from Anderson and Sheppard and a good pair of alligator-and-suede shoes from Cleverley, I head out with Susie to the opening of an exhibition at the Metropolitan Museum of Art where, all evening long, people come up to say, "Good job" and "Glad to hear you clobbered those sons of bitches."

I'm glad to think I have done something good, not just for me but for Warhol. I feel like a winner. But just for a moment.

———

Edward Hayes did little to contribute to the success of the Warhol estate and rendered few valuable services to it. This is the basis of the foundation's argument in the second Preminger proceeding, in which lawyers for Fred and the foundation argue that I am incompetent and money-grubbing and sleazy and shouldn't be paid for the work to which I have now devoted eight years. Again I am confident I will win—after all, the judge has already decided that I had raised the value of the Warhol estate by $400 million—but it is grueling to face attacks like this day after day, especially when there isn't any money coming in and I can't sleep and I lie awake at night anxious about how I am going to get out of this alive and how I am going to support my wife and children and I begin each day full of nausea, dread, and violent stomach upset.

For nearly a year I listen as lawyers for Fred Hughes argue that I took unfair advantage of their client, who was sick at the time I signed my agreement with him. But Fred wasn't sick then. Besides, the fact of the matter is that estate lawyers often work with elderly executors who are sick or otherwise impaired. My basic argument is that I have done my job, I have elevated the value of the estate, and I should be paid for the work I've done.

Murray Kempton, a revered journalist who peddles around town on a rickety bicycle and writes fiery columns full of moral outrage and respect for honest citizens, pokes his head into court toward the end of the proceedings on the value of my services.

"I gather there is a substantial public interest involved here," Kempton says to me during an afternoon recess. "Could be," I say. "I get 2 percent of the value of the estate *one time*; the public gets 5 percent *every year*."

Kempton looks at me and replies, "I think you are about to be awarded a large sum of money, Mr. Hayes."

And I am.

On April 20, 1995, Judge Preminger rules that the foundation must pay me $7,200,000. In a twenty-page opinion, Judge Preminger finds that "Warhol's place in the art world is as secure as that of any artist of his time could be. It is in no small measure due to the foresight, determination and hard work of his executor and his lawyers. In awarding fees, it is often said that the largest determining factor should be the quality of the work and the results obtained. If we mean what we say, the Warhol fees should be on the high end of the scale."

It's a huge win.

I've been validated. The court agrees; the money in the estate is in trust for the public and, by underestimating its value, the foundation has denied the public what is due and so has breached its trust. And I have earned my fee. No way Preminger's decision can be overturned, I think, and with $7.2 million, or $2.4 million more, coming to me, Susie and I will be secure. We can stop worrying about having to sell our house on Eighty-first Street or the house in Bellport and can begin to get out from under. Unbeknownst to me, however, I am about to take another beating.

———

A few days later, the lawyers demand that the appellate court overturn Preminger's decision. Despite the outcome in Surrogate's Court, Carter, Ledyard is still billing away—though now Skadden, Arps, Slate, Meagher and Flom is in charge, a firm that is among the most powerful and expensive in the country and, as I am about to discover, is staffed by some of the most obnoxious motherfuckers in the world.

With all due respect, the lawyers involved—the teams from Carter, Ledyard; Donovan, Leisure; and now Skadden, Arps—are almost all seriously overweight and badly dressed men whose suits are either too tight or too baggy and whose shirts have bad collars and are awful. They wear tasteless, often florid ties, the kind guys think make them look cool. Their shoes are terrible—either those clunky wingtips or tiny little Italian slippers that no man should ever wear. Many of them are very good lawyers, but they are not graceful people. Aside from the lack of grace, I have nothing against these lawyers and no real personal feelings about any of them, except that they stood by (and billed) while their clients tried to mislead the court and the public.

Once Skadden took Gillies and the foundation on as clients, the integrity of the firm was at stake in the outcome of the case against me. How else can you explain the immense outlay of time and money Skadden spent going after me?

Tom Schwarz, a very unlikable man with an unpleasant, fat face, and a large, beefy body always stuffed into a black suit and white shirt with heavy, thick collar and heavy, thick oversized cuffs, is genuinely obnoxious to judges and his own associates. He's Skadden's lead lawyer on the Warhol case, and not long after the foundation's appeal is filed, I meet him in his office. It's clear from the moment I enter his immaculate, colorless, odorless world of purified air and silver pens and polished but badly made shoes that Schwarz and his army of lawyers are going to be very aggressive.

"We'll settle with you for five hundred grand," Schwarz says when I walk in.

No grace, no formality, barely even a "Hello, how are you? Have a seat, won't you?" Just a low grunt from a wide neck bulging like sausage from a too-tight suit. "Five hundred grand."

"You picked a life with little risk," I tell Schwarz. "I chose a life with a lot of risk. Keep your five hundred grand. I'm willing to take my chances before the appeals court."

Clearly offended, Schwarz looks blankly in my direction.

"That's our offer, Mr. Hayes."

"Eddie," I tell him, and I am soon out the door and on my way into the elevator and out of the building.

I don't know it then, but I have just made a terrible mistake. Tom Schwarz doesn't have the vaguest human connection to other people. Everything about him is off-putting—his manner, his appearance, his smug and whiny voice. I never see him smile. He would wear Hush Puppies, for God's sake! I can't possibly take Schwarz seriously as a formidable adversary. But I am actually quite mistaken about this.

I have in fact made another, far graver mistake with respect to Thomas Schwarz. Or "Schwartz," as I misspell his name when I do a background check on him. I don't find much. I don't, for example, find out that he has been the lawyer for the panel that recommended appellate court Presiding Judge Francis T. Murphy Jr. And this turns out to be the biggest—and certainly the costliest—mistake of my life. All because of one lousy "t"!

"This guy is no lawyer," I tell a reporter who covers a pretrial hearing on the appeals for the *Wall Street Journal*. "A trial lawyer's job is to persuade people his position is right. This guy is the least persuasive person in the world."

"That's not what he does," she says. "Be careful with this guy. For one thing, at a place like Skadden, they don't want to *try* cases. The last thing they want to do is get before twelve people or anyone they actually have to convince of anything."

Their MO is instead to use the vast financial resources at their disposal to pressure opponents into surrender, preferably in a forum over which the firm had sway.

Though it's costing me sleep and is taking a heavy toll on my digestive tract, the appeals procedure is fairly straightforward: the foundation submits a brief, I submit a brief, each side argues its position before a panel of five judges, the panel issues its opinion.

———

Argument is set for November 9, 1995, before Judge Murphy and three other appellate court justices. But Schwarz files a motion on October 9 for extended oral argument. Why's he doing this? It makes no sense: oral argument isn't an important part of the appeals process. I don't take Schwarz seriously. This must be something insignificant, not worth thinking about.

I soon receive word that, pursuant to Schwarz's motion, oral argument is put over until December 6. This gives me time to absorb another enormous blow, stemming from Fred and a half-cocked licensing agreement we entered into on behalf of the estate years ago, in 1987, with Schlaifer Nance, an Atlanta company best known for marketing Cabbage Patch Kid dolls. Under the agreement Schlaifer made with the estate the company could design and market Warhol-related merchandise. Six months into the deal, Fred started to go nuts and decided he didn't like Schlaifer's plans to use Warhol images on ripped sweatshirts and junky-looking sequined shirts. By 1989, he stopped talking to the Schlaifer people, who filed a $7 million breach-of-contract suit against the estate. Fred was so arrogant and hostile and crazed at the pretrial conference held earlier this year that Schlaifer decided to jump the sum and refused to settle for less than $12 million. Schlaifer now wins a $3.5 million verdict, including a million-dollar judgment in punitive damages against me personally. It is a stunning blow. I can barely move after the verdict is handed down.

Though the verdicts in the licensing suit, and in the racketeering suit Schlaifer subsequently files, are eventually thrown out, the additional judgment provides a disastrous backdrop for my upcoming appellate argument about the value of the Warhol estate and my fees. My lawyer in the case is Paul Hanly, whose grandfather was John V. Kenny, the mythic boss of Hudson County and New Jersey. Paul's first delicate mission was carrying a suitcase of cash to the Kennedy campaign. He was about ten.

Due to scheduling changes connected to the delay in oral argument on the appeal, the panel of judges who will hear my case has been altered; Judge Murphy will be on the new panel, but the other judges have been replaced by a group that will be presided over by Joe Sullivan, one of the few people I truly despised when I met him years ago in Bronx County Court before his promotion to the appellate court. As a young DA, I watched Sullivan rip into another prosecutor and was so astonished by his manner I said to a nearby court officer, "Boy, that guy is really rough, very harsh." The clerk started laughing and said, "Oh, that's Joe Sullivan. He's married to Judge Murphy's sister, Boss Murphy's daughter. He's tied into the Democratic Party clubhouse."

Sullivan sits sober-faced behind a raised platform at the front of the magnificent wood-paneled room when I walk into the appellate courthouse for oral argument. I sit in the audience; Bob Jossen and his associate Adam Rowland sit at a massive table in front. Archibald

Gillies is here with Vincent Freemont. Fred Hughes is home dying his agonizing death and so can't be present.

Gillies smirks when I sit down. Why is that? Immediately I sense I'm sunk. Schwarz stands, his shiny black suit gleaming like sausage casing, and tells the court that the fee I have requested is excessive. I brought in my brother, he tells the court, and there is the additional impropriety, he says, of my friendly relationship with Surrogate Eve Preminger, as evidenced by my generous contribution to her judicial campaign.

Excessive? I increased the value of the Warhol estate by a factor of four, a jump that would be the basis for a giant bonus for any self-respecting Wall Street guy who turned an account over by that percentage.

Judge Sullivan raises questions about the propriety of my brother's involvement in the case. *You mean, my brother who is counsel to Mick Jagger?* I think. *And Bruce Springsteen, among others? My brother, who knows as much about the world of high-art and big money accounting as anyone? What kind of a moron wouldn't ask someone with his experience to help on a big trust matter?*

Before the Warhol trial, I hadn't spent more than twenty minutes in Eve Preminger's presence; I gave $250 to her campaign at a time when judicial campaign contributions were not even disclosed to contribution recipients!

Deny everything, make counteraccusations, smear your opponent: Skadden's approach to my request for fees is the same approach it later takes against Monica Lewinsky and Paula Jones when Bill Clinton hires the firm to represent him against charges of sexual harassment. Look at Skadden's conduct in the case against Clinton: it had nothing to do either with resolving the matter or with finding the truth; it had to do with the simple, crude fact that the firm had more money and more power and was going to run over and destroy its client's adversaries. If Skadden had tried the case against Clinton several years before, instead of several years after, they represented Gillies and the Warhol Foundation, I would have had a much clearer sense of what was happening.

That night Gillies's smirk haunts my sleep. I can't get it out of my head when I get up the next morning and head to the bathroom to vomit, as I still do most mornings. I'm broke, exhausted, depressed from all the years of litigation and I can't get that smirk out of my mind. Something's up, and it's not good.

—

"Eddie," a reporter I know says on my office phone the morning of February 8, 1996, "you got bad news on the appeal." He's a solid citizen, a neighborhood white boy whose father was a fireman and who dreamt of working his way out of the neighborhood and writing local stories for a local paper.

"Holy Christ, fax me the decision," I tell him.

We disagree with Surrogate Court Judge Preminger's ultimate valuation of Hayes's services is the gist of it.

I nearly pass out when I read the first page of the unsigned two-page opinion. The appellate court halves my fee. Worse, the court demands I give $1.2 million back to the foundation.

I don't have the money.

There's no way I can get that kind of money.

I sweat as I process the opinion and the mess it makes of everything I've done the last few decades.

Blood racing, as it raced when I was a kid running from another beating in the alleyways behind our house, I go home.

I'm at the kitchen table crying when Mike McAlary bursts in. My brother comes in soon after. "We'll do whatever we can," they say.

"There's nothing you can do. I'm ruined," I tell them. "I can't hold on to anything. I'm probably going to go bankrupt."

"I have children, Gail!" I cry when Gail Collins phones. "What am I going to do? How will I take care of my family?"

"Eddie, Eddie, you'll figure it out. If anyone can, you can. You always do," she says.

I love Gail dearly but for the first time I doubt she's being truthful.

Susie is so worn out from the years of litigation, it can't get worse for her. She looks defeated. Maybe for the first time, too.

And then Avery bursts in from school and is joking with Carmen, our longtime Dominican babysitter, as she heads into the kitchen, where she sees us at the table and quickly registers how upset everyone is. She looks scared. "Go upstairs, Avery," I tell her.

I listen to her pad up the steps and decide I better go up and tell her what's happened.

"Honey, we had a very bad decision from the court and it's a very big problem."

Avery starts to cry. "Daddy!" she wails. "What's the problem?"

"We may have to sell the house," I tell her.

"But, Daddy," she says with all the fury in her little-girl heart, "I just got my room the way I wanted it!" Tears drop on her dress.

I look at the pink carpet and cream-colored curtains and Avery's collection of small plastic horses and start to laugh. Very loudly, very hard, and then uncontrollably.

I laugh so hard I can barely speak.

"Avery," I manage to say, "let me see what I can do."

I walk out of her room, past Mike and Steve in the kitchen, and out into the street, still laughing but thinking, *This ain't happening. I'm not doing this. I am not going to be embarrassed in front of my children. My father was embarrassed in front of my brother and me. That is not going to happen with me and my children.*

Inappropriate emotional response is, I later learn, a symptom of extreme clinical depression. Children don't need to consult medical experts to know what's true. At least eight-year-old Avery needs no further study to gauge the measure or the meaning of my laughter.

"Uh-oh," she says to Mike and Steve and Susie when she looks out her window and sees me on the street, still laughing. "Someone is going to get hurt."

Someone does.

And it isn't Mrs. Hayes's oldest son.

CHAPTER 12

"They contracted you out, Eddie," says the neighborhood-white-boy reporter. He's on my office phone again the morning after the appeals court decides against me. "Schwarz was the lawyer for the panel that investigated Murphy when he was up for reappointment to the bench."

"Oh yeah?" I wonder aloud. "Now, why didn't Schwarz disclose that?"

"No idea, Eddie. But I have a good source in the Appellate Division who called last night and said, 'Hayes got contracted out.' They did you, Eddie."

Hayes got contracted out. They did you, Eddie.

There is no way that I am ever going to be able to prove these allegations, but this reporter has impeccable sources within the political and legal establishments, so I have to believe that what he says is substantially true and act accordingly. But I would never have acted as I did if there were not a number of other things that supported my feelings. In the first place, there were never any settlement discussions after the lower court decisions, which is consistent with the idea that Schwarz and Skadden had an unusual sense of confidence. Making motions for an extension of time for oral argument is very rare; the motion was granted just before the appeal was to be heard in an unsigned opinion by a panel headed by Judge Murphy; and the main result of the decision was to get a new panel that pushed Judge Eugene Nardelli, a knockaround guy known for his elegance and independence, off the panel and put Judge Joseph Sullivan on. Further, Judge Murphy's subsequent statement to a *Times* reporter that he didn't remember Schwarz, and Schwarz's refusal to back him up in the press, raised my suspicions. In the months to come, as I battle to exact my revenge and protect everything I own and love and have accomplished, my adversaries will deny these allegations over and over again in the press and in courts of law. I will ignore those denials and press on with my campaign of relentless guerrilla warfare.

There's $1.2 million for me to return that I don't have, not to mention the million dollars in the Schlaifer case, which I also don't have. What about my children and my wife? How will I support them? And my friends—how will I face any of them again? I put down the phone. *They did you, Eddie.* I turn my chair around and look out the window at the City of Ambition I once loved, gray in the morning light. And then I say aloud in my empty office, "You want to go into the street with Eddie Hayes? All right. Schwarz, Sullivan, and especially you, Murphy, you treacherous dogs, let's go. I'm ready."

Exhausted but alert, the way I learned to be as a child when my father woke me up screaming at night, I get up from my chair, blood pumping hard, thinking, just as I did when I climbed up the basement steps of our ranch house in South Carolina, *You'll never beat me, motherfuckers! I will have the best shoes, the best girlfriends, the best everything, whatever it takes. And in the end I will be standing tall and you, motherfuckers, will not.*

I will always be grateful to the reporter who called me that morning and suggested something was bent with Murphy and Sullivan and Schwarz and the appellate court panel. My hero, Michael Collins, believed in making the political very personal by directly attacking his adversaries; when his guys got killed, he went looking for the killers. And that's what I was about to do. By the end of the day, I would know everything I needed to know to attack Murphy, Sullivan, and Schwarz, and a few others along the way.

———

Schwarz, Schwarz, Schwarz—had I not been a moron and spelled it wrong when I ran a background check on him, I would have found that Schwarz and Murphy had a history and that Murphy owed a considerable debt to the sausage-necked Skadden partner.

Murphy I knew about. He was a product of the Chippewa Democratic Club in the Bronx, a powerful political machine that descends directly from Tammany Hall; corruption ran in his blood. Guys in the Bronx joke that you can count on the Chippewa Club to deliver 8 to 10 percent more votes than there are registered voters for favored Democratic candidates in every election.

Murphy's father, Francis T. Murphy Sr., ran the Chippewa Club for almost forty years—doing favors, pulling down patronage positions, arranging contracts, and otherwise conducting standard operating political procedures. In 1957, Murphy Sr. got a special law passed so that his thirty-year-old son could become a judge earlier than existing law allowed. He then saw to it that Murphy Jr. was promoted; in 1973, Murphy Jr. was named Presiding Judge of the Appellate Division, an exceedingly powerful position in the state judiciary. The guys from the big law firms whom he cozied up to love Murphy but he is despised by neighborhood folks, many of whom say Murphy forgot about them as he climbed his way up. But whether they liked him or not, everyone—including the governor—knew Murphy was a formidable guy, one who had to be tolerated and feared.

New York State elects judges, and in areas where one party totally dominates, the selection of judges is one of the last strongholds of the political organizations. Of course, nothing in New York City is really organized, and the political club has become issue- rather than service-based, so now the judges are mostly pretty good, even if they have pictures of Che on their walls. But appellate judges are picked by the governor, who tends to choose them with the eye in the back of his head focused on politics and the enforcement of the state's very restrictive election laws, which favor incumbents and are enforced by the appellate courts.

One of Murphy's jobs as presiding judge is to oversee disciplinary proceedings brought against lawyers, an important—and delicate—role that provides him with new opportunities to exercise and abuse power. After Murphy's appointment as presiding judge, for example, Abe Hirschfeld, the wealthy future owner of the New York Post and a lunatic, charged Andrew Cuomo, a decent and straight-forward guy, with using political clout as the governor's son to get the highway department to build an exit ramp expected to increase the value of some real estate holding he had near a state highway. Apparently the fact that there was no truth to the charge bothered Hirschfeld not at all, but, in a seemingly aberrant moment of late-breaking decency, he decided to retract it. Presiding Judge Francis Murphy Jr., however, had his own problems with Cuomo's father, Governor Mario Cuomo, and over Hirschfeld's objections refused to vacate the complaint; despite Murphy's attempt to use his power with the disciplinary proceedings to needle the Cuomos, the complaint was eventually dropped. But reporters, lawyers, and those interested in the machinations of power in the courts and within the government do not forget the zealous and ingenious way Murphy used the committee as an instrument with which to dog his enemies.

In the following years, Murphy continued to punish adversaries and reward cronies without remorse. But in 1989 his career of unchecked cronyism foundered in threatening and unfamiliar territory when Mike Gentile and Sarah Diane McShea, lawyers who'd worked for Murphy and seen what went on in his office, accused him of interfering with politically sensitive disciplinary proceedings, a serious and apparently substantiated charge—so serious and so substantiated, in fact, that neither Murphy nor his father could stop it from proceeding to a state Commission on Judicial Conduct, which ordered a full-scale investigation.

This episode was hugely humiliating for Murphy and got worse: the Commission on Judicial Conduct forced his chief aides to resign and, in a cautionary letter—the only such letter ever sent to a New York State appellate judge—warned him against even the appearance of interference in any future disciplinary proceedings. It then instructed the Appellate Division, Murphy's court, to take all action necessary to restore "order, respect and integrity." His humiliation must have been lessened, though, by the fact that, despite the reprimand, cautionary letters, and staff resignations, a gubernatorial committee subsequently recommended that he be reappointed presiding judge when the matter came before the governor the following year!

By midday, I have Mike Gentile, the very ballsy straight shooter who worked for Murphy and whose accusations incited the 1989 investigation into the court, on the phone.

"He's a contract guy," Gentile says when I introduce myself and tell him I've gotten slammed by Murphy and want to know a bit about him. "Who was the opposing lawyer?" he asks.

"Thomas Schwarz," I say. "Know anything about him?"

"Schwarz is the one who cleared the guy for reappointment," Gentile tells me."

Oh, yeah, I think, *this is definitely something I can work with!*

The amazing thing, Gentile explains, is that when Murphy came up for reappointment *after* he got the cautionary letter from the Commission on Judicial Conduct, Governor Cuomo reappointed him.

A father's failure to protect his son remains incomprehensible to me and I'll never understand how Cuomo could roll over like this. But I see that his decision to reappoint Murphy has an enormous effect on the disastrous situation in which I now find myself, for it clearly emboldened Murphy. Once Murphy knew that the governor would tolerate his continued tenure on the bench, after he'd been cautioned about abusing the power of the bench and after he'd used that very power to dog the governor's own son, he knew he could get away with anything.

The LexisNexis searches I do at my desk after I hang up with the reporter confirm the second revelation: the lead lawyer on the gubernatorial committee that investigated Murphy and recommended his reappointment as presiding judge was Thomas Schwarz. No "t."

They did you, Eddie. I keep hearing the reporter's words as I bang out searches: "Thomas J. Schwarz," "Francis T. Murphy Jr.," "Commission on Judicial Conduct," "reprimand," and every related search term I can think up. *Hayes got contracted out.*

I start calling guys I know—court officers, reporters, judges, law secretaries. The first call is to Pete, a retired Bronx County Court clerk, a good-looking, fit, black guy who worked in the courthouse for hundreds of years and knows everything about everyone there. I always trusted Pete, who came to me many times during my years in the DA's office and said things like, "Hey, Eddie, a guy I know from church is in trouble. Can you help him out?" "Sure," I'd say, "probation is fine. Let's not press this," and that was it. Pete likes me, knows I'm someone who will give a guy a break, not because he is poor or black but because he is a friend of mine or a friend of a friend's, and I know Pete will have the dope on Murphy, who got his start as a municipal court judge in the Bronx and served there before Governor Nelson Rockefeller appointed him to the Appellate Division in 1971.

I have Pete on the line an hour after I hang up with the reporter. What's the story with Murphy? I ask him.

"He's a fucking contract guy," says Pete.

"What about Sullivan?" I ask Pete.

"He's a stiff guy, a prig."

"He takes a lot of crap from Murphy," says the Bronx DA I phone next.

"Why would Sullivan take grief from Murphy?" I ask.

"He's married to Murphy's sister. He owes a lot to Murphy and the Bronx Democratic machine that Murphy's father ran for millions of years."

Well, that's another little something, isn't it? I think and I press on, phoning guys all over town—court officials, reporter friends, guys at Jimmy McManus's place on Eleventh Avenue.

A friend of McManus's tells me Murphy acts cool and demeaning to Sullivan; though he has a car and driver and lives in the same neighborhood in the Bronx as Sullivan, Murphy refuses to give his brother-in-law a ride home at night or to pick him up in the morning. Sullivan *has* to hate Murphy and his condescension and has to know, too, about all the patronage Murphy's doing on the bench. But Sullivan never questions any of Murphy's dealings; instead he goes along.

I also discover that not only is Sullivan married to Murphy's sister and not only does he owe his career to Francis Murphy Sr. and Francis Murphy Jr., but he has ambitions—to be presiding judge!—for which he needs Murphy's assistance.

They did you, Eddie. I'm defeated, I'm facing bankruptcy like my father, I'm an embarrassment to my own children, and I'm consumed with panic, but I can't get the words out of my mind. *Hayes got contracted out.* As a child in the public library in Jackson Heights, I found solace in history, and at this embattled point in my life I find it comforting to reflect on the military history I studied at UVA, in which the same two mistakes are endlessly repeated: either the victor fails to press home his attack or the vanquished gives up too easily in defeat. I am not going to give up easily. I probably couldn't even if I wanted to. Besides, the lessons I learned from Michael Collins supply a more attractive (and, for a man of my temperament, a more plausible) possibility, that of a fighting retreat in which the vanquished does as much damage as possible on his way down, if only to show that he is a formidable person even in defeat.

I doubt the Michael Collins approach will ease the nauseating knot in my gut or the horror of impending bankruptcy, but I'm sure I can do some real damage on my way down.

I'm sinking fast. The bank is about to foreclose on my house. And I'm heading into bankruptcy, fully expecting to lose everything. Josh Angel, my bankruptcy lawyer, a charming, likable, entirely self-made guy, truly is an angel and couldn't be more reassuring or realistic. He explains that bankruptcy laws reflect some of the best principles on which the country was founded. In most European countries, people who owe are tossed in jail, which works to enforce class status. US bankruptcy laws were designed to protect debtors and to help them consolidate and repay debt, within limits, so they can make a fresh start.

Completely strung out, drained, and in the grip of anxieties that disturb my sleep and waking hours, I badly need a fresh start. It's an effort to pick myself up off the bathroom floor each morning and get out there and try to save my house, my children, and as much dignity as I still have left. It's just as important to me to maintain my place in society, my status as a somewhat substantial guy, a call-up guy. Also, I want revenge.

———

"Don Van Natta here," a voice says on my office phone one morning a few days after Murphy's court hands down its decision against me. *"New York Times."*

Pat Clark, a former marine officer friend of mine who is now a reporter at the *Daily News,* has told me Van Natta, who covers city politics, might call.

I've never met the guy and fail to recognize him as the perfect instrument of vengeance, which in the days ahead he energetically becomes.

"Look, I don't know shit about the courthouse," says Van Natta. "But I understand stuff does go on down there."

"Why don't you come in," I suggest to Van Natta, "and I'll tell you about this Warhol case and what I found out about the appellate judges who decided it."

The next morning a big, tough Dutchman comes up to my office. Van Natta, whose father was a plumber, looks like he has carried plumbing pipe twelve hours a day for the last twenty-seven years and could keep lugging it around for thirty more years without once getting out of breath. He's a McAlary/Dwyer–style commando reporter and I trust him right away—though I'm not sure he won't be intimidated by Murphy (who, although his right-hand man has resigned under a cloud, remains the most powerful judge in New York City) or otherwise deterred from investigating the connection between Murphy and Schwarz and the possibility that the judge manipulated the appellate panel in order to thank a friend who'd done him a favor.

But I badly underestimate Van Natta; he's not intimidated by Murphy or anyone else.

Van Natta looks into Schwarz and his involvement in the investigation of Justice Murphy and also into Sullivan and his relationship to Murphy. Two days later he's on the phone. "You know, Eddie," he says, "it doesn't look good. Something happened here."

Oh yeah! Something definitely happened! I think to myself.

"I'll keep looking," says Van Natta, who in fact looks harder and harder until lawyers for Schwarz and Murphy are on the phone with his editors at the *Times*.

"It's a made-up story. Hayes is a thief and a lowlife. Murphy is a model of decency. There's no story," they tell Van Natta's editor.

Van Natta doesn't back down.

"There's a story," he tells his editor, who, like all other *Times* men, constantly gets calls from people who want stories killed. "Something happened here."

Van Natta presses on. He makes contact with more and more people connected with Murphy and Schwarz, who get increasingly uptight about the possibility that the *Times* is going to run a piece about them.

Schwarz lets my lawyer, Bob Jossen, know that Murphy does not want the story to run. He conveys another message, too: "If it runs, we'll never let you go."

I know what this means. If Van Natta proceeds, Murphy is coming after *me*—and will try to get me disbarred. As the judge who oversees the disciplinary committee, Murphy actually can come after me—he went for Andrew Cuomo—and in fact it's precisely this, using the committee to punish adversaries, that got Murphy, or at least

the administrative aides who took the heat for him, in trouble in
1990.

Soon Schwarz is on the phone with Van Natta, screaming, "Did
Eddie Hayes represent you on a DWI or something?"

It's the wrong thing to say to Van Natta, who basically doesn't
drink and in any case isn't going to fold in the face of threats from a
lawyer whose suits fit like sausage casings. In fact, by the time he's
found out about Murphy and his racket, Van Natta is even more out-
raged by what he sees as judicial impropriety than I am.

But I am completely against the wall, facing bankruptcy and humiliation. Disbarment, a real possibility, is not going to help. Do I
push the story with Van Natta or put it down and save myself more
trouble?

"Fuck it," I tell Van Natta, "let's go."

On Mother's Day 1996 the *Times* runs a huge front page in the
Metro Section headlined "Warhol Decision Draws Conflict-of-
Interest Accusations." The piece explores ethical questions posed by
Judge Francis T. Murphy's failure to disclose his prior relationship
with the Warhol Foundation's lead lawyer, Thomas Schwarz, while
hearing the appeal in the Warhol case. The article quotes a legal
ethicist who agrees that Murphy's conduct is "very egregious."

Reminded that Murphy criticized Judge Preminger for refusing to
disqualify herself from the case because she once attended a social
event at which I was present, Monroe H. Freedman, a legal ethics
professor at Hofstra University, tells the *Times*, "Boy, that's chutzpah."

"This is not my issue," Schwarz says in the *Times* piece, deftly selling his crony down the river. "It's Judge Murphy's issue."

Murphy says the stupidest possible thing to the *Times*. "I don't
have any recollection," he responds when asked about the fact that
Schwarz led an investigation into his conduct; it's a blatantly ridiculous claim that occasions a follow-up *Times* piece citing more experts
who agree there's no way in the world Murphy can justify his failure to disclose his prior relationship with Schwarz or the possible
conflict of interest it raised.

Now I have to decide whether to make a formal complaint against Murphy. Under ordinary circumstances, a judicial committee would immediately investigate the charges leveled in Van Natta's piece, but given Murphy and Schwarz's history with "investigations" that failed to find obvious wrongdoing, I'm actually afraid Van Natta's charges will be "investigated" prematurely and ineffectually.

Vengeance is a long-term proposition; I'm fighting for survival and will keep my mouth shut until the perfect moment arrives.

If the renewed vigor with which Schwarz's army at Skadden go about busting my chops is any indication, neither Murphy nor Schwarz is pleased about the *Times* exposé.

"Hey, Meatball, look what your friends brought over," Susie says one night in Bellport. She drops a packet of subpoena papers on the kitchen table. Skadden's process servers greeted her as she drove our Cherokee up the driveway with groceries—cranberries and oranges for relish—on Thanksgiving Day.

Trying to locate assets and subpoenaing financial records is part of the business of enforcing judgments like the $1.2 million one Murphy's court granted against me, but serving papers on Thanksgiving—that is a bit much. Schwarz and Skadden's servers have been dogging Susie for months in Manhattan, jumping out at her with subpoenas when she was out with the kids or at lunch with friends.

"Fuck 'em," Susie says, ladling caramelized onions over a turkey she's cooking for our low-key, very sober family Thanksgiving. I can barely eat the turkey or anything else and find it hard to talk to anyone. My wife is tough, and though the servers in the driveway and the rest of it don't bother her much, or at least don't seem to, I am close to collapse.

—

Josh Angel successfully buys time on the bankruptcy proceeding, but it's just a matter of weeks until the ultimate collapse. I've been desperate before, of course, and in fact spent the first seventeen years of my life in that state; accustomed to desperation and hard work, I do what I've learned to do during such periods: I stay in shape so my body doesn't give up on me, and I work as hard as I can.

I go to court and take every case I can find, collect as much money as I can, and pay as many bills as possible. I work on every case I get, no matter how big or how small. I am in Bronx Family Court working cases for next to nothing an hour, but they keep my blood moving and they buy lunch. I start in at 7:30 a.m. and come home at 10:00 p.m. My young son thinks I'm the super because he never sees me except when I take out the garbage late at night. I'm so exhausted that I have only one pleasure: I sleep on Johnny's floor so I can be close to him. Sometimes, when I'm lucky, he gets up and sleeps next to me. Other times he just hits me with a pillow and yells at me for not being home earlier.

I look strong and healthy—I actually increase my exercise regimen—and try hard to be pleasing to people but I also make it plain that I'm in trouble. "I got all kinds of problems, but I'm doing the best I can," I let everyone know.

"Your Honor," I tell the criminal court judge who's set to proceed with trial on a small-time misdemeanor case, "I've never asked for anything like this before but I've got a personal-injury case in another court that I need to try first because I need the money. I'm going into bankruptcy." The judge, who hardly knows me, says, "Okay, Eddie"— not "Mr. Hayes"—"I'll give you time." He does and I go and collect a decent fee in the personal-injury case, which I try for a friend of Jimmy McManus's who hurt herself when she slipped in a Korean market on the West Side and couldn't be more grateful.

—

On a Monday morning in 1996, Josh Angel plans to file bankruptcy papers on my behalf. Filing bankruptcy papers is like reading an X-ray that shows terminal cancer; once you reach this point, it's over. I dread spending the weekend before filing at home, without phone calls and the action of the courthouse to keep my mind off what's coming.

New York governor George Pataki, my old law school friend, has invited Susie and me for dinner that Friday night. "This guy will never win," everyone said when he decided to run against Mario Cuomo in the fall of 1993, just as I was sinking into ruin. "No one has heard of Pah-tacky!"

I said, "Well, I know the guy and I like him and I want to help him," and I did.

Solid as our twenty-five-year friendship is, however, it doesn't seem right for a bankrupt to be at the governor's house two days before he goes under.

"Libby, I'm sorry. Susie and I can't make it for dinner," I tell the governor's wife on the phone. My old friend Libby, an attractive, hardworking woman, fluent in four languages, with whom I enjoy regular lunches and frequent conversations about politics, fashion, and New York society, expresses regret—and surprise.

"I'm filing for bankruptcy," I tell her, "and I don't think it's appropriate to be up at the house right before I do."

Fifteen minutes later, the phone rings.

"George says you've got to come up on Friday night *and* spend the weekend," says the governor's wife. "He's *not* going to have you not come. You can't say no."

Okay then.

Susie and I get in the Cherokee and drive up to Garrison to the Patakis' gracious house. The Patakis have four children, all very tall like the governor and his wife; the house, with its high ceilings, great antiques, and its contingent of very fit, tall state troopers in crisp collared shirts, suits them well.

"It's his birthday," Libby whispers as she takes our coats in the foyer.

All weekend long, the governor's crew—Charlie Gargano, Billy Plunkett, Mike Finnegan, strong, old-fashioned guys, solid citizens but genuine tough guys, too, guys about whom you can be confident that what they are supposed to do they are going to do—drop by to pay their respects. I am dying from the bankruptcy. But under the circumstances, the governor's house is not a bad place to be seen and the governor must have known this when he had Libby call back.

"Good to see you, Eddie," he says with a firm shake. "How are you?"

It's his birthday, he's my friend. I don't want to cloud the place up with despair. "I don't know what I'm going to do," I say, and shake my head with as much of a smile as I can manage.

"You'll do it, Eddie. You'll do it," he says, and encouragingly ushers me into the living room.

You'll do it, Eddie. That's all that's said all weekend about my impending ruin. Pataki is capable of great affection, but he is not a man to waste words. A genuine neighborhood white boy, upstate and semirural division, made good, Pataki loves his country, his friends, his family, his dog (I have my psychiatrist on my speed dial; Pataki has his dog on his) and will do right by all of us. Pataki doesn't blow me off even as I am about to go bankrupt—insisting I come up to the house for his birthday is a lovely, lovely thing to do—and I can't express how much this means to me.

"Nice weekend, counselor," Susie says as we drive down the Patakis' Garrison driveway at the end of the weekend. I don't know if she's aware of how many nights I get up and go downstairs and cry in the kitchen or out on the patio behind the house, but she never says anything about it, which is just as well, as I don't know how to talk about what's going on or about how angry and hurt I am.

———

"I know you're mad and you want to hurt people," my mom says when she calls later that night, "but don't do it, Eddie. It will make it worse." She said the same thing when I was a kid and was mad at my dad. I don't know if she means it or not; as my mom, she can't exactly say, "Okay, go out there, kid, and do the guy."

"You're sick, Eddie. You need medication. It can help. You can sleep," says my sister, Barbara. She's become a psychological coun-selor, having known from an early age that she wanted to help peo-ple like us, the victims of other people with addiction problems. But medication seems an unmanly way out. "No thanks, Barbara," I tell her. "I'll work it out."

It doesn't get better. I'm dying, I'm lost, I'm a fucking bankrupt, but my family and my friends knock themselves out for me. Days af-ter I file for bankruptcy, Bill Bratton, another neighborhood white boy, until recently New York City's police commissioner, calls. "Eddie, I got a call from Harry Evans at Random House. He wants me to sign a book deal. It's a big deal, Eddie. I need your help." Fu-ture Philadelphia police commissioner John Timoney—the rough, smart red-haired guy with a big Irish mug who worked as a plain-clothes cop when I was a Bronx DA and who could famously chase down fleeing perpetrators half his age and who clearly had a big ca-reer ahead of him and who is also, at heart, a tough Dublin street kid who just might hurt you—introduced me to Bratton years ago, and Bratton's become a friend. He hires me now, when I can really use the status shot involved with what will be his much-publicized book deal. Read Irish history—it's full of defeats. But look at the guys who took over the General Post Office in 1916 and stood together, shoulder to shoulder, as the British summarily executed them outside the building; like Bratton and Timoney and Mike McAlary and Michael Daly and Jimmy McManus, these were guys who stuck to-gether, who rose up together and who went down together.

McManus basically rolls guys up and down Eleventh Avenue. "You got four dollars? You need a lawyer? Go see Eddie," he tells everyone who comes through his wildly crowded life. He sends over guys with thousand-dollar retainers, just in case. It's his way of thanking me for work I did for free for guys he sent over during better days.

"Alex, I have no security, no equity, no savings," I tell Alex Porter one morning at the New York Athletic Club. "I have a lot of debt. I don't want to lose the house." I ask for a loan.

"You're going to be okay. Don't worry about it," says Porter, and he sends a check up to the office that day.

"Please don't die," I tell Tom Wolfe over and over again as he goes in and out of sleep in Lenox Hill Hospital after the bad heart attack he has on August 9, 1996. It impresses him that I sit by his bed all night. "If I'm not going to spend the night in the hospital with you, what am I going to do?" I ask Tom, who has had me read up on Marcus Aurelius and Stoicism and the idea that it's possible to strip back unnecessary desires and accept life as it comes. I tell him again, "Please, don't die." And he doesn't.

Bruce Cutler and my bond trader friend Tom Guba, both smart, strategic thinkers with helpful ideas about survival, and Gail Collins and Joanna Molloy, who would have had shotguns under their arms if they had been in Ireland in 1916, will do whatever it takes to help, and I would die without them and the others who come through for me now. It was really my brother who got me through the worst of times—he carried me on his back, called me many times a day, lent me money over and over, and made me feel hopeful for the future.

Reinaldo Herrera helps in a memorable, surprising way. Reinaldo is from an aristocratic Venezuelan family and knows so much about how society works that he could have been social secretary to Balzac; he's married to fashion designer Carolina Herrera and, in addition to being one of the classiest people I know, also happens to have a gigantic schlong. ("Reinaldo, I'm never bringing you here again," I tell him on the way out of the New York Athletic Club, where I take him one afternoon. "You're giving all the Irish guys in the locker room a complex for the next hundred years.") At the complete nadir of my life, Reinaldo, who is a close friend of New York socialite Jeremy Rifkin, who exerts influence over the International Best Dressed List, truly comes through for me.

"Congratulations," says Richard Johnson, who is on my phone early one morning.

What, are you crazy? I think, having just picked myself up from the bathroom floor after the morning vomiting ritual.

"It's in the *Post*," says Johnson. "You're on the International Best Dressed List."

I don't know how the fuck Reinaldo did that! I'm barely able to pay for a shoe shine and my friend gets me onto the Best Dressed List to cheer me up!

———

Skadden, which has already spent a fortune going after me, redoubles its efforts after the *Times* runs its piece about Murphy and Schwarz. The head of the firm's bankruptcy department is in court every time the firm makes an appearance or files papers, which is highly unusual in a case of this modest size and suggests the firm's desire to kill me after I have publicly—in the pages of the *New York Times*, no less—made serious allegations about the relationship between a Skadden partner and an acting judge. Skadden clearly takes the view that it would be far easier to destroy me than to answer the charges.

And that's just what they do. In addition to the firm's lead bankruptcy lawyer, Skadden has at least six or seven associates working on the case against me, filing papers accusing me of hiding assets and of criminal activity. One week they accuse me of concealing my professional relationship with Bill Bratton, a relationship Skadden claims is an "asset" and so subject to seizure under the bankruptcy laws, an absurd claim since the Bratton book deal and my involvement with it have been very public. The next week, I'm charged with concocting phone loans to friends like Tom Guba in an attempt to lower the value of my holdings or to put assets into the hands of friends who will return the money later. ("Go to hell," Guba tells Skadden's lawyers at a deposition to which he is summoned.) The firm's unremitting, life-sucking force stops my breath.

———

"I can't see how I can help you, Eddie," Si Newhouse tells me on the deck of his airy country house. "You really are in desperate straits." I'm completely at the end of my rope (the Chase Manhattan

Bank plans to foreclose on my town house) when I ask for help. I don't think there's anything wrong with—or humiliating about— asking a friend for help. I need help. Si, lord of a vast publishing fortune, is in a position to help. "Go see Paul," says Si, referring to Paul Scherer, the chief financial officer of Si's Condé Nast companies, a decent guy who prides himself on financial cunning and is passionate about opera.

"You really are in desperate straits. I have no idea how I can help you," Scherer says when I see him the following afternoon. "But the bank that's foreclosing on you is our bank. So let's think this through." We sit in Scherer's office in the Condé Nast building, then on Madison Avenue, and try to think things through. "Who do you know who can help?" Scherer asks. I tell him I know a lot of people—the governor and his people and guys in the press and in the police department and the courts and everywhere, but what I think I need is a financial whiz who can figure out some way to consolidate my debt so I can come out of this alive.

"Interesting," says Scherer. "My cousin Oscar Cohen is superintendent of the Lexington School for the Deaf in Queens."

"Well! That's great, Paul. Glad to hear that." I'm thinking, *I'm going down the toilet and my family's coming with me, but send our regards to Superintendent Cohen.*

"He's having problems with the budget and he's very upset about it," says Scherer. "He doesn't know anybody in the governor's office and he's afraid the school won't be funded again."

"Oh yeah?" I say, reaching for Scherer's phone. "What's Oscar Cohen's number?"

I dial Scherer's cousin. He's having problems getting some new projects together for his school; he isn't sure he can get support from the governor's office.

Scherer *is* a financial wizard!

"I'll take care of it!" I tell him and walk out of his office into the elevator and then to the nearest pay phone I can find. I call Bill Plunkett, a conservative, devout Catholic from Westchester who has six or seven sons and a wonderful-looking wife who is very close to Pataki, who once worked in Plunkett's law firm.

"Billy, I'm fucking desperate. I'm going to lose my house. I need help," I tell him. "Meanwhile, I have these guys who are interested in a school for the deaf in Queens that may get shut down."

"A school for the deaf?" says Plunkett. "I can't imagine we'd close down a school for the deaf. Why don't you come over right now, Eddie?"

I get in a cab, head over to Plunkett's office across from Grand Central, and he calls someone with an Irish name in Albany who handles school budgets for the governor.

Plunkett talks to Albany. "Are you crazy?" That's what Albany responds when Plunkett says a friend of Pataki's is in the office, scared the governor won't fund a Queens school for the deaf. "We don't take money from blind people or deaf people. What are you, nuts? We're Catholic for Christ's sake! We'll take care of this."

"That ought to make life easier for you," Plunkett tells me. "In fact," he says, "I think we can do better. You call Oscar Cohen, Eddie, and tell him we have a personal interest in whatever he needs."

Scherer calls me later that afternoon. "Eddie," he says, "we're going to take care of your problem." And he does. Soon after learning that Si Newhouse's office would like things to work out for me, the bank decides not to foreclose on my house.

———

Helping Oscar Cohen and the Lexington School for the Deaf works to buy me more time. More importantly, it signals the beginning of a reversal in my now long-running bad fortune.

Having staved off foreclosure on the house, I still have to figure out how to get out of bankruptcy. Judge Cornelius Blackshear of Bankruptcy Court pushes for settlement, but neither Skadden nor Schwarz evinces any interest. Quite the reverse. They don't want to settle; they clearly want to screw me and have no intention of stopping until they do.

Fortuitously, however, appellate court judge Francis T. Murphy comes up for reappointment. This is my moment. If I am going to file a complaint against Murphy, this is the time to do it. I won't file a complaint with the Commission on Judicial Conduct about Murphy's impropriety in failing to disclose the possible conflict of interest arising from his relationship with the foundation's lead lawyer, because I fear the commission will whitewash the matter as they have done so many times before. Instead, I'll file a formal complaint with the Judicial Screening Committee, which determines reappointments and since 1995 has been conveniently filled with Pataki appointees.

"Murphy is really going to come after you if you make a complaint," the lawyer for the committee tells me when I appear to lodge a formal complaint. "You know he's the most powerful judge around."

Yeah, I know. Fuck it. This is my moment. Michael Collins wouldn't let it slide; neither will I.

I do not talk to the governor about the complaint. I don't have to. Pataki knows all about Murphy. The guys around the governor all hate Murphy and can't believe Mario Cuomo rolled over after he jacked up Andrew, and Pataki isn't likely to be well disposed toward Democratic-machine judges, especially those compromised by complaints about improprieties on the bench.

Immediately after I make a formal complaint, Murphy receives word that Pataki will not reappoint him to the bench. Murphy can press his case before the committee; if it finds he is highly qualified for reappointment, it will be difficult for Pataki to decide otherwise. Murphy, however, loses his nerve. Maybe he suspects the committee will find he is not qualified for reappointment, which would be devastating. I don't know. But at 5:45 on a December evening in 1997, an appellate court judge I know phones my office. "Eddie," he says, "I want you to be the first to know. Murphy just resigned."

"Thank you very much. I appreciate your calling." That's all I say. I'm still in bankruptcy but I sense that things are starting to go my way.

"I know what this is like for you, Eddie," my mother says to me that night when I tell her Murphy is out. "Control yourself. Don't get carried away."

———

Once Murphy's down, I can focus on Sullivan, whose ambitions make him an easy target. Sullivan desperately wants to be promoted to the job of presiding judge of the appellate court and is, in fact, the senior guy in line for the job. But he's been passed over three times in a row. It does not help that Richard Johnson is constantly killing the guy with damning stories in the pages of the *New York Post* or that the *Wall Street Journal* runs a big piece slamming him as one of "America's worst judges."

There are those who think Sullivan is a great judge, however, and one of them is Jimmy McGuire, a very decent guy who became counsel to the governor in 1997 and is a friend of mine *and* a friend of Joseph Sullivan and Thomas Schwarz. Mike Finnegan, someone who knows how to hold a grudge and relishes a nice long battle, was the governor's first counsel; McGuire is more of a diplomat, a peacemaker, and he steps in after Sullivan is passed over for the third time, to see if there's a way to broker a deal that will make at least some of his friends happy.

Will I agree to pay the Warhol Foundation $700,000 instead of the $2.1 million that Murphy's court levied against me? McGuire wants to know. Yes, of course I will! It's a sweet deal, very sweet! Thirty cents on the dollar, that's how sweet! The trouble is, I don't have $700,000.

Luck, friends, big blondes, and the promise associated with New York life come once again to my rescue. While Skadden's lawyers have been dancing around in their bad shoes for nearly two and a half years in Bankruptcy Court, New York real estate values have gone through the roof. I don't have money to invest in a plate of good meatballs at a decent New York restaurant but my house on East Eighty-first Street is now worth a fortune, substantially more than I paid for it; at the very least, it's worth enough to secure a $700,000 loan—if, that is, I had anything more than a lot of bankruptcy debt to offer as collateral.

Susie's longtime friend Allison Stern, another member of the big blonde club, has a husband named Leonard Stern, an upstanding Jewish gazillionaire. Though I don't talk much to Susie—or anyone else—about the mechanics of my ruin, I obviously don't need to. Susie, who knows what's what and what to do about it, cooks up a plan with Allison whereby Leonard Stern will guarantee a $700,000 loan. It is a testament to the power of big blondes: Stern does this for Susie and for Allison, and not for me. They save my life.

With the $700,000 I borrow against Stern's name, I write a check payable to Skadden, Arps on behalf of the Andy Warhol Foundation. No further articles about Joseph Sullivan appear in any New York papers after this and I refrain from voicing further opposition to his candidacy for presiding judge. Two months after I accept the terms of McGuire's deal and pay the $700,000 we agree will constitute full and complete settlement of all claims pertaining to *The Andy Warhol Foundation v. Edward W. Hayes*, Sullivan is at last promoted to the position he's sought for more than a decade and, with a strong recommendation from the Judicial Screening Committee, is named presiding judge of the Appellate Division.

McGuire is a very good counsel to the governor. He is a former prosecutor and a straight guy who was mad at me because he thought I was being unfair to Sullivan, who had many supporters. On the other hand, he couldn't understand how I got in trouble for pointing out that someone else had filed an accounting that underreported the assets of a public foundation by 400 percent. And a friend of mine, Earl Mack, who had been the head of the New York State Council on the Arts, interceded with the current chairman, a man named Richard Schwartz, and suggested this unseemly display might best be put behind us.

I lost in the appellate court but worked it out. I emerged from Chapter 11 with 75 percent of my assets, including the houses (now worth millions), and no reason to be embarrassed in front of my children or anyone else. And my son, bless his soul, didn't have to sleep on the floor anymore. As for avenging the dogs who brought me down, if things had gone any further, I might or might not have followed my mother's wise counsel not to get carried away, but I didn't have to decide. In the end, Murphy was out and under a cloud. Schwarz left Skadden, retired from law practice altogether, and went off to serve as president of Purchase College of the State University of New York. Sullivan, whom I tortured in the press for years, got the job he always wanted but served for just a few years before retiring. Fred, of course, was in the throes of a very painful, miserable, and protracted death. A lot of peripheral characters got hurt along the way, including the lead lawyer at the firm that originally represented the foundation, the lead lawyer for Christie's, and the assistant attorney general who was more interested in how much I got paid than in the question of whether the public got its fair share of Warhol's legacy.

In the end, Warhol worked out great for me, but terribly for Bob Jossen and Adam Rowland, my brilliant lawyers. They took enormous risks, spent an unbelievable amount of time on my behalf, and ended up losing money, swallowing fees I could not pay. This, in the end, is what troubles me most about the way the protracted Warhol litigation shook out. I hope, before I'm done, to find a way to make it right with them.

—

In my view, what matters most in life is duty, honor, and glory. I came out of the long battle over the Warhol estate with my castle— the house on Eighty-first Street—intact and with a lot of honor and glory. In *The Bonfire of the Vanities*, Wolfe writes that when you lose your nerve, you lose everything. During the course of the ten-year fight over Andy Warhol's estate, the others lost their nerve and I did not. And I was right about Warhol, whose paintings now sell for millions; whether Archibald Gillies and the others who claimed otherwise like it or not, Warhol is a symbol of our time and a great painter.

During the battle that consumed my life for so long and almost killed me, I took on some of the most powerful institutions in the city—the courts, its most powerful law firm, the art establishment. Not only did I survive, I emerged ready to prosper, my reputation and my place in society secure—and I got vengeance! In the business I'm in, this is the ultimate test: if I can do this for myself—take on everybody and win—I can do it for you, too. I don't know that I'd want to relive the gut-wrenching days and nights as they dragged on and on, but the battle over the Warhol estate made my career. And it made my sense of myself. The people I most admire are those who risk their lives for something they believe in, and though I hope I'll have a chance to do that, I haven't yet. But everything else I had I risked in the struggle. And in the end I think I did pretty well, thank you very much.

CHAPTER 13

I'm in the disaster business.

My practice revolves around misfortune, personal catastrophe, murder, arrest, imprisonment, loss of custody, loss of control. "Trouble is my business," as Raymond Chandler has Philip Marlowe explain. And the thirtieth-floor office space I rent after the Warhol case and the related bankruptcy proceedings (and the attendant acts of vengeance) has a lot of walls that need filling up.

"Bring me a mess of those catastrophe shots," I tell Juan Gonzales, whose photos of car crashes, burning buildings, and snipers shooting up crowds I've seen in the *New York Post*.

Gonzales is in my office the next day with his portfolio, and I pick out dozens of black-and-white photos (including good ones of a mangled woman naked on a stretcher, a neighborhood pizza place going up in flames, and a building falling onto a busy street) and put them up to remind myself that I am in the disaster business and to set the tone in the new office.

Eddie Adams, a client of mine, took the photograph I hang over my desk. It's the famous one of a young Vietnamese man, his face screwed up in agony as a gun rams up against the side of his skull, about to blow his brains out. It's probably the most famous picture from Vietnam and a lot of people think it is a statement about the horror of war. But I know from Eddie Adams what's led up to the scene in the picture and I see it differently. According to Eddie, the guy holding the gun to the Vietcong guerrilla's head was a lifelong friend of the guerrilla's victims, and just before the picture was taken, South Vietnamese officials produced the guerrilla and told the man whose hand holds the gun, "You know, we caught the guy, the one who shot your friend and his family." *Then* he blew the guy's head off. Knowing this gives you a whole different view of the picture: it's a shot not of a cold-blooded assassination, as most people think it is, but of the justified killing of a man who deserved to die. Context. You've got to know about context—history—in order to do well in law, certainly in disaster-related law, and maybe in everything else, too.

—

With Murphy, Schwarz, and Sullivan out of my way and Hughes near death, his body so badly destroyed it can't even muster sufficient strength for even the feeblest of death rattles when his agonies end at last in January of 2001, well, I'm starting to feel pretty strong. My enemies are gone. I'm ready for action.

It does not hurt that one of the first things to come along is a case involving Robert De Niro and some crackpot paparazzo. De Niro is walking somewhere with Uma Thurman when the guy gets right in front of him, hoping De Niro will fall down so he can snap better, more expressive pictures he can sell for even more money than regular pictures of Robert De Niro walking down the street go for, but De Niro sees what the guy is trying to do, grabs the camera, and smacks the photographer.

Tom Harvey, a capable lawyer and former wrestler who is a friend of De Niro's and mine calls the next morning.

"The sleazebag photographer is pressing assault and battery charges against Rob!"

"Bet you anything he calls looking for money."

Sure enough, Harvey phones the next day to say he got a call from LA. "You were right," he says. "Seems like the guy *does* want dough."

"See if he'll take three hundred grand to go away," I say.

Harvey calls the guy back and says, "Meet me at JFK tomorrow morning. I'll be at the gate with a suitcase. Take it, get the fuck out of there, and don't come back."

The next day, the guy meets Harvey in the terminal, takes the suitcase, and, just as Harvey and I planned, is immediately swarmed by a bunch of detectives from the district attorney's SWAT team, who recover the suitcase and cart the guy off. And that's the end of that. Except, of course, for the part about how all the papers run big stories about the paparazzo and his scam and De Niro and his lawyers, Tom Harvey and Edward W. Hayes. Which absolutely does not hurt a guy trying, as I am, to get back on his feet.

I'm back in court full-time, which I love. At this point, I'll go anywhere and do anything in any kind of court. I'm in family, civil, and commercial court, and I'm still taking criminal cases all over the city, in the Bronx, which now is essentially filled with Hispanic immigrants, and in Brooklyn, now teeming with Arab and Russian immigrants and fourteen different types of Indians and Africans apiece; they have to have thirty-seven interpreters on call since every single person down there seems to speak a different dialect. I don't think I meet a legitimate Russian for five years; every Russian hoodlum there is involved in twenty different scams—medical scams, drug scams, insurance scams. Some are just plain out shooting one another; a lot of my clients are so untrustworthy I have to get every dollar from them before they're out of sight or I'll never see a nickel.

Now, more than ever, I make a point of dressing very, very well. It shows respect and is a way of presenting and selling myself to the court. Also, you never know when someone is going to come up in the hallway and say, "I got my kid in jail. Can you help me out?" I'm my own billboard. A lot of the clothes I wear are, in fact, leftovers from the old days, before Warhol, when I traveled to Queens County Criminal Court on the E train, which stops at Fifty-third Street and Lexington Avenue, conveniently across the street from my brilliant tailor Vincent Nicolosi. Often on days when I'd done arraignments, I'd be stopped afterwards by someone in the hall who approached to say, "My son is inside. Can you get him out?" and I'd always say, "How much money do you have on you?" Whatever they answered, I always said, "Fine," and then, on the way back home, I'd put the money in Nicolosi's skilled hand and say, "God wanted me to have a new jacket. Start stitching."

I'm getting guys out of jail and I'm winning cases, I'm in the newspapers and I'm about to get tangled up in some very high-profile and not uninteresting dustups, I'm alive, I'm struggling, still broke half the time, but after the drag-out, knock-down decade of Warhol, I'm keeping everything going.

———

An enormous sea change in the city court system that took place back in 1993 plays a big role in the early days of my resurrection. Judith Kaye became chief judge of the New York Court of Appeals and made it her first order of business to overhaul the city's courts. Kaye and her chief administrative judge, Jonathan Litman, decided that, as the economic center of the world, New York needs to have commercial courts that can handle significant economic matters and do so expeditiously. In civil disputes, most lawyers expect to spend years and years resolving even the simplest cases. Before Judge Kaye's overhaul, the halls of the court were always clotted with long lines of lawyers. A lot of big corporate firm financial transactions involve billions of dollars, and the firms sometimes sent dozens of associates, all of whom billed by the hour, and they'd stand in the hallways in what looked like some kind of orgy of middle-aged men in white shirts and dark suits, hunkering down for a few seasons of endless discovery and motions and oral arguments and filings on the arguments and arguments on the filings and on the motions, and more discovery, and more arguments, that would last for years of hideously expensive billable hours. The commercial courts Judge Kaye created, in dramatic contrast, were set up to resolve commercial disputes, no matter how big or complicated, in a year's time.

I'm standing out among the throng of middle-aged men in crisp shirts and shiny shoes in the hallways waiting to do battle on behalf of high-paying clients who cannot afford or no longer wish to pay for their formerly endless services. I have the smallest waistline, the shortest hair, and the biggest smile in the group and may be the only guy in the whole place who likes his work. And after pushing dozens and dozens of criminal cases through the Bronx justice system each day, as I did in the DA's office, I, unlike the guys in the shiny shoes in the hallways, know how to process cases expeditiously, and I'm good at it.

Inside the courtroom, Judge Herman Cahn has a mountain of papers—filings and briefs—stacked all the way to the ceiling, but he can sum up every case in a minute and a half. Cahn is the quietest guy in the world, never raising his voice or getting upset or surprised by anything, always thinking and always knowing what he is doing. Not incidentally, he is a devout Jew, meaning his people have spent the last thirteen million years studying the Torah and the Talmud, thinking through centuries of laws, and are pretty good at what they do.

"How many depositions do you need?" Cahn asks me and opposing counsel in one of the first of many run-of-the-mill contract cases I try in his courtroom.

"Just one, Your Honor."

"Good. We'll have a hearing the day after tomorrow."

The lawyers for the other side, who are accustomed to putting everything off into an unforeseeable but always expensive future, nearly keel over.

Litigation, formerly a game of outlasting and outspending an adversary, is now a different animal. And an action guy like me, who's used to going to trial tomorrow and would much prefer not to bother with a lot of time-consuming, pointless motions, is not at all troubled by a jumped-up schedule.

Okay, let's go. That's my attitude.

After the hearing, Cahn takes thirty seconds to decide what's what. "You guys owe Mr. Hayes's client $300,000," he says from the bench. *Boom.* Case closed. And I walk out of the courtroom $75,000 richer! Seventy-five grand for two court appearances and a couple of phone calls! Hmmm, this ain't bad. I'll take this any day of the week!

It doesn't hurt that humor is a big asset in the Commercial Division, where all three judges, Cahn, Charles Ramos, and Ira Gammerman, are quite funny. Cahn is witty, though you often don't understand his humor until fifteen minutes after he's made what later dawns on you was a very funny crack. Ramos—who is Hispanic and Protestant and must have been elected because he was mistaken for Puerto Rican—has little patience for lawyerly pedanticism, and the humorlessness most lawyers bring to the bar doesn't play well with him. In truth, most courtroom lawyers would be well served by charm and humor, though precious few possess much of either. A lot of lawyers, in fact, seem genuinely unable to talk to people. (The difference between me and these guys may be that they spent too damn much time studying in the library, while I was always trying to fuck the librarian, and so *had* to develop the ability to talk to people, which really is a big help in a courtroom, and most other places, too.) Gammerman, also a wit, chews the plodding, humorless lawyers right up.

Eleanor Green—a red-headed assistant with three big, strong sons, a great work ethic, a good smile, and no deference toward me whatsoever—joins my office staff, as does Rae Koshetz, who was deputy commissioner for trials of the NYPD for fourteen years. That means she was the head judge for the NYPD and can read and write well, probably because she was writing opinions all those years for hardheads who didn't like big words or long sentences. I do what Eleanor tells me to do—I am not good at schedules—and having Rae means I can submit papers on cases.

A man named Peter Flanigan made me join a program called Student Sponsor Partners, which sends poor kids to parochial schools. I pay for them and give them work—they have to find God on their own. But now my office is full of kids named Rajit, Jeans, and Manny, who mostly make deliveries, answer the phones, and make trips to tailors and to see my cousin Richard, who works in the world's best button store. It's fun to have them there and I get lots of good Dominican food.

Together, the Commercial Division judges show me that no matter how complicated cases seem, most come down to a simple formula: X owes Y money; X signed a contract, has to honor it, and if he doesn't the court will make sure he does.

—

Before the Warhol slamdown, I stayed away from family court and divorce cases. I thought they were messy and when I was younger and single I knew I would end up sleeping with all my clients, which might be a problem. Besides, most lawyers hate family court. The courtrooms are dingy and full of overworked people with badly abraded nerves after bearing witness to human nature at its basest, listening every day to tales of greed, treachery, and abandonment, not to mention awful stories about the mistreatment and abuse of children.

But after Warhol I start taking family court cases, initially because I'm taking any case that pays five dollars, but soon because I find family court work rejuvenating and consequential and human. I like the clients, most of whom haven't killed anyone (which for me is a new thing) or stolen millions of dollars (which is refreshing after the revelations of Warhol). They are usually nice women down on their luck, and I find it gratifying to get them extra money or court protection, whatever I can to keep chaos at bay. Also, I'm winning, getting good results, and I'm always on time, careful about returning phone calls and exercising the basic discipline involved in being a lawyer. Eventually I start getting high-end divorce cases. The remuneration is better but the satisfaction I find in making things easier for someone in terrible shape is the same as it is when the client is a working mom with two kids, two jobs, and a husband who's threatening her and making her miserable. Initially I misread the culture of family court and think the jobs of the lawyers and judges are the worst, most miserable ones on earth. But I am wrong: family court jobs aren't miserable, they're difficult, which is what makes them valuable. As Ernie Peace said when I was a kid, an easy life is not the same as a good life. My life in court now, especially in family court, isn't easy, but it is good, very good, to be back in the game.

And then there's the other stuff. The cases that get in the papers.

———

"Eddie, Puffy's in trouble. I need your help."

Sean "Puffy" Combs's publicist is on the phone in the middle of the night telling me the rapper and his girlfriend, Jennifer Lopez, are in police custody.

"They were arrested driving away from some crappy club on the West Side. A bunch of people were shot. Puffy didn't have anything to do with it. He was going through a red light when they stopped him and there was some fucking gun in the car. But he had nothing to do with shooting anyone."

Puffy's flack Dan Klores is a good publicist, an old friend of Mike McAlary's and someone I've known for years. Why is he calling *me* in the middle of the night a couple of days after Christmas, during a holiday when most lawyers are sitting out in Aspen or St. Croix? He's probably called at least nine other guys before he calls me.

"I need you, Eddie," Klores says.

Okay then. *I'm there.*

"They're in Midtown North."

Klores gives me a few other details: the gun in the car was stolen and unlicensed, Puffy's bodyguard, Anthony "Wolf" Jones, who was in the car with him and J.Lo, had dope on him and has been charged with drug possession. I lace up some custom brown suede shoes, pull a blue and brown plaid jacket from Anderson and Sheppard (I'm very partial to brown and blue) over my khaki pants, and I'm on my way. Gotta look sharp for Puffy, no mean clotheshorse himself.

The Midtown North Precinct building, a shithole under normal circumstances, is a total shithole over the Christmas holiday. The place is home to the absolute dregs of humanity, cops who need sleep and evidently some job counseling since any officer on the force with any resources whatsoever uses them to get a few days off at Christmastime. Don't even think about the people desperate enough to get hauled in over Christmas, guys far enough gone to actually get arrested by a cop so lowly he can't get off the holiday shift and would much rather feel sorry for himself, maybe with a honey-glazed cruller in the patrol car, than go out in the cold and bother with some lowlife dumb enough not only to *cause* trouble but to attract so much attention *doing it* that the officer *has* to go out into the fucking cold and fool around reading the motherfucker his rights, getting him into the car, and hauling his sorry ass into the shithole precinct building on West Fifty-fourth Street.

"Edward Hayes," I tell the clerk behind the desk in the front office, which is painted that sick green color that, by law, all government offices must be painted in order to cast the absolute worst light on all who pass through. "Here to see Puff Daddy and J.Lo," I tell him, and he grumbles into the corner from which an officer pulls himself off a folding chair and takes me into a smaller room (green, of course) down the hall.

You cannot handcuff Jennifer Lopez to a fucking pipe!

J.Lo is in the green room, sitting on a folding chair, her little wrist wrapped in a metal cuff bolted to a pipe.

Someone got the bright idea it would be a good idea to handcuff the nation's biggest Latin star to a steam pipe!

"Do you fucking know what is going to happen if some photographer from the *Post* comes in here and sees this? You might want to rethink this," I tell the officer, "because there are going to be some very upset people in the world."

The officer is not so sleepy as to miss my point and, as he gets up and fiddles with the cuffs, I go looking for Puff Daddy, whom I find, not cuffed, in a chair in an adjacent (green) room.

"Call my mother and tell her I'm okay," Puffy says when I tell him that Dan Klores called and that I'm here to help.

He doesn't seem to give a fuck that he is in jail or that he's been arrested or that any of this might cause trouble for his billion-dollar Bad Boy record company. All he cares about is his mother! I've never seen a guy in prison more concerned about his mother than this guy. "Man, you got to call my mother!" he says when I ask what happened. "Tell my mom I'm okay."

Puffy's entourage is waiting out front. "Could one of you guys give Mr. Combs's mother a call?" I say, and as I head back inside, past the green room in the front, I see J.Lo (no longer cuffed), standing next to a sleepy-eyed officer, checking her skirt in the dim reflecting glass of a plated institutional-style door. She looks at me, smiles sort of, turns back toward the folding chair, and gives her buttocks a little twitch as she does. None of the three detectives standing next to me can speak for a full thirty seconds: never have I seen a woman turn or twitch her tail with as much skill as J.Lo put into that quick and staggeringly effective move.

Man, she's always working it! Even in the precinct house, facing criminal charges, the lady is working every chance. (This is, of course, precisely what I am doing here and the reason I—and not any one of the nine or nineteen or however many lawyers Dan Klores called before he dialed my number—am here now. As J.Lo's career—and maybe, in some much smaller way, what is about to be the second act of my own career—suggests, working it all the time is not the worst thing to do if you're looking to get ahead.)

Charges against Lopez are eventually dropped, and Puffy and Wolf (a genuine tough guy who did not get his nickname by accident) will, after a highly publicized trial, be acquitted of all charges. (Though I am initially retained to represent Wolf, I have to recuse myself because when I go outside to get someone to call Mrs. Combs a member of Puffy's entourage says something to me about the gun, thus making it possible I could be called as a witness, which, were I representing Wolf—who, incidentally, is later murdered in Atlanta—could create a conflict.) Klores has hired me to represent Puffy and J.Lo while they are in custody; I do my job, get a nice fee, and remind myself once again that it is nice to be in the center of things and gratifying—as well as remunerative—to use my resources to help, even just a little. And as 1999 winds down, I'm pleased, really pleased, that J.Lo is uncuffed and released and I've saved not only her (spectacular) ass but the officer on duty, who certainly would have lost his job had there been evidence of whatever bad judgment led him to cuff one of the country's biggest stars to a pipe. Puffy's mom can sleep easy, which puts the rap mogul's mind at ease, and all is well with the world, if only for a moment. *Ba rum ba bum bum.*

———

I'm still taking calls at three in the morning a year and a half later.

"Eddie, Lizzie's been in an accident. There's a problem."

It's Allen Grubman, a sterling example of a knock-around Brooklyn Jew that I've always loved. Pretty much the country's leading entertainment lawyer, Grubman is convinced that everyone sees him as a greedy Jew and is always talking about his obsession with money and eating, but he has a lot of very fine qualities: he's brilliant, witty, and, though he is very good at making money, a much better man than he pretends to be. I love guys who are better than they let on! A heavy guy, Grubman has tiny little feet and I'm always telling him he should get custom-made shoes, which, three years into our friendship, he actually does, though the $2,300 pair of English shoes he has made are too small, even for his dainty feet!

"You sonofabitch, Eddie," he says, laughing. "What am I gonna do with these tight suede shoes?"

Grubman's got a great laugh and a great smile. "Give 'em to the homeless, Allen," I say, and Grubman laughs his great big street-tough Brooklyn Jewish laugh.

He's not laughing when he phones me that morning in July 2001.

"Lizzie has a problem," he says. "A number of people have been hurt at a nightclub."

Lizzie Grubman, Allen's thirty-one-year-old daughter, is a loud-mouth who hangs out at late-night clubs with rappers and drinkers;

on the occasions when Allen and his elegant, classy wife, Debra, had Susie and me to their houses in New York and in the Hamptons, Lizzie and I never got along well.

"Where is she, Allen?"

He gives me a number, I dial, and I soon find out from her friend, Andrew Sasson, that Lizzie ran over sixteen people in the parking lot of a club called Conscience Point where the summer crowd goes to drink and hang out.

Sixteen people! I think. *That's impossible. You can't run over sixteen people! Five maybe, but sixteen people you can't.*

"I swear to God, Eddie, it was an accident," Lizzie says when I get her on the phone. "I didn't mean to do it. I don't know what happened."

"Have you been drinking? Are you using drugs?"

"No, I'm not messed up. Everyone is telling me I'm messed up," she says. "Eddie, I'm not messed up."

She's not messed up. I can tell from her voice.

Andrew Sasson gets on the phone.

"Is there anyone else in the house?" I ask him, and he tells me there is a well-known actress there. "Is she sober?"

"Not really."

"Get her out of the fucking house. Tell her to stand in the driveway. Otherwise, everything we say she is going to repeat to somebody."

Sasson has a lawyer named Eddie Burke whose father is a Suffolk County judge and who is well connected there. I tell Lizzie that we'll try to work something out and that she should keep her mouth completely shut. Then I call Burke at home and tell him to go to the house because the cops are going to show up there soon, which they do, though they don't yet arrest Lizzie since she clearly isn't drunk. Lizzie left the scene of an accident, which isn't good but also isn't unreasonable in light of the fact that she'd run over half the parking lot and was legitimately afraid any guys left standing might want to rip her apart.

Allen and Debra stop by my house in Bellport on their way home from the Hamptons the next morning; later in the early afternoon, Lizzie, who has since been arrested and released, stops in, too, and we spend a loud day together.

Allen's partner's wife is sick, his ex-wife (Lizzie's mother) is dying, and his daughter is in big trouble. Allen, who is used to being in control, is in bad shape. The huge talent he represents gives him a lot of clout—real control—in the entertainment business and he is not accustomed to the relative powerlessness of a complete crisis.

"She didn't do anything wrong."

"She didn't do *anything* wrong?"

"She fucking made a mistake! What is the problem? What is wrong with making a mistake?"

Allen goes on and on like this.

"Eddie," he says at last, "they are just coming after us because we're rich Jews! This is ridiculous."

"No, Allen," I tell him. "They are coming after you because she ran down the whole fucking neighborhood."

Lizzie's arrival intensifies the craziness. The first thing that happens when she comes into the house is that she and Allen start screaming at each other.

"You're not listening to me," Allen complains.

"You're not saying anything," Lizzie retorts.

"Lizzie, you've got to listen to what we are telling you."

"You're always telling me what to do. You listen to me!"

"Listen to me, Lizzie, you didn't do anything wrong—"

"Daddy! *I'm not listening to you.* I didn't do anything wrong. I made a mistake. I didn't *mean* to hurt anyone."

"I got the police records," Eddie Burke says on the phone. "They say she called one of the guys out there 'white trash' before she ran him down."

"White trash!" I say. Ohhh, fuck. *That's* a problem. *Goodbye, Lizzie!* I think. *You're going to jail.*

Allen digs his heels in. "I can fight 'em. I'll spend more money than they have. They can't make a case."

Spoiled rich girl runs over locals and tries to duck responsibility:

it's very *Bonfire of the Vanities*! Politics and class war are going to drive the case against Lizzie Grubman as forcefully as it shaped the hunt for Sherman McCoy.

"Allen," I say, "you're taking the wrong approach. Look at the names of the people she ran over. At least half of them are Catholic. The witnesses are Catholic. The prosecutor, Jim Catterson, who is running for reelection, is Catholic. Catholics believe in confession, penance, and redemption."

Allen fumes.

"As a Catholic, the most important thing to do is to say, 'I'm sorry.' God will forgive you if you say that. But God will *not* forgive you—and neither will anyone else—if you call people 'white trash' and then run them down with your Mercedes SUV and insist that, no, you didn't do anything wrong and, yes, night is day."

Allen looks like he may have an aneurysm on my porch.

"Stop saying she didn't do anything wrong. Make sure the reporters who cover this, who, incidentally, are going to eat Lizzie for breakfast so often she'll be an entrée on the Atkins diet, see this for what it is—a political opportunity for a prosecutor seeking reelection. Then wait for Catterson to make a mistake. Because he will make a mistake."

By day's end, Allen and I aren't speaking anymore.

But Catterson is indeed kind enough to make a mistake, sending a detective to strong-arm Andrew Sasson—who is dependent on state authorities to get the liquor license renewal he needs to stay in business with his own Hamptons club—into saying Lizzie was drunk at Conscience Point, even though she most definitely was not drunk, which accounts provided by witnesses and detectives on site at the time verify. By the time Allen's wife gets him and me talking again after a couple of months, I know exactly how to use Catterson's mistake to Lizzie's advantage.

In Suffolk County, judges are elected in real elections in which character matters. It's not the same as in Manhattan, where judges like Murphy are selected by the Democratic Party and stay on the bench forever. These Suffolk judges sweat blood to get elected and work hard to protect their integrity and the dignity and independence of the judiciary. At the very least, the prosecution of Lizzie Grubman is, given Catterson's aspirations, partly political and as such does not serve the local judiciary's interest in remaining above the fray, eschewing scandal or the appearance of any conduct that could compromise its integrity. This, as I see it, provides an opportunity for Allen Grubman, who comes to me the following summer.

"It's serious, Eddie," he says. "They're going to force this to trial."

"Enlist the judiciary, Allen," I tell him. "Get the judge to take control of this situation, get the story out of the newspapers, which are beating Lizzie's brains in every day, and move it toward conclusion. The incident has been blown out of proportion to serve the political needs of a prosecutor during election season. Get the court to step in and restore dignity."

Allen, who is best with people in matters involving money and, except in those matters, really shouldn't talk to people at all, winds up doing a brilliant job handling the insurance companies and the civil claims arising from the accident at Conscience Point. ("If the people Lizzie ran down get paid for their trouble, they'll be a lot less mad," I advise him.) And though I am not Lizzie's lawyer of record—I couldn't handle Allen *and* Lizzie—I know a lot of judges, lawyers, and elected officials in Suffolk County and I'm Allen's friend and adviser and, after talking to a number of people about the situation, I know what has to be done. Someone—Allen or his representatives—needs to go to the judges and say, "This is out of control. We have done what we could. We know she is going to jail. But bear in mind, she is a hardworking woman and her father didn't start out with money. He earned it. The Hamptons are an important part of Suffolk County life." And at the end of the day, the judge says, "Okay, let's move this along. Plead or go to trial."

The lawyers Allen hires, Eddie Burke and Stephen Scaring, take over and Lizzie gets sixty days and does community service. It's over, and she emerges from the whole thing a much kinder, softer person.

Getting your brains beat out every day may be a good thing for someone who is just a bit of a spoiled brat: almost nothing unspoils you faster than a good beating in full view of the entire country. I grow to like Lizzie very much, and best of all she and Allen become devoted to each other.

Accept the truth and go from there. That's almost always my inclination. I learned as a child that some things in life are just plain fucked up. You can't spin it, you don't like it, nobody likes it, but that's how it is and the only real question is: What can be done about it? A lot of lawyers profit, or try to profit, from spinning the truth; my inclination with Lizzie—and almost everyone I represent or advise—is to accept the truth and proceed. It's a strategy that usually works out well, as it does for Lizzie and Allen, who now graciously concedes that my instincts were right from the start. For me, her case is also a good example of something I learned in the Bronx DA's office and at various points in private practice (certainly with Warhol)—that media, legal, and political pressures sometimes overlap in ways that can work to my advantage.

—

If I am going to talk, I like to be paid for it. After Warhol, while I'm working to get back on my feet, and throughout my involvement with the Grubmans, I get calls from producers at Court TV who are looking for lawyers to comment on the trials they televise. Will I come in and talk about this bitter divorce trial? Will I agree to talk about a child molesting trial in California? We've got a murder case, Eddie. Can you come on and talk about the issues involved? I've always liked reporters—and attention—so yeah, sure, I'll be on TV as a reporter and commentator. But after a while I get tired of going down and talking for free. Court TV's ratings are in the toilet in 2000, but its president, Henry Schleiff, has started to turn the place around.

"Eddie, you've got the voice of the people," he says. "Come work with us. We'll give you a regular show. You can say whatever you want."

Schleiff understands that trials are part of popular culture and that broadcasting them has both entertainment and didactic value, and he is as good as his word. I'm on every Friday with Rikki Klieman, an action girl who has married a bunch of Irish guys, including Bill Bratton, and is lively and outspoken and smart. "The guy killed his friend. He should die." "Having a good body is like having money in the bank." Commenting about murder cases, divorces, everything that comes up, I say whatever I want, and though some of the producers flinch when I do, neither Schleiff nor anyone else at Court TV ever objects to my saying what I think. The most important thing I learn about television is from Charlie Rose, who tells me to ask the questions the *viewers* want answered.

One of my favorite things about talk radio is that any one of zillions of nutcases in the world can say absolutely whatever they want, and a lot of them do. John Batchelor and Paul Alexander, two guys I know from knocking around with journalists, get a show about politics and current events going on WABC Radio. "Can you fill in and do a show on politics and crime?" Batchelor asks. I give it a shot, love the immediacy of talking to listeners who call in, and in short order start to appear regularly, for an hour, on Wednesday nights. I invite political analysts, police chiefs, guys who are expert in shooting people in snow to come on and talk about everything from polling techniques to crime scene investigations to sharp shooting in Afghanistan. "Pollsters undercount young voters." "Would you like to see me in a bikini?" Listeners phone in all the time and say all kinds of wild things.

—

"My friend is in jail. He gave Bill Clinton's brother $300,000 for a pardon."

I'm enjoying some good fresh yogurt in my office at 7:30 one morning after having done a radio show the night before, when I pick up the phone.

"I heard you on WABC last night. I thought you'd want to know about this. My friend's name is Guy Lincecum. His mom put the money up."

The yogurt, from the Union Square farmers market, is so fresh and good I'd really rather not talk to this guy calling me first thing in the morning with a cockamamie story about the Clintons and inmates in the Texan prison system.

"Sure," I tell him. "You got copies of the checks?"

"Yes, I do," says the voice.

"Sure. Good. Okay. Here's my fax number. Fax them over, I'll take a look, okay? Thanks for calling." I get back to the yogurt.

The fax whirs a moment later and I look at facsimile copies of canceled checks made out to a friend of Roger Clinton.

Holy Christ! This looks like the real thing!

I get the number for Guy's Lincecum's mother, Alberta, who wrote the checks. She's sick and old—I can hear it in her voice—and she tells me that her son, a convicted thief, met Roger and a friend of Roger, and she got the money and wrote the checks because Roger Clinton said he could talk to his brother and get Guy pardoned, but he would have to be paid first.

I do not want to get involved.

Whoever does get involved is going to be in the center of a big political rat fuck. He'll be asked to go on all the right-wing talk shows. It's a lot of craziness I don't need.

Clinton was not a bad president. But after Monica Lewinsky showed him comfort and kindness, he had his proxies attack her in the media and say she was a stalker and other terrible things designed to ruin her name. That was disgraceful. I have done a lot of bad things in my life, but I would never do that. Don't let a woman suck your dick if you aren't going to show her respect. I finish my yogurt. *Clinton may have been a good president,* I think to myself, *but what he did was wrong, and you know what? Fuck him.*

Before the hour ends, I'm on the phone with the US attorney's office, and the following day a big *New York Times* story runs about Roger Clinton, Guy Lincecum, presidential pardons, abuse of power, and old, sick Alberta Lincecum. The tawdry incident fuels a fast-growing scandal about the fire-sale pardon giveaway that took place before Clinton left office.

Clinton took advantage of a young woman, and his brother took advantage of a sick old woman. Guy Lincecum never got his pardon and never got out of jail and his mother never got her money back, but there is a measure of satisfaction, possibly even for Alberta Lincecum, in knowing that though big, powerful people took advantage of other, weaker people and got away with it, they were at least held accountable in a very public forum, the *New York Times,* and did not escape moral opprobrium for their conduct. In helping bring Roger Clinton's shameful and usurious conduct to light, I feel I did a good thing.

———

Goddamn! Everything is going well!

I'm behind the wheel of my gray Jeep Comanche on a lovely summer night after a lovely day with Governor Pataki at Charlie Gargano's house in the Hamptons. The Lincecum case, of course, gives rise to interesting conversation on a perfect day during a good season, and I'm speeding home to see my wife and children, who are doing well. It's all good.

I'm sailing down the road listening to Bruce Springsteen and thinking how happy I am, when suddenly I'm sobbing in my seat.

I cry so hard I can't see, so hard I have to pull to the side of the road. I get out of the Jeep and stand there crying like a baby as BMWs and Land Rovers whiz past. Then, after what seems like ten full minutes of this, I finally choke back the tears, look down at my English spectator shoes, and say out loud to myself, "Eddie, this ain't right."

Something is definitely wrong.

I'm doing all these good things, I've fought hard to restore my status, and now I'm doing well, making money and enjoying terrific friends. Why am I crying by the side of the road?

"Absolutely, there is a genetic component to depression that is often passed down, generation to generation," says a Cornell psychopharmacologist at a dinner party *New York Observer* owner Arthur Carter and his wife, Linda, throw a few days after my sobbing fit on the way home from the Hamptons. I start thinking, in a way that is perhaps more manic than not, about my father drowning himself with drink and about the Irish in general. They can't *all* be prone to depression and drunkenness just because they live in a place where it rains too much. It occurs to me for the first time that depression and what may be associated, drunkenness, have a genetic basis.

Two days later I'm in Dr. Michael De Meo's office in the Kips Bay section of Manhattan.

"Edward Hayes," I say, holding out my hand. "I need help." I explain that my responses to things that happen in my life are often inappropriate. "I cry when I should be happy. I laugh when I am enraged," I tell him.

Dr. De Meo has the matter-of-fact manner of a financial adviser or a dentist, which I find enormously reassuring.

"Do you have trouble sleeping?" he asks.

"For forty years, yes."

He proceeds down a list of questions that he explains will help diagnose the problem.

"Ever experienced uncontrollable rage?"

"At least six times a day."

"Have trouble concentrating?"

"I haven't concentrated on *anything*, besides Dominican women, for more than fifty seconds in my whole life. No, not true. There have been a few African women who've held my attention. Also some blondes."

Dr. De Meo looks at me in a way that is neither sympathetic nor unsympathetic and continues the questions.

"Do you ever have trouble talking to people?"

"All my life."

"Do you ever have thoughts about hurting yourself or others?"

"Twelve times a day. At least."

Halfway through his questions, Dr. De Meo puts down the questionnaire and says, once again in a manner neither sympathetic nor unsympathetic, "You know you are crazy."

"Nobody ever said I was fucking stupid, Doctor! I know I'm crazy." And I start to cry, just like I did all those years ago when I first went to see the psychiatrist on Central Park West and just like I did when I won cases in the Bronx and every other time in my life when things were going well.

"I don't know why I get like this. It's not fair. I didn't do anything." I'm crying and saying the same stupid things I said to my mother when my father beat me. "Why am I getting hurt? I didn't *do* anything."

The doctor speaks softly, in that clinical, soothing way doctors sometimes do.

"You have a major depressive disorder, Mr. Hayes. It's not uncommon. I think medication can probably help you."

He tells me about brain chemistry and how it's possible that an imbalance in brain chemicals, particularly in the levels of a neurotransmitter called serotonin, causes depression. A new class of medication, SSRIs (selective serotonin reuptake inhibitors), drugs like Celexa, increases serotonin levels in the brain and restores the balance of brain chemicals, which in many people works to relieve or eliminate depression and depressive symptoms.

I don't want medication.

Throughout my life, I've always had two weapons at my disposal: intelligence and anger, the white, burning feeling that took hold when my father slammed me around and that resurfaced again and again throughout my adult life, that rose up in a furious blast and blotted out all thoughts other than *I am going to get you.* Antidepression medication will kill that anger, I think, and leave me defenseless.

I am already medicating myself, anyway. Just as my father did with drink, I self-medicate with work, danger, and risk. I am addicted to risk and excitement. I read more about all this and begin to wonder if operating, as I always have been, in a state of adrenalized fury doesn't work to invigorate neural chemicals that have otherwise malfunctioned. I wonder if the incredible crash I often feel after I succeed at something—winning a case, trouncing an enemy, or even something simple, like enjoying an afternoon with friends—is chemically induced. Whatever the reason, for me success is always a prelude to terrible depression; I never, in all my life, have enjoyed more than a single moment of pleasure without anxiously reaching out for more problems, dangers, risks. Which, if you think about it, really is kind of messed up.

I call Dr. De Meo a week after our meeting.

"I'll take the pills," I tell him.

Within two weeks, and for the first time in as long as I can remember, I don't begin the day with a sick knot in my gut or, worse, vomiting on the bathroom floor, and I get through the day without the near-constant sense of humiliation and rage I've had since childhood. By the end of the month, I sleep through the night, maybe for the first time in a decade, and go to sleep calm and full of pleasure, my wife at my side, my children nearby, money in the bank, and the promise of engagement and maybe, but not necessarily, danger in the day ahead. Not a bad way to feel as I move toward the third and fourth quarters of a life I couldn't even have dreamt about as shoes landed, tossed from my father's forceful hand, onto the floor of that South Carolina basement so many years back.

CHAPTER 14

Geez, I'm well dressed today!

I leave my house in a beautiful fawn-colored lightweight wool suit, the kind of ginger-colored suede shoes that you can wear after Labor Day, a blue and brown shirt, a blue and brown tie and silk pocket square from Seigo, an elegant tie shop near my house. I'm on my way downtown to see Susan Bender, a lesbian lawyer whose office is in Lower Manhattan, to try a case together in court. I always tell Susan Bender how much I want to go to bed with her. I worship the ground she walks on; I don't know why, but I do. Will the fact that I am particularly well dressed today be lost on Susan, who, in addition to being completely fabulous, is also very butch, I wonder as I step out of the Cortlandt Street subway station, six blocks from the World Trade Center, a little after nine the morning of September 11, 2001.

Oh my fucking God! What is that?

Smoke fills the streets, and dust. People are everywhere, running, screaming, looking up toward the top of the World Trade Center, where what looks not simply like a fire but more like an inferno or a volcano blasts heat onto the street. People jump out windows and disappear into clouds of dust and fire near the street.

I stand in the fawn suit just watching this fucking unbelievable volcano burn. Guys who can't get closer to the buildings in cars leave them in the street and run toward the buildings. Clean, fit, athletic guys, neighborhood white boys, off-duty and uniformed firefighters and policemen *run* toward that inferno. I'll never forget the image.

The guys running into those buildings are overwhelmingly Catholic. Most of them probably grew up as I did in white-boy neighborhoods around the city and were raised with the same Catholic ideas—*God loves you. Sacrifice yourself for others. God knows. And He will take you into His arms and find for you a glorious place in heaven*—as those I learned, or, more accurately, absorbed into my skin, at St. Joan of Arc church in Jackson Heights. Those burning buildings are white-boy heaven.

When the buildings finally fall, there are cops inside who could have left but did not leave. There are also plenty of firemen who could have gotten out but instead said, "No, I won't leave," and were crushed to bits when the towers imploded.

Remember, and be haunted by, this: a number of the hundreds of rescue workers who lost their lives on September 11 took last rites before they *ran* into those buildings.

Pat Brown, a fire captain and decorated Vietnam hero, ran inside the North Tower, wouldn't leave, and died inside. Pat, who was someone I knew, slept with more strippers than anyone on earth, and you never saw so many good-looking girls (at least not at three in the afternoon) as were present at his funeral. Those girls, like the rest of us, were very broken up. Paddy Brown, a committed bachelor, never shared all of himself with anybody but he did share a very nice piece of himself with a lot of people.

Tom Guba, my old bond trader friend, had a lot of friends at Cantor, Fitzgerald and at his annual Fourth of July party I got to know many of them fairly well. Between the firemen and the police officers and the Cantor, Fitzgerald traders, there are a lot of funerals in the days and weeks after September 11, many of them attended by state and city officials, notably Rudy Giuliani, then mayor of New York, whose brave and admirable behavior rightly attracted national atten-tion. It later turned out that he was actually there, with the fire com-missioner, in a command center alongside the World Trade Center and that *he left before the buildings fell.*

How could Rudy have left the location with his fire commissioner and let all those firefighters keep going inside to die? Why the fuck didn't Rudy say, "I'm getting out. You get out, too. Because there is no way you can rescue anyone now"?

If I were a relative of one of those dead firefighters or cops or even of one of those dead bond traders or anyone else who died in either of those buildings, this would be the first question in my mind after *Oh my God, how could this happen?*

In fact, it's one of the first questions asked again and again in the churches and graveyards where families memorialize or bury loved ones and at what are about to become an endless series of meetings convened by family members seeking various kinds of redress from bureaucrats and officials such as Rudy Giuliani.

———

New York is a good place for someone like me, someone who likes and can take a beating. In fact, the whole damn place is made up of people who have it in their blood to take beatings, since every-one who's here came or had parents or grandparents or great-grandparents who came because they had gotten too many beatings someplace else and wanted to get out. But the inclination to take it into the streets, to fight and push and shove for what they need or think they want must follow them here; how else can you explain why absolutely no one ever seems to advance themselves without massive conflict. The September 11 attacks on the city and on the Pentagon introduced, of course, a new order of conflict, and it is but a matter of time before we know for sure which interests will profit, as some inevitably do, from misfortune, trouble, and war. I know for certain already, however, that the main thing about the two big cases I handled after 9/11 is that they affirmed and solidified my general sense of how things work in the city, my belief that what is best about New York tends to emerge—as do the characters who survive and prevail here—only after struggle and conflict.

———

"Look, we have a problem. We can't get anyone to help us."

You cannot imagine how much I love Kathy Vigiano, who is on my phone in January 2002. Kathy Vigiano is every girl I grew up with.

I met her as a consequence of the worst mistake of character analysis I've ever made in my adult life. In 2000 I backed Pat Lynch, a personable Brooklyn police officer, for the presidency of the Patrolmen's Benevolent Association. In addition to promising drastic reform of the police union, Pat said I'd play a central role in negotiating on behalf of the union if he got elected. But when he was elected, he forgot my help, and the various offers he'd made me. The good part of the story is that Pat had a dedicated, hardworking woman doing the computer work in his campaign office, Kathy Vigiano. When I went to Pat's office at nine at night to help during the campaign, Kathy was always there working away. She's a lovely, lovely person and she loved her husband, Joe, an emergency service police officer who belonged to the same gym I did on Long Island, and who was on duty on September 11, one of the many who went into those buildings and didn't come out.

Kathy's father-in-law, a decorated former marine, lost both Joe and another son, John, a firefighter, who was also on duty that day and who also went into one of the towers and did not come out. Mr. Vigiano had just two children, both gone now, and I remember looking at him at Joe's funeral and thinking that he looked crushed, destroyed, as if he, too, had been smashed to bits by a falling building.

"We're having trouble getting money from the relief fund," Kathy says on the phone, referring to the fund that Giuliani, then mayor, and the city raised for the families of those who died in the tragedy. There's a lot of money, some $100 million. Instead of transferring the money directly to the families, Kathy explains, Rudy and city officials made plans to transfer it to a not-for-profit fund controlled by city-selected fiduciaries.

"Come in tomorrow morning," I tell her. "We'll figure it out."

Kathy arrives with Frank Dominguez, a published poet whose brother Jerome, a biker with nipple rings and a job as an emergency service policeman, also died on 9/11. Jessie Ferenczy, Jerome's fiancée, comes too, as does Gerry Gilliam, a terrifically outspoken and straightforward Mississippi woman who lost her son, a black police sergeant.

Kathy and Frank and Jessie and Gerry and who knows how many others have funeral expenses, not to mention bills to pay and fatherless children to feed, and they explain they're having trouble getting the city and Rudy Giuliani, who is no longer mayor but still controls the funds, to release money. If you control the sums of money involved, you control a lot of people and there are a lot of favors involved, which may or may not have something to do with Rudy and the city's tightfisted hold.

"The money was collected for us," Kathy says that day in my office. "We don't want to have to keep going to Rudy Giuliani or anyone else for the rest of our lives to get what's ours in the first place."

"I don't see why you should," I tell her and the others.

"No one will go up against Rudy," Kathy says.

Especially in the aftermath of 9/11, during which Rudy behaved like a true hero and a true leader, he is, more than ever, a force to be reckoned with. He is also a figure of increased national prominence.

"Kathy, I'll get you the money."

———

The next day I write to Michael Cardozo, the corporation counsel, who as lawyer for the city of New York has responsibility for the funds the city collected on behalf of the families.

"I represent a large majority of the families of the twenty-three New York City Police Department officers who died at the World Trade Center on September 11, 2001," I say in my letter. "There has been a good deal of public discussion about whether New York City should transfer the money it collected on behalf of the families to a New York State not-for-profit corporation set up under the control of ex-mayor Rudy Giuliani. My clients disagree with the way this situation is being handled." I ask that the assets not be transferred into any new funds but be distributed at once to the family members for whom they were intended.

New York is not only a city defined by constant conflict but a city whose history is full of strange incidents in which the same characters turn up again and again. Cardozo was president of the New York City Bar Association when Francis Murphy resigned from the Appellate Division rather than suffer removal after scandal surfaced in the pages of the *New York Times* and elsewhere. I never met Cardozo, but I did have a long-standing feud with him, one that began shortly after Murphy's resignation. Cardozo, who supported Murphy throughout his life on the bench, took a very public position against what he considered Murphy's forced resignation. You have some nerve saying Murphy was forced out, I told Cardozo in a letter I dispatched at the time. You never investigated the allegations made against Murphy, and you should have!

And so we meet again, Cardozo and I, and in no more congenial a fashion than when we clashed years earlier.

"This fund was raised for a specific purpose by the city for city employees. Further, New York City set itself out as the custodian of the fund for a very specific group of individuals. It is not fair, and I believe it is actionable, for New York City to now walk away from the promises it made to the donors to the fund and to the people who are its recipients," I tell Cardozo in a follow-up letter.

Though he refuses to return my calls or to answer my letters, Cardozo's response is: No. I can't get involved. I am not getting involved.

You can't take the position you're not involved! Your old law firm is handling the fund, is my position.

Cardozo's old firm, Proskauer, Rose is Rudy's current firm and as such is working with the city to transfer the $100 million for the families into a fund it will create.

Why am I willing to take this on? The true answer is, I like Kathy

Vigiano. And Frank Dominguez and Jessie Ferenczy and Gerry Gilliam. These people have become good, long-lasting friends of mine; whatever they want I'll do. Also, it doesn't seem right to delay payout to the families who genuinely need help and in fact have gotten some from a generous public.

As a public relations battle, the fight for money for the families just about takes care of itself. All I have to do is keep putting the widows out there and make sure a lot of people hear them say, "We lost our husbands. We're not children. We have children on our own. They lost their fathers. We need help!"

Then I send letters to Rudy and Cardozo and leak the letters to the *Post*, the *Daily News*, and the *New York Times*, all of which run pieces that work to increase both the pressure and the PR fallout on Rudy and the city.

And then, almost as if God himself, tired of casting the extras in the ongoing urban drama, decided just to go ahead and have some of the extras play double roles, Dan Klores turns up as the publicist for Rudy Giuliani. In this capacity, Klores, in response to the constant barrage of 9/11 widows' statements, has been calling me every name in the book in the local papers. This goes on for weeks, during which time it does not get easier for the widows to feed their families or pay their rent.

After a month of this, Eliot Spitzer, the New York State attorney general, a tall, handsome, bright guy who is a very fast runner, steps in.

"I'm not going away," I tell Spitzer at his office in the Federal Building in Lower Manhattan. "Somewhere in the state there's got to be a town populated only by cops. I am going to find it. And then I'm going to find a Surrogate's Court judge in that town to rule that this money is going to these widows."

Spitzer, who acts impressively throughout, looks at me as if I am the most reasonable man on earth and as if there is nothing in the world he would rather do than listen to me go on all day about towns full of cops and about judges who will do exactly what the 9/11 widows want.

"Listen, Mr. Spitzer. You can tell every state politician who opposes me that I will personally bring these grieving widows to every single campaign stop they schedule for the rest of their lives."

"Mr. Hayes, I don't know what, as a matter of law, is right in terms of setting up a fund for families who lost loved ones on September 11. But I personally believe that a judge should hear testimony on this and that we should, and will, schedule a public hearing."

That's a fucking brilliant idea if ever there was one! I practically dance out of Spitzer's office. A hearing! *Well, guess who's going on the witness stand?* Yesss, the widows. And guess who isn't going to allow this to happen? That's right. No judge will let this happen. And Rudy Giuliani won't let this happen, because it won't look at all good to try to keep money out of the hands of women whose husbands gave their lives in the service of others.

Next morning, I get a call from Dan Klores. "Do you want to have breakfast, Eddie?" he says. "How about tomorrow?"

"Sit down," he says when I meet him at the Regency Hotel. "You really want that fucking money, don't you?"

"The widows want the money. I said I would get it for them. I have to have that fucking money."

"Look," says Klores, and he makes a fair proposal right there at the table, before we've even ordered eggs. No question Klores is acting on Rudy's behalf. I accept his proposal on the spot.

I like it about Rudy first that he came to understand (though not without significant pressure and threat to his reputation) that he had been wrong not to establish a fund that would be immediately accessible to the families and second that, as soon as he realized he had made a mistake, he set it right and agreed to turn over all the money on a specified date. He fully lived up to his bargain.

Rudy saw he made a mistake and changed course, which is not a bad thing to do. Though it's better to be right about something in the first place and refuse ever to give essential ground, it's good to change your mind when you're wrong. All in all, Rudy behaved like a great man during those difficult months after 9/11 and was a wonderful mayor before.

Repenting for wrongs, central in Catholicism, is of particular interest to me when my brother calls to say my father is sick, very sick,
from heart problems caused by obesity.

"Look, I can't forgive him for what he did. I'm not going to sit
there with him while he dies," I tell my brother. "But call me if *you*
need me."

There were times I actually said, "Look, Dad. I am Catholic. You
did it. Admit what you did. Admit you were wrong. I will forgive
you." But my father was not genuinely sorry for what he did. He always denied he ever did anything wrong. He was sick, he said, he
couldn't help himself; that's as far as he ever went toward acknowl-
edging wrongdoing. It's true, he was sick. But sickness goes only so
far in explaining what he did to us.

"Look," I told him when we last spoke, just after my wedding. "I
am not going to forgive you for anything. The violence went on well
past the point where you were sick. You did wrong. Confess.
Repent."

He never did. I never forgave him.

I wish I had loved my father, I wish I could have saved him as I
have saved so many others. He is the only person in my life whom I
have walked away from. He was never there for me and I did it because I thought he would bring me down with him. But when he
died, I went to his wake and it was full of crying men whom he had
helped with their alcohol problems. They told me that and told me
how proud I should be of him. When I went with Susie to his
funeral the next day, I broke down sobbing and couldn't stop. I
thought of him alone and helpless in the woods of the world, chased
by the wolves of his addiction. Years later, I went to see his girlfriend, a lovely woman named Marion Dolan, at the Mary Manning
Walsh Nursing Home on York Avenue in Manhattan. She was glad
to see me. When I left, I cried. A social worker said that I must have
loved my father very much, and I turned to her and said that I had

hated the bastard more than anything in the world. I will never ever have peace. I have never been to my father's grave. And I'm not going.

———

"I'd like to see you, Eddie."

Victoria Newhouse, a convert to Catholicism and the wife of me-dia magnate Si Newhouse, is on the phone.

Victoria is exceedingly polite, like a killer who has guns cocked at your head and knows, as Victoria knows, that you have to do whatever she asks and who figures, what the hell, she might as well be polite.

"Daniel Libeskind is our guy for the World Trade Center site re-development project."

Okay, if you say so.

I know there is a heated competition for the commission to rebuild the Trade Center but I don't know who Daniel Libeskind is or what Victoria is talking about.

"We'd like you to help, Eddie."

Well, if you say so.

"What would you like me to do, Victoria? I will talk to the gov-ernor about this if you like."

Victoria says, "Oh no, I don't want you to do that. That would be improper. I don't want even the vaguest taint of impropriety."

Not the vaguest taint of impropriety? Jesus Christ! There's never been a building contract in the history of the world that didn't have a taint of impropriety!

"Victoria," I say, "it's almost impossible to have a building con-tract that's completely clean. Tell me what you want me to do."

Victoria says that she is going to send over some architecture books and would like me to take a look and then we'll talk.

Twenty minutes later, a library of books about Daniel Libeskind, Frank Gehry, and other leading modern architects arrives at the of-fice door. I read them all and also a packet of materials about the project and quickly see that plans for the rebuilding are primarily concerned, as is much of my life and maybe everyone else's, with ideas about memory and reconciliation.

Victoria invites Susie and me for dinner with Libeskind and his wife, Nina, the following week. Going to the Newhouses' is like going to the Museum of Modern Art; they have so much great art they actually rotate pieces on display. They also always have fantastic food at their house, which I like. I'm at one end of the table with Daniel; we don't say a word about architecture but instead talk about kids and schools. Personally, I don't like to get involved with people who don't have a strong connection to their kids. The Mafia feels the same way; family connection exerts a kind of control: people who care about family and worry about embarrassing themselves in front of their children are more likely to behave better. The Libeskinds have three kids, one a physicist, one a classic Jewish brainy guy who knows about everything, and a teenage daughter who is smart and feminine and close to her family. I like the Libeskinds and there is also a lot to be said for the veal chops the Newhouses serve for dinner.

Before dinner ends, Daniel, who grew up in the Bronx but was born in Poland, tells me about his Hasidic uncle and his Orthodox grandparents and the eighty relatives killed during the Holocaust. Judaism is clearly pretty central to this guy's life; I like people who have some religious content in their life, which, like family connection, often works to moderate behavior.

The Libeskinds come to my office the next day; they want the contract for the master plan for the World Trade Center site.

"Can you help us with the governor?" they want to know.

Probably. Yes, I can.

But first I want to know more about Libeskind and his plans, which I study with some care. Essentially his idea is to transform what was a moribund space into a lively cultural center, full of plazas and public spaces and museums and street life, and to build better access roads to the site, at the center of which he envisions a wedge of light that, every year on September 11 between 8:46 a.m., when the first plane hit, and 10:28 a.m., when the second tower fell, will shine into a plaza at the angle it shone on that morning in 2001. The wedge of light will, with other ingenious aspects of the Libeskind plan—chief among them the centrality of the New York Harbor, views of the Statue of Liberty, and the 1,776-foot Freedom Tower—speak to the past and connect the site and its history to a lively present full of culture, life, and possibilities.

You know what? I think when I've finished more books and know more about Libeskind and what he has in mind. *I like this guy!*

I call the governor. Everyone calls the governor—every powerful person, every big contributor, everyone who gives big calls him looking for favors, looking for help. Which is one reason I never push anyone—or anything—on him.

Instead I call and say, "You know what? This Libeskind guy is a very good architect. He is a Jew from the Bronx. He is a family man. He is a little nuts. But all these guys are a little nuts. He's a decent guy, he loves his wife, loves his kids. I like the guy and you'll like him too, I'm telling you."

"Good, Eddie." The governor doesn't waste words.

"Let me send you some pictures," I say, and I call the Libeskinds back into the office so we can figure out what to send Pataki, who, as the highest state official, has fundamental responsibility for and control of the architectural competition for the World Trade Center rebuilding project and the Lower Manhattan Development Corporation's decision as to who will build what on the site. I give the Libeskinds Pataki's autobiography and Daniel thumbs through the pages while we talk.

"See this haystack?" Daniel says, pointing to a photo of Pataki standing next to a haystack in Hungary. "That's the kind of haystack I grew up with in Poland."

"Is that so?" I say.

"Yes, yes!" says Libeskind, who gets excited in the unabashed way children do and, possibly as a result, has a magical ability to generate great enthusiasm around him. "See the shape, the roundness, the lushness of the haystack. I've thought about the simple shape of the stack a lot over the years and about how simple shapes convey meaning."

"Do you have any pictures of you and your haystacks?" I ask. He does. Libeskind sends me copies of the pictures, which I immediately dispatch to the governor with a note that says, "Look familiar?"

I also send the governor a framed picture of the view of New York Harbor from Libeskind's planned Freedom Tower. The old World Trade Center towers blocked the water view and I know that Pataki, who has a house by the river, has strong feelings about the Hudson.

A week later, the governor is scheduled to go to the Winter Garden at the World Financial Center, across from the site, to view the proposals.

"I'd like to go and show the governor your proposal," I tell the Libeskinds. "Fine," says Nina, "so long as we pay you for your time." I tell her no. "I don't want to take money from you. I'm doing it because I think Daniel's Freedom Tower is the right building for New York and I don't want anyone to say I'm doing it for money."

I soon find myself squatting on the Winter Garden floor, in a three-buttoned navy blue suit with peak lapels and a white-collared lavender shirt, lavender tie and pocket square, and alligator shoes, in front of Daniel's Freedom Tower model.

"You got to take a look from here!" I tell the governor and the people around him. "Look at the view of the river! Look at the way the tower spirals up! Look at the spiral in relation to the Statue of Liberty and the sweep of her arm! There is a visceral connection! People will feel the connection! And look, the building is oriented toward the river that connects New York to the world!" I'm very excited.

Apparently the governor is, too.

"I think the Libeskinds will win. I like them. I like their proposal," he tells me when I get up off the floor.

The Libeskinds and I are fully confident as the committee moves toward its final decision that Studio Libeskind will get the commission for what will be the largest, most important architectural commission of the century.

But my office phone rings at 7:30 the next morning and Nina Libeskind is on the line.

"We lost," she says.

"Don't fuck around with me. It's too early in the morning."

"We lost," she says again.

I pick up the *Times*. It's true: the selection committee has chosen the proposal from THINK, an architectural group headed by Rafael Viñoly, for the site of the former World Trade Center. It seems hopeless for the Libeskinds and I don't know what to do, but I start dialing, getting people who know selection committee members out of bed. All the people I speak to are afraid to make a fuss or just feel it's simply too late: the committee has decided.

All right then. I'm calling the governor.

"I thought you liked Libeskind."

"I do like Libeskind. I like his proposal, too," Pataki says. "But I have a committee. They made their choice. What am I supposed to do?"

"This is your business, not mine, governor. But choosing the building for the Trade Center site is the most important thing you'll ever do in public life. Nobody will remember all those fucking bills you passed. They are just going to see those buildings. You've got to do what *you* think is right."

The governor calls back an hour later.

"How am I going to do this? I appointed the selection committee. I thought they were going to choose Libeskind's proposal."

"No one even knows who's on your goddamned committee! But everyone knows who *you* are. Who are you comfortable with? That's who you have to go with."

I keep my mouth shut after I say this, which turns out to be a good move.

"You know, you're right."

Bippity bop! Looks like we're getting somewhere.

The selection committee schedules an urgent meeting later that afternoon with the Libeskinds and the THINK team, both of whom are given thirty minutes to explain their respective plans to the governor and to Mayor Bloomberg. Libeskind takes just five minutes to explain his plan. "If I can't explain it to you in five minutes, it's probably not worth building."

At five that afternoon, the office phone rings once again. "Governor George Pataki on the line for Ed Hayes."

Showtime!

"You tell those people they owe you a lot. It was those goddamned haystacks. I couldn't get those haystacks out of my mind."

Haystacks!

I hang up, certain that Libeskind won't disappoint the governor and satisfied I've done something good. Thanks to Celexa, I no longer exhibit inappropriate emotional responses, so I don't cry or fall apart as I used to on so many other occasions when I felt proud of what I'd done.

I didn't help Libeskind get the World Trade Center commission because I have connections or am a backdoor operator (though I have connections and *am* a backdoor operator) but because I understand something about people and their aspirations for greatness and also because, after my association with Tom Wolfe and Andy Warhol, I have an appreciation of genius. I understand Pataki and his aspirations and I sense that Libeskind, like Wolfe and Warhol, is a true genius. I knew how to bridge a connection between these men and their shared ideals—with haystacks, of all things.

Any schmuck can be an operator. It's not hard. You go in, offer someone a political contribution of some kind—best if it's cash money—and ask for something in return. But to be a big-time operator, the kind of operator I've always wanted to be, you have to understand the power of shared ideals, of beauty, longing, love, and vulnerability, which I think I do.

"We're not going to do this job unless you are our lawyer," Nina Libeskind tells me a few days after Studio Libeskind wins the competition to rebuild on the World Trade Center site.

If she wants me to be her lawyer, I tell her, there are two things you have to know: (1) you have to pay me, *a lot*, (2) your troubles with this project are just beginning. I convey this in polite but direct terms.

Nina agrees, but she can't possibly know how right I am about what is ahead, nor can she or I imagine how the rebuilding will involve all the usual power players—lawyers, politicians, bureaucrats, and moguls—in a classic, expensive, contentious New York cluster fuck, out of which something enduring, or at least successful, will hopefully emerge, as it so often does in this city of endless shovers, pushers, strivers. But I'm right: the Libeskinds' troubles and my machinations on their behalf have not yet begun.

—

"Daddy, I got pinched."

My fifteen-year-old daughter, Avery, is on the phone one spring afternoon shortly after the Lower Manhattan Development Corporation names Libeskind master-plan architect for the World Trade Center site.

My daughter is rebellious and political and she's been downtown demonstrating against the war in Iraq. She's an action girl, which I like. Let her get in trouble.

"The police told us to disperse. I was with my girlfriend. She was scared and she grabbed my arm. A big cop came up and said, 'I told you not to do that,' pulled us over, and said he was taking us into custody."

"Where are you now, Avery?"

"They took us into custody. Then a fight started and there was a lot of screaming and yelling and, while the cops were dealing with that, I started running."

"Okay, baby, what happened?"

"The police said, 'Come back. You are under arrest.' "

"Okay, kid, what did you do?"

"I just kept running."

"Good girl! Now where are you? You better come here. Come to my office."

My very good-looking, very ready daughter says she can't do that.

"Daddy, I have to find my friend."

"Avery, if your girlfriend was arrested, there is nothing *you* can do. If she is not arrested, you're apt to run into the cops that grabbed you before and they are going to be genuinely annoyed to see you again and they *will* arrest you."

"Daddy, I can't leave my friend," she says and hangs up and goes back for her girlfriend.

I couldn't have been prouder: my daughter cared enough to go down and demonstrate, escaped from the cops, and risked arrest to go back for a friend. *That's my girl!* God, I'm proud of that kid.

Avery has wonderful friends, a good sign of character and something else I admire about my daughter. I adore Avery's friends. The guys she brings home are substantial, attractive guys who are physically and mentally strong and who work hard. Avery sometimes tells boyfriends that Bruce Cutler is her godfather; some of her friends don't know who he is, but their parents usually do and are sometimes terrified.

"Daddy, I have a friend who has a problem," Avery tells me at breakfast.

"Tell me what it is, honey," I say over bananas and organic cereal.

"She's gay and into the punk scene, and her parents really don't like her, and they do awful mean things to her and they're going to throw her out of the house. She's having a terrible life. Daddy, I'm afraid for her. I'm afraid something might happen to her."

"Avery, why are you telling me this?"

"Well, Daddy, could you maybe help her?"

Can I help your fifteen-year-old gay friend?

"Is she a close friend of yours?"

"Yes, Daddy. She is a *very* close friend."

"Avery, I am not going to let anything bad happen to a close friend of yours. If your friend has a problem, bring her to me. I'll make it right."

Avery looks at me with her gorgeous blue eyes, her face full of light.

"Daddy! I told her you would say that!"

This is definitely getting a little ridiculous!

I always wanted to be a stand-up guy, someone you could call out to, and here at last I am, the guy troubled fifteen-year-olds on the Upper East Side of Manhattan turn to when they need help!

—

By 2003, the conflict surrounding the World Trade Center rebuilding project has devolved into a dramatic clash between ideal-ism and crass commercialism. Helping Libeskind will require negoti-ation through more forceful channels in the city's power structure than I've ever battled before.

Three things about Libeskind really impress me: he runs seven miles a day, he has great kids, and he has the biggest, best library you have ever seen. He has every major literary, philosophical, and his-torical book written in the last five centuries in English, French, Dutch, Italian, German, and who the fuck knows what other lan-guages. He is brilliant, has a singular vision, and, on essential points respecting his vision, will not back down, no matter what. Which does not mean he won't compromise. Architecture is compromise. It just means there are core issues tied to his fundamental vision for which he is willing to sacrifice everything. Libeskind based his plan for the site on ideas about memory and the future; Pataki liked the plan precisely because it reconciled the tragic with a fundamental optimism; the 1776 tower is central to Libeskind's vision and he won't give up on its fundamental design for any amount of money or in response to any amount of pressure, bullying, thumb screwing, or anything else. A Polish Jew, Libeskind grew up in the Bronx; I'm an Irish Catholic guy from Queens and a Tough-guy school graduate. Libeskind and I share similar values. He's a tough little Jew. I like him. And I love Nina and the fact that his office is full of the most diverse, international group anywhere outside the United Nations; he's got Germans, Frenchmen, a Baluchi, and the lovely and very voluptuous Carla Swickerath, who runs the place.

Pataki's office remains central to the rebuilding; John Cahill, Kevin Rampe, and Joe Seymour, all Irish German guys, are the key state players. These guys will never jerk anyone around. If any of them, especially Cahill, a movie-star-handsome former triathlete, is mad at you, he'll tell you in no uncertain terms.

The Port Authority, which owns the site and has an obvious interest in the rebuilding, is an unbelievably powerful institution that isn't accountable to anyone. It was created to manage transportation and infrastructure issues in the New York/New Jersey area and was intended to be free of political influence. Not a bad idea, of course, though the trouble is that the Port Authority does not report to anyone or any institution, political or otherwise. The guys who run the place—which controls millions and millions of dollars in public monies—don't have to listen to anyone and they don't.

The real problem with the rebuilding project is that Larry Silverstein, a wealthy corporate developer, owns the lease to the sixteen-acre parcel of land on which the towers stood and though Governor Pataki and the LMDC named Libeskind master-plan architect for the project, Larry Silverstein wants his own architect, David Childs, of Skidmore, Owens and Merrill, to design the building that will replace the towers. A good, hardworking architect, David Childs is a corporate guy who designs good corporate buildings for big corporate clients, and like most big corporate guys, he doesn't have much use for refined ideas. He's accustomed to running over everything and everyone in his way. Childs, however, is not the problem. Larry Silverstein is the problem.

Silverstein's primary concern throughout negotiations on the rebuilding is to maximize his profits. He wants to build the largest possible structure with the maximum allowable rentable units. The clash between Jews and Catholic white boys that underlies so much of New York history surfaces quickly in what becomes the endless controversy over rebuilding plans at the WTC site. The image of the fireman with the ruddy Irish face and thick neck and short, stocky white-boy build running into the burning tower after taking last rites on the sidewalk never leaves my mind, nor do I forget all those white-boy funerals I attended in white-boy enclaves all over Long Island and New Jersey. I feel a special responsibility to do everything I can for the families of those who died, to remember their bravery and honor their memory in the most enduring and uplifting way. The tower that Daniel Libeskind proposes for the site and that the LMDC hired him to design is intended to do just that, and I know its beauty and its power to incite memory and hope will last forever while whatever pecuniary gain Larry Silverstein manages to sweep into his pocket will not.

A self-identified Jew, Daniel Libeskind operates at all times in his professional and personal lives with both a sense of history and an awareness—and appreciation—of how much this country has done for him, something, it seems, that Larry Silverstein does not share.

It's evident from the start that, despite his agreement with the governor and the LMDC, Silverstein is not particularly interested in proceeding with Libeskind's Freedom Tower. In the spring of 2003, for example, Silverstein offers Libeskind big money if he agrees to accept David Childs's design and serve as consultant for the project. Libeskind, who has not only his artistic integrity but also his own sense of responsibility to the families of those who died on 9/11 and to the people who endorsed his plan, declines.

Silverstein proceeds with his plans until a big showdown in the summer of 2003 at the LMDC headquarters in Liberty Plaza, where the Libeskinds, Childs, Rampe, and Larry Silverstein's representative, Janno Lieber, spend hours in the sweltering, windowless office trying to figure out who's designing the building the governor has authorized zillions of dollars of the public's money for. Discussions go on and on and on and it gets hotter and hotter and these guys are getting nowhere and I want to go home.

"Pass me the phone, Nina," I say, and I dial Lisa Stoll, the governor's director of communications, who knows the governor's positions on almost everything.

I put the phone on speaker so the others can hear.

"Eddie Hayes here, Lisa. I'm with Rampe and Janno and Nina Libeskind. Does the building we put up here have to look like the building in Libeskind's master plan? And does Silverstein have to hire Libeskind to design the building for the site?"

"The answer to both questions is yes."

"Thank you very much, Lisa." Kevin Rampe, Janno Lieber, and Nina Libeskind get the message.

Libeskind has to stay on the project, and the building on the site has to look like the building in his plan. If Silverstein wants the governor's support, that's it. These are the terms. Silverstein signs an agreement accepting them.

The trouble, we soon discover, is that an agreement doesn't mean anything to Larry Silverstein, who seems to see all agreements as part of a new negotiation. Everything he agrees to, he tries to take back. It makes you nuts. Evidently it does not occur to him or to Janno Lieber that this is an unusual way to do business.

The next thing that happens is that Silverstein and Childs decide to build a tower on top of the Port Authority terminal. The building they have in mind would be especially valuable, and the rents especially high, because tenants could enter straight from the PATH train terminal without having to go outside. The trouble is that the building is not in the master plan, the one the governor's office expressly indicated we should follow, and it will keep light out of the plaza that is central to Libeskind's plan.

I already have a good idea that John Cahill is a straight-shooting white boy. I go to his office and walk him over to a table full of models of towers over the PATH terminal.

"You know, John, I really think this is a good idea, this tower here on top of the station. Because when my mother and your mother get off the train and look up, it's a good thing that they will be able to see immediately that looming over them, in the space over their heads, are all the men who are going to control their lives and that, while they spend their whole day working without daylight, someone very rich is sitting up there, above their heads, on top of that building."

Cahill listens carefully, his movie-star-handsome face expressionless, intent.

"I think *not*, Eddie."

"Right, Johnny Boy. Fuck that."

"That is *not* going to happen."

"I didn't think so, Johnny!"

Cahill is the nicest guy in the world, but he is a tough customer; if he says he's not going to do something, he's not going to do it. Shoot him, beat him for a week, he still isn't going to do it. That's it.

Silverstein is going to make a lot of money, no matter what. And his position is better after the buildings come down than it was before because, per the master plan, the site will be dramatically improved, full of museums and cultural centers that will attract crowds, not to mention better roadways to get people there and more commodious plazas and public spaces in which to remember what happened and to enjoy music, street life, and other urban pleasures. So why's he screwing with everyone for a little extra money? The guy just negotiates and renegotiates every agreement and can't seem to stop himself from endlessly trying to get the better of every deal, even those deals that have already been negotiated and renegotiated. The guy is a problem.

More meetings. More agreements. More indications that Silverstein does not intend to include Libeskind or his ideas in the rebuilding project. After one of many interminable meetings, I get Cahill on my cell phone. "Johnny, this guy is beating you and us like a drum. He doesn't give a fuck what happens here as long as he makes money."

Silverstein now goes to the governor and shows him a model for the building Childs has designed. But the model he shows Pataki is not built to scale. And it's 50 percent bigger than the building he agreed to build. Time to get Cahill on the phone again.

No matter what is going on in the state of New York—or for that matter in the world—you can always reach Cahill on Saturday mornings at the Catholic Youth Organization basketball game in Westchester, where he lives; he's at that CYO basketball game every single fucking Saturday of the year. His cell is always on in case one of the kids' parents need to reach him. (I think they play CYO basketball in Cahill's parish all through August!)

"Johnny, I don't think the model Silverstein showed you guys was to scale. Imagine what the local planning board would think if some guy came to them and got permission to build a house that, it later turned out, was 50 percent bigger than the zoning regulations allow and 50 percent bigger than indicated on his plans. This is exactly the same kind of thing. You gotta check this out."

There've been a lot of times when Cahill told me to go to hell. He's a very fair guy. When he finds out I'm right about the scale, he sees we've got a real problem.

Things are so bad, Cahill has to call in Charlie Gargano, an elegant, charming tough-operating guy who is very close to Pataki. Gargano calls Silverstein and tells him, "Whatever you build on that site has to be consistent with the master plan." Silverstein is so hardheaded he doesn't give a shit. He really doesn't care what anyone thinks. So finally Pataki calls Silverstein and says, "It's over. You've got to build something consistent with the plan. End of discussion." Pataki may be the one person Silverstein actually cares about, not because he likes Pataki, of course, but because the governor has power over state funds and, as Silverstein well knows, in the end the only tenants he's likely to get in any of those towers are state organizations and agencies that Pataki also controls.

Okay, won that one: the tower Libeskind designed will rise above Ground Zero.

Now, after all the designing and the conferencing and the model building and the redesigning, Libeskind wants to get paid. Silverstein says nope. He won't pay and he won't pay, and this goes on for four or five months.

"We're going to have to sue this guy," I tell Libeskind.

"No, we don't want to sue him. It's going to be bad."

"You don't have a choice."

We sue the guy, and seventy-eight days later he pays us. But not before making a bunch of disingenuous statements about how he wanted to mediate all along. *Of course you wanted to mediate! You can drag mediation on for eight months and then ignore what the mediator says!* Thanks, but no thanks, we'll sue, and after we do then we'll mediate. That's what we decided and it worked out nicely.

Though not all of the details were exactly as they were in the master plan, until April of 2005 it looked like the 1776-foot Freedom Tower that would rise above Lower Manhattan would conform in all essential ways to the building Libeskind proposed. But then it became clear that the New York City Police Department would not accept the agreed-upon design, as the proposed building presented security problems. The governor reassured the public that the master plan would be followed and appointed John Cahill to manage the redesign process. Libeskind will continue to fight to protect his vision; I like it about him that he keeps pushing for what he wants. During the protracted battle over the site plan, he could have taken an easier way out and probably would have made more money if he had. Ideas are actually more important to Libeskind than money, though, and the apparent outcome in the battle over how best to memorialize the people killed on September 11 shows that in the life of the city ideas matter more than money, at least some of the time. Work your ass off and you can get ahead here; a couple of buildings blew up but New York is still a place where Polish-born Jews from the Bronx and Irish neighborhood white boys both can elbow their way through crowds of other ceaseless strivers and, if they manage not to back down when presented with obstacles, really get somewhere. That's what I learned from the big cases I took after September 11.

———

"Meatball, I'm inviting your friends to dinner on Wednesday. Make a list."

I owe a lot to my wife, Susie. In her midfifties, she is gorgeous, doesn't have an ounce of fat on her, is a great mother, a good cook, and a wonderful friend, is a lot of fun, and provides endless comfort, and she makes a mean meatball.

I don't care about birthdays or holidays. Maybe because when I was a kid holidays meant my father's spending more time at home and so having more opportunities to cause us grief. But Susie really does make a nice meatball with pignoli nuts and raisins and if she wants to have a bunch of people over for dinner on Wednesday, my fifty-seventh birthday, that's okay with me.

Sheila and Tom Wolfe—dressed as always in an elegant, nicely tailored cream suit with a wide waistband that shows off his still-small waist, and custom spats, silk tie, and matching pocket square—are the first to arrive. Wolfe's last two books, *I am Charlotte Simmons* and *A Man in Full*, both grapple with the question of what is a man and what is a woman and posit a fairly traditional view of gender in which women enable men to realize their full potential; it is absolutely true that Tom Wolfe would not be where he is without Sheila, a wonderful, elegant woman and a brilliant editor, anymore than I would be where I am without Susie Hayes.

"Counselor," says Tom, extending his lean, elegant hand.

I collect cactuses and James Truman walks in with a particularly nice weird cactus.

Bruce Cutler arrives with Allen and Deb Grubman, who bring an Hermès scarf I'm able to exchange later virtually for an entire closet of clothes. Police Chief Ray Kelly, and Kelly's longtime friend and colleague Charlie DeRienzo follow.

Pretty much the liveliest collection of self-made men and women you can find anywhere on earth, we sit down at my kitchen table to feast and celebrate. Avery and Johnny both flit in for some head tousling and hellos. God, I'm proud of those kids. I look around at my friends—Allen, the quintessential Brooklyn Jew, and Deb, everything a quintessential Brooklyn Jew could have dreamt of, and Tom, the son of an *Agriculture Magazine* editor from Richmond, the grandson of a Confederate infantryman captured by Union soldiers at Wilkes-Barre, Sheila Wolfe, a Bronx Jew who looks terrific in leopard-skin miniskirts, and Bruce Cutler, the son of a policeman and another Brooklyn Jew, Truman, an upper-class Brit who came here to strike out on his own, and Kelly, an Irish white boy who rose to the highest rank in the white-boy pantheon, and DeRienzo, his Italian right-hand man, and Susie from the wrong side of the Stockton tracks with her high school degree from a juvenile home—and it's hard not to think, *Holy shit, this is the screwiest amalgam of people in the world right here in my kitchen!* The Bronx, Brooklyn, British public school, and agrarian Virginia: these people simply could not have come from more different places. But the connection among us is obvious as we eat

Susie's great dinner and talk about sex and Tom's new book and the election and the Phil Spector murder trial. These are lively-minded people, all of them, and they are all funny and live hard, take risks, and keep themselves ready and open to experience. It's hard to imagine such a cast of characters brought together anywhere outside of New York City, which is one of the things I love best about this place.

"Toast, toast," says Susie, filling glasses with champagne, looking strong, lean, and gorgeous in tight jeans and a tank top.

The Irish, inclined as they are to drink and florid rhetoric, aren't known to scrimp at toast time; theirs is a tradition of endless invocations to lift glasses in praise of brave men, glorious women, histories full of wars (all merry) and songs (all sad).

I keep my toast simple.

I look at the assembled group, at my wife, at the great food, and I think of how I got to this table in this house—bought with money I earned working on the estate of a weird-looking gay guy from Pittsburgh who came to New York with a couple of pencils, serious drawing skills, and a very strong desire to be rich and famous—here on a perfect tree-lined street in the greatest city on earth. I lift my glass and say:

"No man has ever benefited more from friendship than I have."

"Thank you."

"And pass the meatballs."

That's it.

ACKNOWLEDGMENTS

I didn't want Susan Lehman as my partner. She is a liberal, she is a product of the Jewish intellectual class, she wears a lot of dark colors.

But my editor, Gerry Howard, sent me a piece she wrote in which the opening line was "It's hard to kill a pig." It was a story about testing electric chairs used to kill people. Now, Howard is a nice Irish fella with good taste in books. I like him, he wanted a book about the life I know. He's a pleasure to do business with and his company delivers the checks just when they promise to. He liked her. So I said I'd meet her.

And, you know what? She has three kids. She doesn't have just one kid, which is sort of giving up on the future of the human race; she doesn't have two kids—I have two, and there really is going to be a shortage of white people pretty soon if we don't do better than that. She has three kids and she works hard at taking care of them.

And she likes knock-around guys. She worries a lot sitting around by herself, while I tend to worry about things after I do them. Still, she is not against doing things; she is just neurotic about doing

things. I'm neurotic about *not* doing them. It has made for a good combination.

Anyway, I figured that I'd take the chance. It has been a lovely experience.

Gerry Howard has a whole theory of life based on books. Like a
detective who knows his job is to protect the social order, Gerry
Howard knows that, for depth of experience, get a book. A movie is
here and it's gone, but a book is like a brick set in the building of
your life. You learn something, you roll it around in your head, you
keep lots of books around—your life gets better. I really hope this
book does well, because Gerry loves the people he grew up with just
like I do and I hope that love does right by him.

Edward Hayes grew up in the Irish-American enclave of Jackson Heights, Queens, and graduated from the University of Virginia and Columbia Law School. He worked as an assistant district attorney in the Bronx before moving into private practice as a defense attorney. He now practices law in Manhattan for a wide variety of influential and/or notorious clients, as well as for the families of police who died in the 9/11 tragedy. He coanchors *Both Sides* for Court TV and broadcasts once a week on WABC Radio. He is an inductee into the International Best Dressed List's Hall of Fame.

Susan Lehman, a former criminal defense lawyer, was senior editor at Riverhead Books, *Talk*, and Salon.com. She has written about law, crime, and entertainment for a range of publications, including the *New York Observer*, the *Washington Post*, the *Atlantic Monthly*, *GQ*, and the late *Spy* magazine. She produced television for Court TV and was a consulting producer for CNBC's *Topic A* with Tina Brown.